FACHBUCHREIHE
für wirtschaftliche Bildung

Lehrerhandbuch

Wirtschaftliches Handeln international

Economics and Business Basics

Lehr- und Arbeitsbuch für den bilingualen Unterricht

4. Auflage

von

Stefan Bader, Ulrich Bayer, Theo Feist, Viktor Lüpertz, Elena Rätzke

VERLAG EUROPA-LEHRMITTEL
Nourney, Vollmer GmbH & Co. KG
Düsselberger Straße 23
42781 Haan-Gruiten

Europa-Nr.: 94063

Verfasser:

Stefan Bader	Oberstudienrat, Dipl.-Hdl.
Ulrich Bayer	Studiendirektor, Dipl.-Hdl.
Theo Feist	Prof. a. D., Dipl. Kfm.
Viktor Lüpertz	Prof. a. D., Dr. Dipl.-Volksw.
Elena Rätzke	Oberstudienrätin, Dipl.-Kffr., M.Sc,

Lektorat:
Dr. Viktor Lüpertz

Die digitalen Begleit- und Zusatzmaterialien können Sie unter **vel.plus/page/94063-4** herunterladen.

Enthalten sind u. a.
- Arbeitsblätter
- Planspiele, Rollenspiele, Experimente
- Zusammenfassende Übersichten

Zur ausführlichen Begründung einzelner Lösungen wird verwiesen auf
Feist, Lüpertz, 66 Stolpersteine aus Wirtschaftslehrbüchern, Verlag Europa-Lehrmittel, Best. Nr. 23599

4. Auflage 2021

Druck 5 4 3 2 1

Alle Drucke derselben Auflage sind parallel einsetzbar, da sie bis auf die Behebung von Druckfehlern identisch sind.

ISBN 978-3-7585-9068-9

Gestaltung, Umschlag und Satz: Punkt für Punkt GmbH · Mediendesign, 40549 Düsseldorf
Umschlagkonzept: tiff.any GmbH, 10999 Berlin
Druck: Totem, 88-100 Inowrocław (PL)

Learning area A
Basic economics and human behaviour

for chapter 1 Motives for economic activity

INTRODUCTORY EXERCISES

IE 1 Individual and collective decision-making: the NASA game

Instructions on how to play and further materials for both games can be found in the teacher's digital resources.

IE 2 Basic economic and ethical problems

1. Individual results

   Example of an inexpensive energy provider as of May 2020:

Variable consumption price (Verbrauchspreis)	EUR 1,395.00 for 5,000 kWh per year	27.90 cent per kWh
Fixed basic price (Grundpreis)	EUR 195.40 per year	EUR 16.28 per month
Total price without bonus (Gesamtpreis ohne Bonus)	EUR 1,590.40 per year	
Immediate bonus on first instalment (Sofortbonus auf Abschlag)	EUR 100.00	
Immediate bonus (Sofortbonus)	EUR 153.37	
New customer bonus (Neukundenbonus)	EUR 136.63	
Total price with bonus (Gesamtpreis mit Bonus)	EUR 1,200.40 for the first year	

   Didactic note:
   Students get a first insight into the pricing policy of enterprises such as the differentiation between variable consumption prices and a fixed basic price as well as the incentive effect of a bonus for new customers.

2. Overall price per year, duration of price guarantee, duration of contract and cancellation period, headquarters of the energy provider, types of energy production (e.g. nuclear, wind, water or solar energy).

3. Economic problem: Usually, customers choose the energy provider with the lowest price. From a consumer's viewpoint, there is no difference in quality for energy (homogenous good).

   Ethical problem: An energy provider might offer cheap prices for energy that is created by burning fossil fuels (oil, gas) which are bad for the environment. If customers choose energy from renewable sources (solar power, wind power), they might have to be willing to pay a higher price.

for chapter 1 Motives for economic activity

TASKS FOR APPLICATION AND PRACTICE

Task 1 Classification of needs

	Classification regarding:	
	Urgency	**Type of need satisfaction**
a) Pretzel	Basic need	Individual need
b) Cigarettes	Cultural need	Individual need
c) Legal certainty	Cultural need	Collective need
d) Beach chair	Luxury need	Individual need

Task 2 Needs and goods, benefits and preferences

1. Lea is hungry, she has a feeling of deficiency (= **a need**).
   A burger (= **a good**) can satisfy her need.
   Lea prefers a burger over a pizza (= **preference**).
   Lea might expect the burger to satisfy her need better than a pizza (= **provision of a benefit).**
2. Needs can be satisfied with goods. The individual value attribution determines the personal preferences and therefore the choice which goods are used to satisfy a person's needs.

Task 3 Wants and needs of young people – working with a graph

1. Structure:

   The upper part of the graph (bar chart) shows the income and the lower part the expenditure of 6- to 19-year-olds in Germany in the year 2019. The according sums in euro are shown as horizontal bars. The longer a bar, the higher the value.

   Informative value:

   The graph shows how the overall income and the overall expenditure of young people in Germany are composed. The income is mainly created through regular net income, followed by pocket money. The expenditures are shown in more detail. More than 20% of the income is spent on clothing and fashion, followed by leisure activities such as going out to clubs, bars etc. Since the income exceeds the expenditures, about 2.5 billion euros are either saved or used to pay for debts. Overall, 6- to 19-year-olds seem to be an interesting target group for enterprises due to their purchasing power. This might explain the manifold advertising activities of enterprises in different media targeted at young people.

2.–3. Individual results

Task 4 Relative and absolute scarcity

Relative scarcity: In relation to the population's needs, firewood is a scarce good. As long as trees and forest exist, however, this resource will renew itself. Therefore, it is a good with relative scarcity.

Absolute scarcity: In relation to the population's needs, petrol is a scarce good as well. The naturally occurring stock of crude oil is limited though and will hence be used up some time in the future. Therefore, it is a good with absolute scarcity.

Task 5 Economic and ethical questions (I)

Socrates probably means that people long for (too) many goods while not really needing them. Wilhelm Busch says that human needs are unlimited and that people will never be satisfied.

The satisfaction of the unlimited needs of people with limited resources and goods is an economic problem (problem of scarcity). This may lead to distribution problems which are solved through rising prices in market economies.

In ethical terms, it is questionable when resources are wasted for goods that aren't really needed and possibly only available for certain population groups who can afford them.

Task 6 Economic and ethical questions (II)

Individual results

Task 7 Economic and social consequences of a ban on tobacco advertising

1.

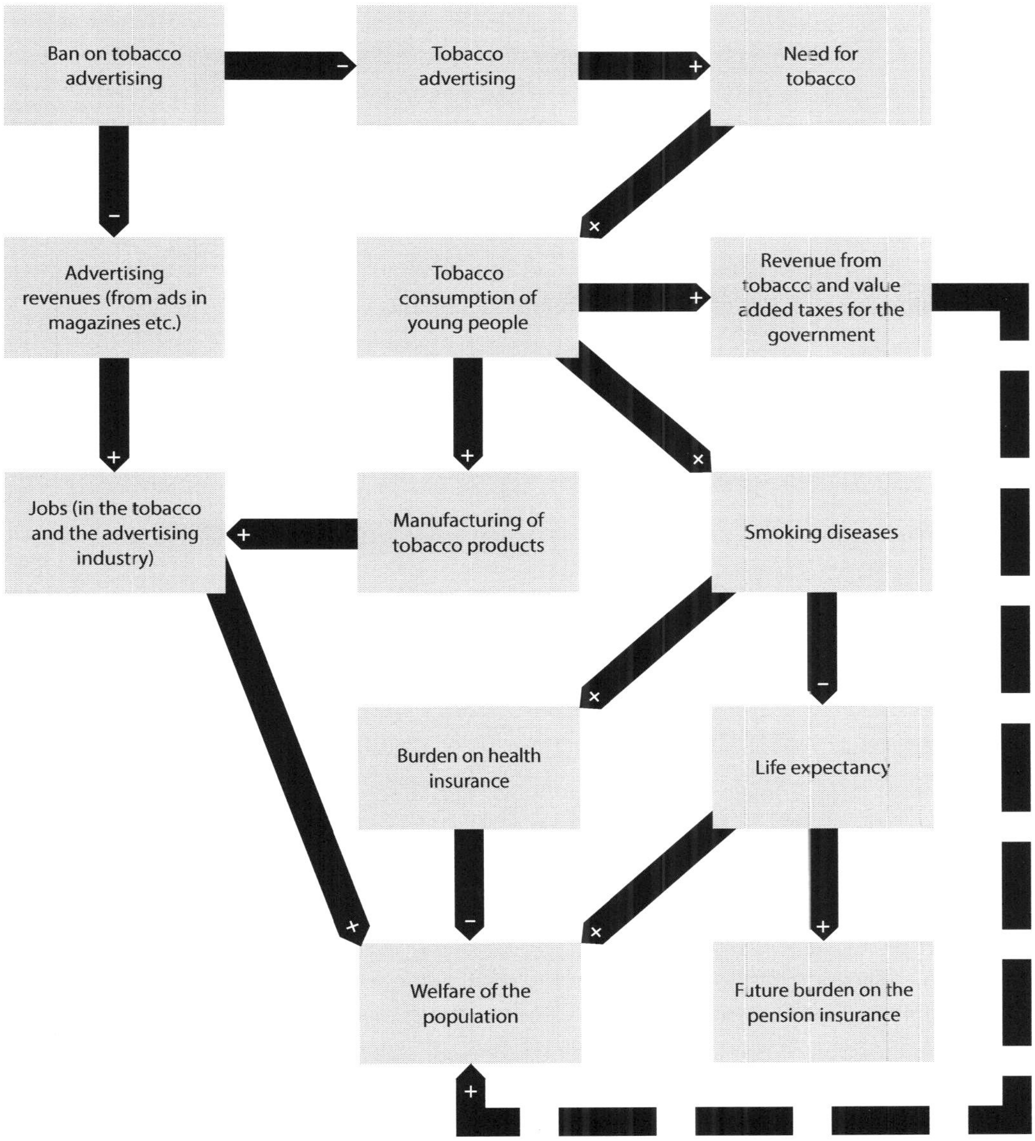

2. The flow chart shows different economic parameters such as the welfare of the population, jobs and governmental revenue.

   A ban on tobacco advertising has a negative impact on the number of jobs in the tobacco and the advertising industry. Therefore, unemployment in these areas may increase which can affect household income and hence the population's welfare. The government's revenues generated from sales tax and tobacco tax decrease leading to lower financial means that can be used to fulfil the government's tasks. The ban has a positive impact on the health and life expectancy of the population and hence the overall welfare of the population.

   Conclusion: The given flow chart shows that economic goals (e.g. employment) and social goals (e.g. health) can be in conflict with each other.

   Didactic note:
   It is essential that students weigh the dangers of smoking against the limitation of freedom rights that occur if advertising or products are banned.

3. Flow charts visualize complex issues regarding their chain of effects. They do not only show direct effects of a change but also indirect ones. The informative value of flow charts depends on the elements (parameters) used. Important elements may be missing due to different reasons (e.g. clarity, neglect, goal of the depiction). The choice of parameters can impact (manipulate) the informative value of flow charts.

Task 8 Differentiation between maximisation and minimisation principle

Maximisation principle: Driving the longest distance possible with a given tankful of petrol.
Minimisation principle: Using up as little petrol as possible for a defined distance.

Task 9 Behaviour according to the economic principle (I)

1. Maximisation principle: Paint as much of the wall as possible with a 5-litre paint bucket. (Application 1)
   Minimisation principle: Use as little paint as possible for a 30m^2 wall. (Application 2)
2. Individual results
   Example for planning a holiday:
   Maximisation principle: With a defined budget of €500, I will try to book the best hotel possible.
   Minimisation principle: I want to stay in a 3-star hotel. I will try to spend as little money as possible on a hotel of this type.

Task 10 Behaviour according to the economic principle (II)

1. a) Maximisation principle: A defined input is used to reach the best output possible.
   b) No application of the economic principle since not both factors (input and output) can be optimised at the same time.
   c) Minimisation principle: A defined output is supposed to be reached with as little input as possible.
   d) No application of the economic principle since not both factors (input and output) can be optimised at the same time.
   e) Minimisation principle: A defined output is supposed to be reached with as little input as possible.
   f) Maximisation principle: A defined input is used to reach the best output possible.

2. a) The quantity learned does not necessarily reflect its quality.
   c) If the student underestimates the difficulty of the test, he might not study enough to pass the test.
   e) The cheapest fodder might not have the best quality. The hens might become ill or their meat might not have the expected quality.
   f) If too many hens are kept in the hall, they might become ill or their meat might not have the expected quality.

Task 11 Behaviour according to the economic principle (III)

The city could apply the minimisation as well as the maximisation principle, though plans based on a certain budget (i.e. the maximisation principle) are more likely.

- Minimisation principle: Build a planned school (defined output) with as little money as possible (minimised input).
- Maximisation principle: Use a certain budget, e.g. 20 million euros (defined input) to build the best school possible (maximised output).

Both applications have advantages and disadvantages.

	Advantages	Disadvantages
Minimisation principle	▪ A well-planned school fulfils the purpose. ▪ The city might be able to save money for other purposes.	▪ The school's quality might not be the best. ▪ Cost may rise during construction and additional costs may occur in the future.
Maximisation principle	▪ A defined amount of money is used in a purposeful way for the city's people. ▪ A school with great facilities creates a productive and agreeable learning environment. ▪ The city can plan their overall expenses more accurately.	▪ Might be a waste of tax money since more money than necessary is spent. ▪ The money might still not be enough to create adequate facilities.

for chapter 2 Basic issues and methods of economics

INTRODUCTORY EXERCISES

IE 1 Basic economic questions of an economy – economic factors of production – capital accumulation – labour productivity

PDF DIGITAL+

1. The following decisions must be made:

   What goods should be produced in what quantity?

   Should the production include collecting fruit and berries, catching fish, planting potatoes, building huts or building a water pipeline?

How should the goods be produced?

Should the fish be caught by hand, or should boats, fishnets or fishing rods be produced?

For whom should the goods be produced?

Should everybody receive the same share of the production output despite the fact that some people did not contribute to e.g. building a boat? Do the people unable to work (the injured) receive the same share of the production output as all the others? Will the food rations be differentiated according to age and work input?

Who decides what, how and for whom the goods should be produced?

An economic system, i.e. the fixing of rules, is necessary to solve e.g. the following problems:

What is to be done if some people want to cultivate wheat and some others want to cultivate potatoes on the scarce soil?

What is to be done if some people want to build a boat while others are not willing to reduce the production and consumption of their daily food rations while the boat is being built?

How shall the production output be distributed?

2. The example of the island describes a model of a natural economy. The silver coins do not have a function in this situation. Probably none of the survivors would agree to give away a share of their collected berries against silver coins. As long as the silver coins are not accepted as general means of exchange, they are useless for their owner. Only in case of a rescue and return to a monetised economy could the silver coins become useful again.

3. (35 kg · 2,400 kJ) = 84,000 kJ per day
   84,000 kJ/12 people = 7,000 kJ/day per person

4. a) The collection output is divided in half. Therefore there are only 3,500 kJ left per day and person.
   b) Per day and person, 6,500 kJ must be provided by catching fish.
      6,500 kJ · 12 people = 78,000 kJ daily food requirement by fish
      78,000 kJ : 3,900 kJ = 20 kg edible share of fish
      The daily output of fishing must be 30 kg.

5. a) Tree trunks:
      Before: 3.5 cubic metres per person and day After: 5 cubic metres per person and day
      Increase: 42.9%

      Fish nets:
      Before: 1 square metre per person and day After: 1.5 square metres per person and day
      Increase: 50%

   b) The productivity of labour increases through division of labour, specialisation, better work organisation.

6. a) **Increase of labour productivity:**

      Before: 84,000 kJ/10 collectors = **8,400 kJ per person**
      After: 15 kg share of edible fish and 3,900 kJ per kg results in 58,500 kJ per day
      (42,000 kJ berries + 58,500 kJ fish) : (5 fishermen + 5 collectors) = **10,050 kJ per person**
      Increase: 19.6%

b) The productivity of labour increases through formation and use of capital. Moreover, fish with 3,900 kJ per kg is a richer source of nutritional value than berries with 2,400 kJ per kg.

c) **Payoff of the production detour and the decision not to consume for a limited period of time:**

Before: 84,000 kJ/12 people = **7,000 kJ per person**
After: (42,000 kJ berries + 58,500 kJ fish) : 12 people = **8,375 kJ per person and day**
Increase: **1,375 kJ per person and day**

d) **Days it takes to make up for the decision not to consume:**

Amount of forgone consumption while building the boat: 3,500 kJ · 5 days = 17,500 kJ
Increase of the nutritional value by increased fish consumption: **1,375 kJ per person and day**
Calculation of days: 17,500 : 1,375 kJ = 12.73
On the **13th day** the forgone amount of consumption is evened out.

Visualisation of 6 c and d:

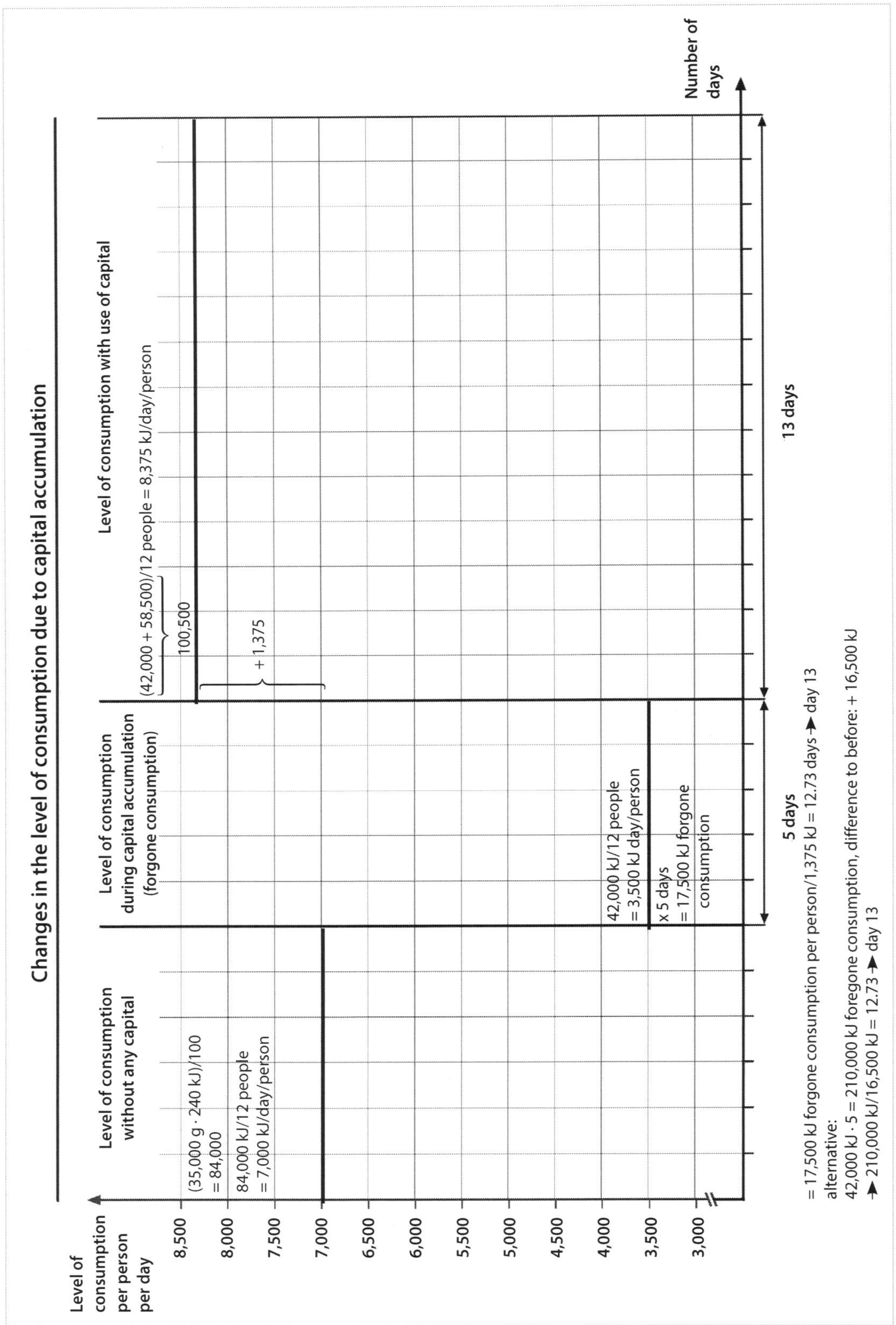

IE 2 Free-rider problem with public goods – payoff matrix

1.

		Neighbour Jones	
		Agreement ($S J_1$)	Rejection ($S J_2$)
Neighbour Smith	Agreement ($S S_1$)	300 / 100	– 200 / 600
	Rejection ($S S_2$)	800 / – 400	0 / 0

2. **$S S_2$/$S J_1$:** Smith does not pay. Nevertheless, he has a benefit of 800 monetary units (MU) because Jones pays the full amount.
3. **$S S_1$/J_2:** Jones does not pay. Nevertheless, he has a benefit of 600 MUs because Smith pays the full amount.
4. **$S S_2$/$S J_2$:** None of the two pays because both hope that the respective other one will pay. In this case the street light will not be installed. There is neither a benefit nor a loss as compared to the initial situation.
5. Smith and Jones will both decide not to pay on a voluntary basis. That is because with **any** possible behaviour of the other one they would always be better off as if they had paid themselves. With this behaviour everybody will have a chance to become a "free rider" and thus a chance to benefit from the street light without paying for it if the respective other one pays.

   The problem of taking all the benefits without contributing to the costs is typical of public goods because nobody can be excluded from using them (the principle of exclusion does not apply). With bigger and more anonymous social groups, the "free rider" behaviour will more likely occur.
6. Public goods have to be provided by the government. When it comes to public goods, markets will fail because too few people are willing to provide a financial compensation in return.

for chapter 2 Basic issues and methods of economics

TASKS FOR APPLICATION AND PRACTICE

Task 1 The features of economic models

In IE 1, a model economy is used to simplify the complex interactions and influencing factors in a real economy. Premises: There is only a limited number or economic agents (twelve survivors), there are only certain resources available, the people are willing and able to cooperate.

In IE 2, a model is used to simplify a complex situation that involves more economic agents in real life and that is usually influenced by many factors. Less important influencing factors are ignored (e.g. an alternative use of the money or the financial situation of the agents). Premises: Only two strategies are possible (no compromise), the individual benefit has a certain monetary value in euros.

Task 2 Categorisation of goods according to tangibility, durability and intended purpose

				Intended purpose	
				Consumer goods	**Producer goods**
Tangibility	Material goods (real assets)	**Durability**	**Durable goods**	1 b) vacuum cleaner	2 e) drill
			Non-durable goods	3 a) sugar	4 d) wood
	Immaterial goods (services)			5 c) cinema ticket	6 f) payment of an external tax consultant

Task 3 Classification of goods based on excludability and rivalry in consumption

	Rivalry in consumption	Non-rivalry in consumption
Excludability	**Private goods** d) jeans	**Club goods** b) public pool f) streaming service
Non-excludability	**Common goods** c) water from the village well	**Public goods** a) fireworks e) open-air concert

The free-rider problem usually occurs for public goods. Since fireworks can be seen without paying for them, the willingness to pay for them is quite low. The music from an open-air concert can also be heard outside the festival area, therefore people might just listen to it from a distance without buying tickets.

Task 4 Types of goods

a) Uncongested country road	2) Public good
b) Uncongested toll road	4) Club good
c) Congested country road	3) Common good
d) Congested toll road	1) Private good

Task 5 Education as a public good?

Two criteria need to be fulfilled for it to be a public good: Non-excludability and non-rivalry in consumption.

Non-excludability is not given since students who do not have the necessary school-leaving certificates or not the required marks are not accepted to the school (= are excluded).

Non-rivalry in consumption is given since many students can attend the school at the same time if we ignore the fact that the capacity of rooms and teachers will limit the number of students at some point.

Consequently, "attending at a vocational secondary school" is not a public good but a club good.

Task 6 Production factors of Christmas trees

All factors of production are used in the production of Nordmann firs:
1. Land: The soil and the climate contribute to the growth of the firs.
2. Labour: Mr Winter takes care of the firs and cuts them down for sale.
3. Capital: The chainsaw is used to cut down the trees and a tool is used to put the net over the trees for transportation.

Task 7 Differentiation between the production factors

1.

	Land	Labour	Capital	Human capital
Wild berries	Soil (forest soil), climate	To go into the forest, to collect/ pick berries	A basket to carry the berries, work gloves to protect hands	The knowledge which berries are edible and where they can be found
Bread	Soil (farmland), climate	To cultivate and harvest wheat, to bake bread	Tractor, oven	The knowledge how to cultivate wheat and how to bake bread

2. Real capital denotes the capital goods such as machines and tools (basket / tractor, oven) used in the production process. They are derived factors of production since they had to be produced beforehand. Human capital is also a derived factor of production. It involves the skills and knowledge that had to be learned (to know which berries are edible / to know how to cultivate and harvest wheat and to make bread).

3. The production factor information can be very important for the success of the production process. If people collecting berries do not know where to look for them in the forest, they might not find any. If a baker is not informed about the type and quality of the flour he is using, the bread might not turn out as planned. The production factors human capital and information cannot always be clearly differentiated.

Task 8 Resources used in smartphones

1. Smartphones are made with precious metals such as gold, silver, aluminium, palladium and copper. Overall, more than 40 different materials are used to create a smartphone. The case consists of plastic and glass. The microchips are made from silicon. Rare-earth metals are used in such as small quantity that they cannot be won back in the recycling process. Overall, the resources used belong to the production factor land. Their value motivates companies to take care of old smartphones.

2. Group A: Consumers

- Consider the expected durability of the phone when purchasing it (e.g. can the battery be replaced?)
- Have a defective smartphone fixed
- Use smartphones for a longer time instead of replacing them every other year
- Don't throw away smartphones but make them available for recycling

Group B: Companies that sell smartphones

- Offer a recycling service for their customers
- Reuse resources from the phones
- Offer sustainable smartphones such as the *Fairphone*
- Mention environmental aspects during sales talks

Group C: The government

- Educate the population about the resources in smartphones
- Set incentives for companies and consumers to recycle
- Create legal regulations (requirements and bans) concerning recycling
- Subsidise environmentally-friendly smartphones

Task 9 Human capital – workers' qualifications

1. Due to increased qualification and skill training, the production factor labour is rarely used in its original form (= unskilled labour). That is why the (highly) skilled labour is referred to as human capital. Obviously, the company considers "training" to be important. Furthermore, the applicants must have finished school.

2. Just as for the formation of regular capital, the formation of human capital (through school, university degrees, job training) requires a reduction of consumption. While attending a university or being in a job training, one might have to give up a well-paid job. This "production detour" pays off if the skills gained lead to a better paid (and possibly more productive) job compared to a job one could have had without the skills learnt.

3. School buildings, school furniture and equipment (desks, computers...), books, teachers, ... These expenditures are financed by tax revenues or deficit spending. There are no school fees for publicly-maintained schools in Germany.

4. As long as their children are students, parents receive child benefits and/or tax allowances as well as other benefits (such as subsidies for public transportation), which are financed by the community. As long as students do not have their own income, their health insurance is free of charge or they get a cheap insurance rate. Moreover, students are covered by the statutory accident insurance for accidents that happen in connection with their education. Students in need are eligible for state aid according to the Bundesausbildungsförderungsgesetz (BAföG). German universities which are financed by tax revenues do not charge their students. All of these expenditures must somehow be financed. Furthermore, with citizens in training, the state faces opportunity costs such as a reduced contribution to the GDP, forgone tax revenues and forgone social insurance contributions.

   The production detour pays off, however, if students contribute more to the GDP after finishing their education than they would have without their education.

5. Individual results concerning the following qualifications:
   Team spirit, motivation/commitment, reliability/punctuality, communication skills

6. Since knowledge becomes obsolete ever more quickly in an information society, it is essential to be able to familiarise oneself with new problems and to learn the skills needed quickly. The so called "soft skills" (or "key skills") are an important precondition for this.

for chapter 3 Economic behaviour and its consequences

INTRODUCTORY EXERCISES

IE 1 Ultimatum experiment – fairness and egoism (role play)

DIGITAL+

Instructions on how to play with two people or with the whole class and additional materials can be found in the teacher's digital resources.

IE 2 Environmental goods as common goods – consequences of egoistic behaviour

DIGITAL+

1.

		Restaurant Jones	
		Payment (S_{J1})	No payment (S_{J2})
Restaurant Smith	Payment (S_{S1})	1,500 / 1,500	4,000 / – 1,000
	No payment (S_{S2})	– 1,000 / 4,000	0 / 0

- S_{S1}/S_{J1}: Both decide to pay. Each pays 2,500 MU and hence makes a profit of 4,000 – 2,500 = 1,500 MU.
- S_{S1}/S_{J2}: Smith pays 5,000 MU while Jones decides not to pay. Smith makes a loss of 4,000 – 5,000 = 1,000 MU while Jones makes a profit of 4,000 MU.
- S_{S2}/S_{J1}: Smith decides not to pay while Jones pays. Smith makes an additional profit of 4,000 MU and Jones a loss of 4,000 – 5,000 = 1,000 MU.
- S_{S2}/S_{J2}: Neither Smith nor Jones pays. The water treatment plant isn't built. Their situation doesn't change compared to before. They make neither a profit nor a loss (0 MU).

2. Smith and Jones will both decide not to pay on a voluntary basis. That is because with any possible behaviour of the other one, they would always be better off than if they had paid themselves. They have a chance to become a "free rider" and thus a chance to benefit from the water treatment plant without paying for it if the respective other one pays. The problem of taking all the benefits without contributing to the costs is typical of common and public goods because nobody can be excluded from using them (the principle of exclusion does not apply). With bigger and more anonymous social groups, the free-rider behaviour will more likely occur. As a consequence, public goods have to be provided by the government. When it comes to public goods, markets will fail because too few people are willing to contribute to their provision.

3. a) Yes, the free rider problem plays a role because every car driver hopes that the other car drivers will get a catalytic converter installed in order to reduce air pollution. The single car driver would then benefit from a cleaner air (less respiratory diseases, reduced greenhouse effect) without having contributed to it.
   b) Yes, the free rider problem plays a role, same argumentation as in a).

4. Environmental problems are not solvable on a voluntary basis. In most cases promoting an environmental awareness will not be sufficient, if environmental-friendly behaviour is associated with increased costs. That is why government action is required, e.g. instructions, bans, criminal law, liability law or compulsory levies. Background information about the prisoners' dilemma can be found in the teacher's digital resources.

IE 3 The fisher game – the concept of sustainability

DIGITAL+

Instructions on how to play, worksheets and a key can be found in the in the teacher's digital resources.

for chapter 3 Economic behaviour and its consequences

TASKS FOR APPLICATION AND PRACTICE

Task 1 Behaviour of the economic man

a) An economic man would have a look at all the currently offered new cars. He knows what he needs (e.g. annual mileage, car size) and would make his decision based on certain criteria (e.g. mileage per 100km). Then he would check where to get the cheapest car (minimisation principle).

b) An economic man also wants to maximise his personal benefit during the holidays. If he knows that he prefers the mountains over the beach, he will try to find the cheapest offer for a certain holiday in the mountains. Depending on the cost, he might also choose to book a holiday at the beach, if his overall benefit – concerning further criteria such as travel time and price – lead to a higher benefit in the case of a holiday at the ocean.

c) An economic man would be interested in the future income. He would decide on a subject in which he can expect to earn a high income with his skills. It is unlikely that he will decide on his "dream job" if this job is connected to a much lower income.

d) At first sight, the economic man is not interested in giving blood. It involves some effort (time needed, trip to the place of the donation) and the donor is not compensated for it. However, other aspects might be relevant for the maximisation of his personal benefit: He receives a free health check-up on his blood and a free lunch.

e) Individual results. Some thoughts:
   - The economic man does not have a girlfriend.
   - His girlfriend is an economic man, too, so neither of them expects to give or receive gifts.

   Note: The model of the economic man is mainly relevant for economic decisions (e.g. purchasing decisions) since they are based on quantifiable criteria (e.g. a price in euros).

Task 2 Personal economic behaviour

Individual results. Example:

a) When I bought my last pair of hiking boots, I considered the price and the quality of the shoes. I compared several shoes online and in shops downtown before I decided on a pair.

b) When I went to party last Saturday, I bought a present at a gas station on the way to the party. That was more expensive than in a regular shop and there was not much choice but I did not really feel like shopping around.

Task 3 Outcomes of self-interested economic behaviour

1. Win-win situation. Inventor Joe makes a profit with his sales. The customers benefit because they are now better protected from accidents.
2. Lose-lose situation. The employees do not receive higher wages which might worsen their financial situation, e.g. if prices increase due to inflation. The business also loses. It might save costs but due to the lower motivation of the employees, the quality of their work might suffer or they might switch jobs. This will harm the business sooner or later.

3. Win-lose situation. The customer wins since he receives free advice for his purchasing decision.The specialist shop loses. Despite the sales advice, they couldn't make any profit with this customer. Nevertheless, they need to pay the cost of the sales staff.

Task 4 Self-interested behaviour and the rationality trap

1. Since standing up means better vision for the football match, all ticketholders would stand up after a while. An individual ticketholder would, however, not see more compared to the situation before everybody stood up. What seems advantageous from an *individual's* point of view ("stand up in order to see more") is disadvantageous from the community's point of view ("standing for the whole match without having better vision.)[1]
2. If many consumers started "panic"-buying, the extent of price increases for foodstuffs would grow – or price increases would even be triggered in the first place, because the quantity demanded would exceed the quantity supplied.
3. If many people acted like this, the crisis in the automobile industry (and in other industries) would become worse, because enterprises would sell less due to lack of demand, which in turn would cause dismissals and shutdowns.
4. If many companies followed this example, the rising wages might be used as an occasion to increase prices. A general increase of prices, however, would make the rise of wages non-effective due to a decrease of purchasing power.
5. If many companies lowered the pay of their employees, consumption expenses of employees would decline. As a consequence, the sales of companies would decrease which would mean lower profits. This in turn might lead to dismissals or even shutdowns.

Task 5 Individual and collective rationality

1. OLDI will extend its opening hours. This decision results in a daily profit of at least €7,000. No matter whether WIDL extends its opening hours or not, OLDI will always be better off if it extends the opening hours (€7,000 instead of €5,000 if WIDL decides on "yes" and €15,000 instead of €10,000 if WIDL decides on "no")). WIDL will also decide to extend its opening hours, based on the same considerations. Therefore, strategy combination 1 will be realised.
2. Both enterprises have made rational individual decisions since their profits were maximised under the given conditions (€7,000 each). Neither enterprise is willing to risk more for a higher profit. If they had agreed not to extend their opening hours, they could have reached higher profits (€10,000 each). In that case they would have had to make a rational collective decision.
3. Both firms know that a collective (cooperative) behaviour will lead to higher profits. OLDI might not extend its opening hours the first week and check whether WIDL does the same. If that is the case, there is no need for OLDI to change the opening hours in the future, unless WIDL changes them – but then OLDI can react to the new situation.

> Background information:
> If a (prisoners') dilemma with a strategic conflict in which individual rationality prevents successful cooperation is repeatedly played (reiterated) and the players don't know when the last round will be played, the following strategy has proved to be especially successful: "Cooperate in the first round and then choose the strategy that the other player chose in the round before." This behaviour is called "Tit for tat" (An eye for an eye, a tooth for a tooth).

1 See P. Bofinger, book "Wir sind besser als wir glauben, Wohlstand für alle", Munich 2005, p. 108.

Task 6 Dilemma situations

DIGITAL+

Exercises and information about dilemma situations and economic and ethical decision-making can be found in the teacher's digital resources.

Task 7 The environmental impact of air travel

DIGITAL+

Background information:
The burning of kerosene (aviation petrol) creates climate-damaging exhaust fumes. They are mainly composed of water vapour, carbon dioxide and nitrogen oxides. The effects of these gases are three times as high at this height as on the ground and so worsen the greenhouse effect. The airplanes' vapour trails intensify the atmosphere's warming since they reduce the reflection of heat into space. Air traffic is turning into the number one climate killer amongst means of transportation. Flying is the most energy-consuming way to travel. A trip by bus or by train only uses about one third of the energy a flight needs.

1.

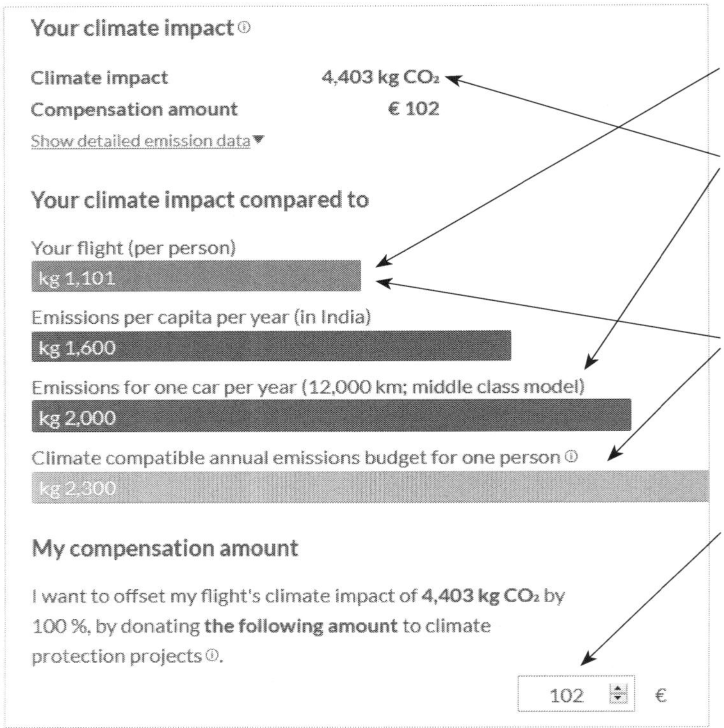

a) CO_2 emissions per person on this flight

b) Difference between the CO_2 emissions per person to the emissions of a mid-sized car

$4{,}403 - 2{,}000 = 2{,}403$ kg

c) CO_2 emissions of the flight as a percentage of annual CO_2 budget of one person

$1.101/2.300 \cdot 100 = 47{,}9\%$

d) Donation to offset emissions.

2. Passengers do not have to pay the amount atmosfair suggests. The payment depends on their personal willingness. The following thoughts might contribute to the decision:
   - The understanding that air travel harms the climate immensely and that this harm should be balanced out
   - The persuasiveness of atmosfair's figures: In the given case, a single flight uses up almost 50% of the yearly climate-neutral budget of a single person. This flight corresponds to a mileage of a middle-class vehicle of about 6,000 km. The compensation's cost is not very high in relation to the flight's cost.
   - Individual financial situation
   - Trust that atmosfair will really invest the donated money in climate protecting projects
   - Willingness to forgo consumption in the value of the donation
3. On a voluntary basis, passengers pay a certain amount of money (EUR 102 for the four people in the case at hand) as compensation for the greenhouse gases they cause by flying. The

money is paid to the non-profit organisation atmosfair gGmbH. They invest the money e.g. in solar, hydrogen, biomass power or in projects which are aimed at saving energy. Their goal is to achieve greenhouse gas reductions which have a similar effect on the climate as do the emissions of the plane. The projects take place in developing countries. In fact, the damage done by flying cannot be reversed. However, preventing environmental damages in other places might at least achieve a kind of balancing.

4. - **External costs:** The costs of burdening the environment are not taken into account when the airlines calculate their prices. In fact, the community bears these costs (= social costs). The same is true for aircraft noise. Railway companies, on the other hand, have to bear most of the costs (e.g. for their traffic routes) themselves. Apart from shipping, rail has the lowest social costs of all means of travel.
   - **Subsidies:** Air travel is strongly subsidised:
     - Tax exemption: Commercial air traffic is exempt from mineral oil tax, eco-tax and value-added tax on international tickets. Railway companies add these taxes to their prices and pay them to the government.
     - Other subsidies from the state include exemption from property tax for airports, tax breaks for investments in aircraft funds, forgoing cost-covering take-off and landing charges.
   - **Other reasons:** Charter and low-cost airlines often cut cost on the back of their staff. Furthermore, they take off from local airports that are hard to reach.

for chapter 4 Use of the production factors labour and capital

INTRODUCTORY EXERCISE

IE 1 Capital accumulation and forgone consumption

1. | | | | | |
|---|---|---|---|---|
| Labour productivity | = | Number of fish caught / hours used | | |
| Old labour productivity | = | 1 fish / 3 hours | = | 0.33 fish / hour |
| New labour productivity | = | 14 fish / 6 hours | = | 2.33 fish / hour |
| Percentage change in labour productivity | = | ((New productivity – old productivity) / old productivity) · 100 | | |
| Percentage change in labour productivity | = | ((2.33 – 0.33) / 0.33) · 100 | = | 606.06% |

   His labour productivity would increase by impressive 606.06%.

   Sam should create a net in order to catch more fish per hour.

2. Minimisation principle: He could catch as many fish as before (in this case 2) within fewer working hours (in this case 51 minutes instead of 6 hours).

   Maximisation principle: He could spend the same time as before working (in this case 6 hours) and catch a much higher amount of fish (in this case 14 fish instead of 2).

3. There are several options:

   Option 1: He could catch fish with his bare hands for three hours per day, so he has one fish per day to eat. He could use the remaining three working hours per day to create a net. This way it would take him: 21 hours / 3 hours per day = 7 days to create the net.

   Option 2: He could catch two fish per day for a couple of days. He could eat one and save the other. After 3.5 days, he would have a stock of 3.5 fish and could start working on the net full time. If he works 6 hours per day on the net, it will take him 21 hours / 6 hours per day = 3.5 days. Overall, it would also take him 7 days until he has the net.

4. Sam has to forgo the consumption of 7 fish in order to benefit from more fish later, this is called saving. The increase in the stock of physical capital (in this case the net) is called investment. A production detour is made because the producer good (the net) must be produced first in order to increase productivity.

   Visual representation of the situation before, during and after the production detour:

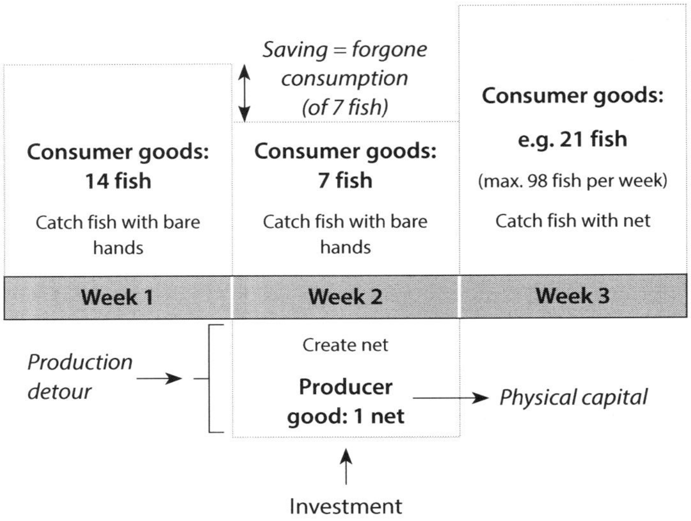

5. The purchase of a delivery van is an investment that needs to be financed. This could be done with the help of a bank loan. The money needed for the investment cannot be used for consumption purposes. The delivery van may contribute to a higher level of consumption goods in following periods, though.

for chapter 4 Use of the production factors labour and capital

TASKS FOR APPLICATION AND PRACTICE

Task 1 Forms of the division of labour

a) International division of labour
b) Occupational division of labour
c) Original division of labour
d) Economic division of labour
e) Social and technical (operational) division of labour

Task 2 Economic division of labour

1.

Primary sector	0.7%
Secondary sector (22.9 + 4.9 + 2.7)	30.5%
Tertiary sector (16.1 + 4.7 + 3.8 + 10.8 + 11.0 + 18.2 + 4.0)	68.6%

2.

Architect	Other services
Construction approval granted by the district administration	Public services, education, health
Bricklayer	Construction
Carpenter	Construction
Production of roof tiles	Manufacturing
Construction loan granted by the bank	Finance and insurance service providers
Cable connection for the TV	Information and communications
Homeowners' insurance	Finance and insurance service providers
Hedges for the garden	Agriculture, forestry and fisheries

Task 3 Internal division of labour – labour productivity

1. Labour productivity = apple juice in litres /number of workers

   Old labour productivity = 5,000 litres/10 workers = 500 litres per worker

   New labour productivity = 9,000 litres/6 workers = 1,500 litres per worker

   Percentage change in labour productivity = ((New productivity – old productivity)/old productivity) · 100

   Percentage change in labour productivity = ((1,500 – 500)/500) · 100 = 200%

   Labour productivity has increased by 200%

2.

Management	Workers
■ Increase in labour productivity ensures future competitiveness of the company. ■ Prices can be held stable or even decreased. ■ Remaining jobs can be secured. ■ The labour costs per liter have decreased from €0.16 to €0.064.	■ Increase in labour productivity meant a loss of several jobs. ■ Higher sales and profits can lead to pay rises. ■ Productivity has increased by 200% while wages increased only by 20%.

Task 4 Types of investment in a company

1. Gross investments (overall increase in capital goods and inventories):
   €100,000 + €1,000 + €10,000 = €111,000

   Net investments (gross investment – depreciation): €111,000 – €20.000 – €500 = €90,500

2. Capital investments (increase in the stock of durable production goods):
   €100,000 + €1,000 = €101,000

   Inventory investments (increase in the stocks of non-durable production goods, semi-finished and finished goods): €10,000

   Capital investments are increases in durable production goods such as machines. Inventory investments are planned and unplanned increases in the stocks of non-durable production goods such as raw materials as well as in finished and semi-finished goods.

3. If a company doesn't invest over a longer period of time, the used up or depreciated capital goods aren't properly replaced. Replacement investments are necessary to maintain the company's competitiveness.

   Capital-widening investments (e.g. in larger or more productive machines) increase a company's capacity. This can either increase the company's competitiveness or it could lead to difficulties, if the company isn't able to use the new capacities properly and hence encounters economic difficulties.

   It is essential that appropriate investment decisions are made according to the company's goals and current situation.

Task 5 Types of investment in an economy

1. Preconditions: Reduce consumption (= saving) because goods cannot be consumed and invested at the same time.

   Purpose: Improvement of the need satisfaction level by being able to produce more consumer goods (production detour). Investments can increase labour productivity and thus enable a higher production output with the same level of labour input.

2. a)
   1) Capital investments (Building investments)
   2) Capital investments (Machinery and other means of production)
   3) Inventory investments (Changes in inventory)
   4) Replacement investments (Amount of depreciation)

   b)

	Gross investments (250 bn + 170 bn + 11 bn + 350 bn =)	781 bn euros
–	replacement investments:	– 350 bn euros
=	net investments	= 431 bn euros

Task 6 Opportunity costs in everyday life and business situations

a) If I spend the afternoon at the lake, I forgo a good grade on my next exam.

   If I spend the afternoon studying for the next exam, I give up a great tan and recreation time.

b) If Sam turns it into a fitness room, he has to give up a place to relax and retreat to with his friends.

   If Sam turns it into a chill-out area, he gives up being in shape / the opportunity to save the membership contributions to the fitness centre.

c) If Sara buys the outfit right away, she gives up some extra money she could have saved.

   If Sara doesn't buy the outfit right away but researches online to find a cheaper version of it, she gives up time she could have spent differently.

d) If the car producer spends the money on further research concerning combustion engines, he gives up the opportunity to expand his range of products / to reach new customers.

   If the car producer spends the money on research in order to enter the electromobility market, he forgoes the opportunity to keep his existing customers happy / to anticipate future developments in the market (concerning CO2 / pollutant emissions, fuel efficiency etc.).

e) If the company uses traditional advertising, they might miss out on a younger target group who doesn't watch "regular" TV anymore but streams films and reads magazines online.

If the company uses an influencer / social media, they will forgo an older, and possibly more affluent target group that doesn't use social media as much.

Task 7 Production possibility curve and opportunity cost

1.

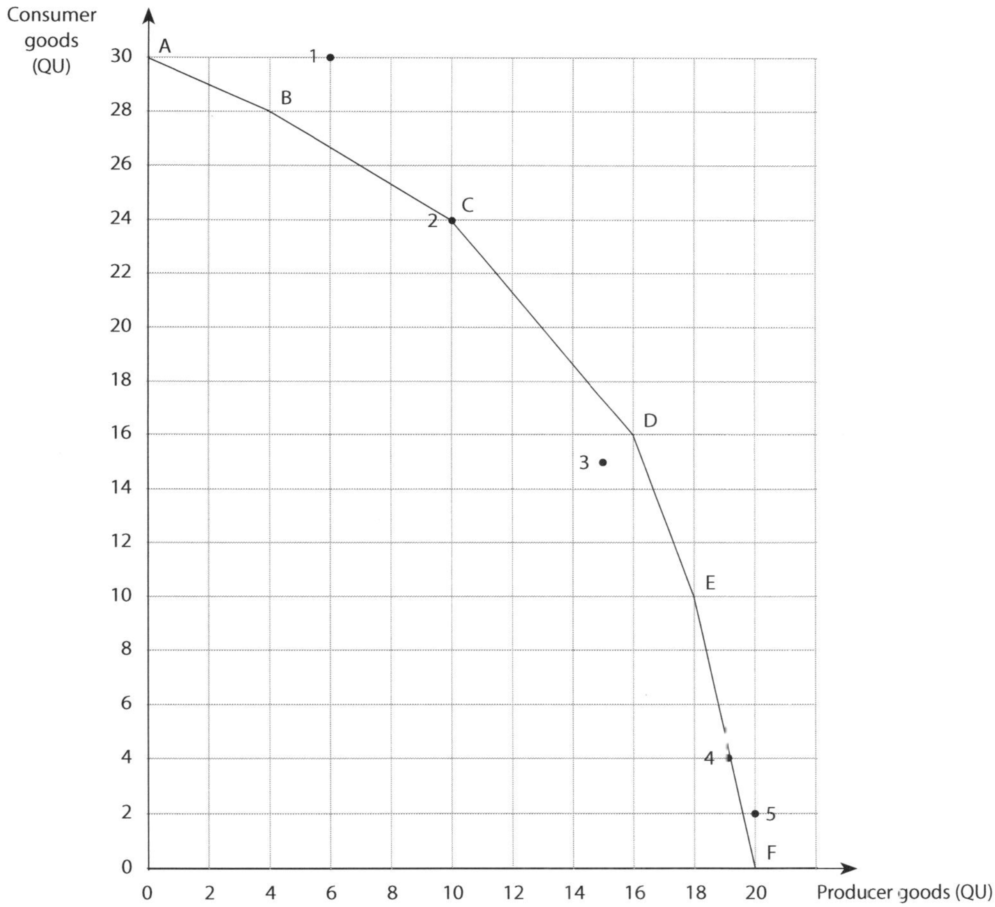

2. See graph: convex shape. Explanation: It cannot be a linear shape since the changes (decrease of consumer goods / increase of producer goods) are not constant. It must be convex since further decreases of the consumer goods leads to diminishing increases of the producer goods (see subtask 5).

3.

Combination	Consumer goods (Quantity units)	Producer goods (Quantity units)	Possible combination?
1	30	6	No, since 30/0 (alternative A) is the maximum.
2	24	10	Yes, combination is on the curve (alternative C).
3	15	15	Yes, combination is below the curve (below 16/16)

4	4	19	Not quite clear from the table (since no data is available between alternative E and F).
5	2	20	No, since 0/20 (alternative F) marks the possible maximum.

4. All combinations located on the production possibility curve (e.g. A, B, C, D, E, F) are efficient combinations of goods. The full production potential of the model economy is realized at these points. All available factors of production are used to their full extent.

   If a combination is located below the production possibility curve, e.g. (6/16), the factor allocation is inefficient. The factors of production are not used completely. The economy's aggregate output could be improved.

   (Combinations above the production possibility curve, e.g. (6/20), are neither efficient nor inefficient. They are simply not possible with the given factor endowment.)

$$\text{Opportunity cost (of producer goods)} = \frac{\text{Forgone amount of consumer goods (good 1)}}{\text{Additional amount of producer goods (good 2)}}$$

5. From option A to option B: (– 2)/(+ 4) = |–0.5| ➤ In order to produce one additional unit of producer goods, 0.5 units of consumer goods have to be given up. The opportunity cost of the production of one additional producer good is 0.5 consumer goods.

Option	Consumer goods (Quantity units)	Producer goods (Quantity units)	Opportunity cost
A	30	0	
B	28	4	– 2/+4 = | – 0.5 |
C	24	10	– 4/+6 = | – 0.67 |
D	16	16	– 8/+6 = | – 1.33 |
E	10	18	– 6/+2 = | – 3.0 |
F	0	20	– 10/+2 = | – 5.0 |

Increase of opportunity costs ↓

The law of increasing opportunity costs is fulfilled, since the values increase from option A to F. If the output of producer goods is increased, the productivity of the used production factors will decrease as they are withdrawn from the production of consumer goods for the sake of producing producer goods (e.g. due to retraining, familiarisation, adaptive difficulties of workers). That is why for every additional quantity unit of producer goods, more and more production factors will be needed. Since these production factors are taken from the production of consumer goods, the output of consumer goods will decrease.

6. An increased output of producer goods would go hand in hand with a reduced consumption of consumer goods. However, producer goods are an investment, because those goods are production factors (= capital) which enable the national economy to produce more consumer goods in the future. Thus, there will be an improved supply of goods by means of a production detour in the future.

   The increase in the production of producer goods entails an expansion of the production factor capital. More or better production factors increase the production potential of an economy. Therefore, the production possibility curve shifts to the right / outwards.

7. In general, an expansion of the production potential would result from an improvement or expansion of the factors of production, e.g. more capital, improved technologies, higher qualifications of the workforce, more labour force due to immigration...

for chapter 5 Distribution of goods

INTRODUCTORY EXERCISE

IE 1 Fair income distribution (group work/role play)

Detailed instruction and materials including a key to the exercise can be found in the teacher's digital resources.

DIGITAL+

for chapter 5 Distribution of goods

TASKS FOR APPLICATION AND PRACTICE

Task 1 Distribution principles: payment of temporary workers

1. **Workers (group A)**

Hourly wage?	Principle of performance	Principle of need	Principle of equality
Clearing tables outside	e.g. €9	e.g. €9.50 – €12	e.g. €10
Preparing beverages and cashing up inside	e.g. €11	e.g. €9.50 – €12	e.g. €10

- Based on the **principle of performance**, all the workers inside receive higher hourly wages because theirs tasks require more responsibility and care. Furthermore, they should have "people skills" to deal with the customers.
- It is difficult to apply the **principle of need** in this case since there is no further information on the individual workers' personal backgrounds. A single mother might need a higher wage than a student living at her parents' house who just wants to earn some pocket money.
- Based on the **principle of equality**, all temporary workers would receive the same wage, e.g. €10.

Hint: As of January 2020, the minimum wage in Germany, which also applies to the hospitality sector, is €9.35 per hour (https://www.dgb.de/themen/++co++6ca263de-fb0e-11e9-bdcf-52540088cada).

Employers (group B)

Individual results, e.g.

Information sheet: Payment of temporary workers

- During the first four weeks, temporary workers receive a uniform hourly wage of €9.35.
- After this probationary period, the hourly wage is increased to €12.
- Temporary workers working inside receive an extra 20% added to their wages.
- Tips are be collected and shared equally among all temporary workers at the end of the day.
- The legally required breaks don't count as working time.

2. Individual results. Distribution conflicts might be mentioned: between the temporary workers who work inside and the ones who work outside; between the temporary and the permanent staff; between more and less efficient workers.

Task 2 National distribution conflicts between different population groups

a) Employed people profit while businesses / entrepreneurs suffer due to higher labour costs and therefore lower profits.

b) Pensioners profit, while higher pensions might put more financial pressure on employed people as well as companies since both will have to pay higher contributions to pension insurance into the social security system.

c) Better childcare support could relieve (working) parents. The state needs to finance it, though, so all tax-paying citizens might be burdened with higher taxes.

d) Higher unemployment benefits improve the lives of unemployed people. The transfer payments are financed through higher contributions to the social security system (unemployment insurance). These contributions are paid by the employed part of the population as well as by their employers.

e) Higher profits are the main goal of companies / entrepreneurs. These higher profits could be reached through cost reductions, e.g. a reduction in labour costs. This would negatively affect the employees.

f) A higher minimum wage would benefit workers in the low-wage sector. However, it would negatively affect the corresponding industry / employers since labour costs increase and profits decreases as a consequence.

DIGITAL+

Task 3 International distribution conflicts (I): land speculation

Individual results. Information is available in the teacher's digital resources.

Task 4 International distribution conflicts (II): The distribution of water

Individual results

Hinweis: Die Themenblätter der Bundeszentrale für politische Bildung können kostenfrei über die Website www.bpb.de als Klassensatz von 31 doppelseitigen (identischen) Arbeitsblättern im Abreißblock bestellt werden. Dazu die Bestellnummer 5969 in die Suchmaske eingeben. Hinweise und Hintergrundinformationen für Lehrkräfte sind inbegriffen.

DIGITAL+

Das Heft steht alternativ auch als Download zur Verfügung und ist zusätzlich im digitalen Lehrermaterial enthalten. Dort finden Sie auch weitere Informationsblätter zum Thema.

Task 5 International distribution conflicts (III): meat consumption and its consequences

1. Description: individual results

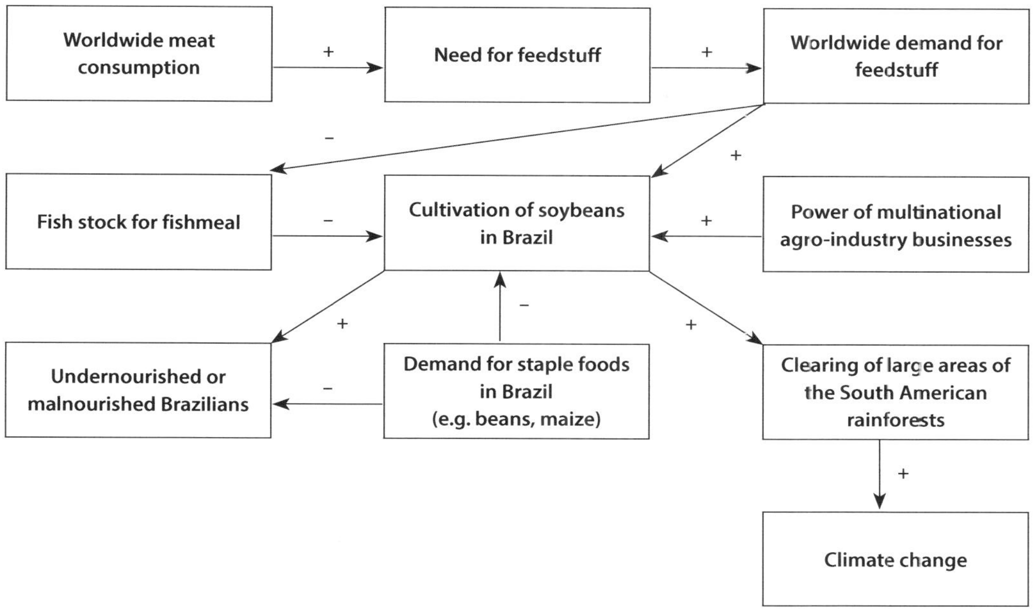

2. Individual results.

for chapter 6 Economic processes as a circular-flow model

INTRODUCTORY EXERCISE

IE 1 Monetary economy as a result of specialisation

1. Exchange transaction for five goods: 4 +3 +2 +1 = 10
   Bread for butter; bread for milk; bread for meat; bread for eggs (= 4)
   Butter for milk; butter for meat; butter for eggs (= 3)
   Milk for meat; milk for eggs (= 2)
   Meat for eggs (= 1)
2. Possible exchange transactions for…

5 goods:	$(5^2 - 5)/2$	=	10
6 goods:	$(6^2 - 6)/2$	=	15
10 goods:	$(10^2 - 10)/2$	=	45
100 goods:	$(100^2 - 100)/2$	=	4,950

n = amount of goods ⇢ $\frac{n^2 - n}{2}$

3. a)

Rate of exchange	Bread (250 g)	Butter (250 g)	Milk (1 litre)	Meat (1 kg)	Eggs (1 egg)
Bread (250 g)		1 : 2	1 : 1	4 : 1	1 : 12
Butter (250 g)	2 : 1		2 : 1	8 : 1	1 : 6
Milk (1 litre)	1 : 1	1 : 2		4 : 1	1 : 12
Meat (1 kg)	1 : 4	1 : 8	1 : 4		1 : 48
Eggs (1 egg)	12 : 1	6 : 1	12 : 1	48 : 1	

b) Bread (as well as milk) has a higher value than butter and eggs, since one loaf of bread yields 2 units of butter or 12 eggs. Since 4 loafs of bread are necessary to get 1 unit of meat, meat must have the highest value.

4.

Bread (250 g)	Butter (250 g)	Milk (1 litre)	Meat (1 kg)	Eggs (1 egg)
6 coins	6 / 2 = 3 coins	6 / 1 = 6 coins	6 · 4 = 24 coins	6 / 12 = 0.5 coins

5. In a barter economy, goods are exchanged for goods. Therefore, an exchange rate is needed for every single exchange. It is difficult to keep track of all the different rates. Furthermore, matching exchange partners need to be found for every transaction.

   In a monetary economy, money acts as an intermediate exchange good and a reference value. In all exchange transactions, goods are exchanged for money. This exchange for money simplifies the exchange transactions. Furthermore, it reduces the amount of transactions needed to receive the intended exchange good.

for chapter 6 Economic processes as a circular-flow model

TASKS FOR APPLICATION AND PRACTICE

DIGITAL+

Task 1 From barter economy to monetary economy

Instructions how to play and the role cards can be found in the teacher's digital resources.

1. Miriam, Gülcan, Sergej and Sam are successful. Mona and Latitia are not successful.
2. First exchange: Sam – Gülcan, now Sam owns a gaming console, second exchange: Sam-Sergej, now Sam owns a suitcase, third exchange: Sam – Miriam, now Sam owns a notebook.
3. It was a rather time-consuming process that needed some coordination. It would probably not work well in reality because the value of the things is very different, and it would be difficult to coordinate all the exchanges.

Task 2 The functions of money

1. a) Payment function, account function (reflects the value of his service)
   b) Payment function, exchange function, account function
   c) Asset function
   d) Account function

2. a)

1.	He is filthy rich.	d)	Er stinkt nach Geld.
2.	To have money to burn.	e)	Geld wie Heu haben.
3.	Money has no smell.	b)	Geld stinkt nicht.
4.	Money doesn't grow on trees.	c)	Das Geld wächst nicht auf Bäumen.
5.	Money is the root of all evil.	a)	Geld ist die Wurzel allen Übels.
6.	Time is money.	f)	Zeit ist Geld.

b) Individual answers, e.g. He is filthy rich has a negative connotation since "filthy" means "schmutzig, dreckig". It seems the person is dirty or a bad person because he / she has money. The idiom is used for people who show their wealth, e.g. through their branded clothes or their behaviour (which isn't always seen positively by others).

c) Individual answers, e.g. ein Schweinegeld verdienen; Geld allein macht nicht glücklich; das Geld zum Fenster rauswerfen, …

3.

Does Bitcoin fulfil the following characteristics of money?	Yes	No
Is it generally accepted?		x (some shops accept Bitcoin but not all of them)
Is it divisible?	x	
Is it portable and transferable?	x	
Is it durable?	x	
Is it limited and difficult to counterfeit?	x	

→ Bitcoin fulfils the criteria to a certain extent.

Task 3 Flow of money in a market economy

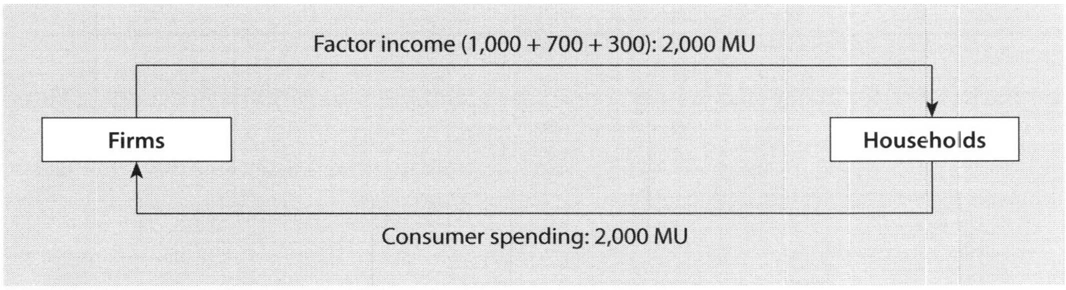

The flows of production inputs and outputs have the same value as the flows of money (in this case 2,000 MU). Therefore, it is sufficient to focus on the flow of money.

Task 4 Flow of production inputs and outputs in a market economy

1. It is an economic division of labour since different businesses (in different sectors) contribute to the production process of the sofas.

2.

	Calculation (value inflow = value outflow)	Interpretation
4	Fabric manufacturer: Outflow: 70 Inflow: 60 Missing inflow: 70 – 60 = **10**	The fabric manufacturer receives furniture worth 10 MU from the furniture manufacturer (flow of production outputs).
3	Furniture manufacturer: Outflow: 10 + 160 = 170 Inflow: 80 + 70 = 150 Missing inflow: 170 – 150 = **20**	The furniture manufacturer receives boards worth 20 MU from the timber producer (flow of production inputs / outputs).
1	Furniture shop: Inflow: 160 + 40 = 200 Missing outflow: **200**	The furniture shop sells furniture worth 200 MU to the consumers (flow of production outputs).
2	Timber producer: Outflow: 20 Missing inflow: **20**	The timber producer receives production factors such as labour worth 20 MU from the consumers (flow of production inputs).

3.

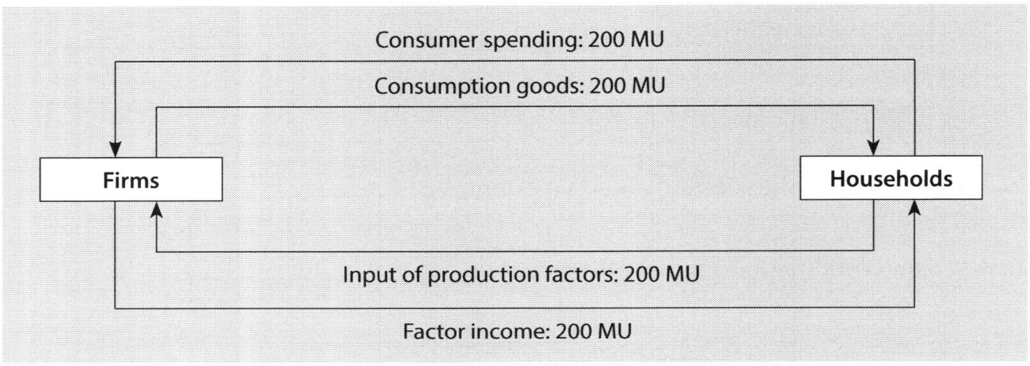

4. The households might increase their consumer spending. If the firms do not supply a larger amount of goods to be purchased, prices might rise. The households could also save the extra money. This would increase the banks' ability to grant credits to firms and households. The depiction of savings would require a more complex model.

for chapter 7 Economic systems: coordinating human behaviour

INTRODUCTORY EXERCISE

IE 1 Price determination at a commodity exchange (simulation/role play)

Instructions on how to play and a key to the simulation can be found in the teacher's digital resources.

DIGITAL+

for chapter 7 Economic systems: coordinating human behaviour

TASKS FOR APPLICATION AND PRACTICE

Task 1 Allocation function in a free market economy

1. In a market economy, the prices take on the allocation function: scarce goods fetch higher prices, and higher prices mean higher profits for enterprises. Therefore, companies will focus their resources on these goods in order to maximize their profits.
2. Prices take on the signalling function. A high price is a signal of scarcity.
3. Prices take on the incentive function. High prices stimulate consumers to substitute scarce goods for goods that show less scarcity. Enterprises are stimulated to substitute scarce factors of production for more cost-effective factors of production.
4. Prices take on the balancing and plan-coordinating functions. If at a certain price the quantity demanded is higher than the quantity supplied, the price will rise. As a consequence, the quantity supplied will rise until quantity demanded and quantity supplied are balanced. If the quantity supplied is higher than the quantity demanded, the course of the process will be the other way around.

Task 2 Distribution of goods through the pricing system

DIGITAL+

Hinweis zur Umsetzung:

Eine kurze digitale Umfrage mit Auswertung in Prozent ist z. B. möglich über die Apps socrative und plickers. Nach der Auswertung der erreichten Prozentwerte können einzelne Schüler um eine Begründung gebeten werden. Es folgt ein Vergleich mit den Ergebnissen einer empirischen Untersuchung, bei der die Einstellung der Durchschnittsbevölkerung mit der von VWL-Studenten im Hinblick auf das Preissystem verglichen wurde.

Vgl. W. Pommerehne u. a., Semper aliquid haeret?, Studium der Nationalökonomie und Einschätzung der Fairness des Preissystems, in: WiSt, Heft 8/1993, S. 405 ff.

Im Folgenden wird auf den Vergleich mit der Durchschnittsbevölkerung und auf mögliche Beweggründe der Befragten eingegangen.

1.

I think the price increase is:	Completely fair	Acceptable	Unfair	Extremely unfair
Average population	2%	14%	38%	46%
Class				

Most of the average population (84%) assesses the price increase as being unfair or extremely unfair. Only 2% find it completely fair.

2.

I think the price increase is:	Completely fair	Acceptable	Unfair	Extremely unfair
Average population	5%	16%	45%	34%
Class				

Due to the scarcity situation being explicitly mentioned, acceptance among the average population increases: 21% instead of 16% find the pricing system fair or acceptable.

3.

I think the price increase is:	Completely fair	Acceptable	Unfair	Extremely unfair
Average population	3%	16%	42%	39%
Class				

This situation leads to similar results as the water scarcity in situation 2, showing that the type of good doesn't necessarily affect assessment.

4.

This system sounds fair to me:	Pricing	Traditional system	Principle of chance	Government intervention
Average population	28%	77%	12%	44%
Class				

"First come, first served" seems to be the preferred principle (77% of the population deem it fair). In traditional economics, this principle is considered to be inefficient. It is suggested that the use of a pricing system leads to a more efficient allocation of scarce resources. Efficient in this sense means that the thirstiest hikers would be willing to pay the highest amount and would therefore receive some of the scarce water. "First come, first served" might also be preferred because it allows poorer people who might not be able to acquire it at a higher price, to also purchase a certain good if the pricing system is used.

Government intervention is considered the second-best approach, even though a majority of 56% don't deem it fair.

The pricing system and the principle of chance considered unfair by the majority (72% and 88% respectively).

Task 3 Basic economic questions using the example of a bakery

	Free market economy	Centrally-planned economy
1.	The bakery. It reacts to the customers' demand.	The state tells the bakery how much bread and what kinds they have to produce.
2.	Miss Smith decides both. She needs to have enough money to do so, though.	The state determines the distribution of the bread to its citizens. Everybody, including Miss Smith, receives some bread.
3.	Mr Jones decided to work as a baker and the bakery decided to hire him. Both contractual parties agreed to it.	The state allocates the workforce to different jobs.

4.	Mr Samuels and the bakery agree on a contract.	No individual contract is possible/necessary.
5.	The Wholebread Bakery owns it (private ownership).	The oven is provided and owned by the government/the community (public ownership).

Task 4 The function of prices in a market economy

Function:	Signalling	Allocation	Plan-coordinating	Incentive	Control
a)	X				
Explanation:	The higher price signals the scarcity of tomatoes. The lower price signals a lower scarcity of cucumbers.				
b)				X	
Explanation:	The higher price leads to a more economic handling (lower consumption) of the tomatoes. She substitutes the vegetable with cucumbers.				
c)		X			
Explanation:	Due to the higher price of tomatoes, the farmer directs his available product on factors into the area with the highest profit expectation, in this case the production of tomatoes.				
d)			X		
Explanation:	The price brings the production plans of the farmers and the consumption plans of the customers into balance. Only certain farmers and customers are able to fulfil their plans.				
e)					X
Explanation:	Since prices affect the profits of the suppliers, they determine their economic behaviour. An inefficient farmer suffers losses or even has to leave the market.				

Task 5 Market power in different types of markets

1. In general, reactions of competitors and customers need to be considered.

Ski lift (Max):

There aren't any competitors. The customers have no choice but to pay the higher price if they want to ski in this resort. This may lead to higher profits for Max.

Ski school (Lea):

There are two competitors. The customers' behaviour depends (among other factors) on their pricing decisions. If they don't increase their prices, customers might decide to book their skiing lessons instead of Lea's. A loss of customers would have a negative impact on her profits.

If Lea's competitors also increase their prices, customers would probably pay the higher price at all of the schools and Lea may – up to a certain extend – make higher profits than before.

Restaurant (Carl):

There are many competitors and hence many alternatives for the customers. If they don't raise their prices, customers might decide to choose these cheaper restaurants instead of Carl's. This would lead to lower profits for Carl. (If Carl's restaurant has an especially attractive location or excellent food though, customers might still prefer his restaurant over the cheaper ones and hence the higher prices would lead to higher profits for him.)

2.

	Type	Characteristics	Market power
Ski lift (Max):	Monopoly	One supplier – many consumers	Very high
Ski school (Lea):	Oligopoly	Few suppliers – many consumers	Medium to high
Restaurant (Carl):	Polypoly	Many suppliers – many consumers	Low

3. They could come to an agreement regarding a common (higher) price that would benefit all of them. Since customers cannot avoid booking their classes since there aren't any other, cheaper, ski schools in the resort, they would all achieve higher profits up to a certain point. Price-fixing agreements are, however, forbidden in Germany.

Task 6 Price determination at a commodity exchange

1. Supply (sellers' plans)

Price per tonne in €	A	B	C	D	Total quantity supplied
60	–	–	–	80	80
100	–	–	60	80	140
120	–	20	60	80	160
180	40	20	60	80	200

Demand (buyers' plans)

Price per tonne in €	E	F	G	H	Total quantity demanded
60	60	20	40	80	200
100	–	20	40	80	140
120	–	–	40	80	120
180	–	–	–	80	80

Aggregated quantities

Price per tonne in €	Supply	Demand	Quantity traded in tonnes
60	80	200	80
100	140	140	140
120	160	120	120
180	200	80	80

The broker will fix a price of €100 per tonne (equilibrium price). At this price, the highest executable volume of 140 tonnes (equilibrium quantity) is traded. The quantity supplied and demanded match at this price.

2. The broker must follow the principle of the highest executable volume, i.e. the price at which most orders (highest quantity) can be traded must be set. At a price of €180, only 80 tonnes would be traded. Quantity supplied: 200 tonnes; quantity demanded: 80 tonnes; excess supply (gap in demand): 120 tonnes.

   At a price of €60, the quantity supplied would be 80 tonnes and the quantity demanded 200 tonnes. This would lead to an excess demand (gap in supply) of 120 tonnes.

3. und 4.

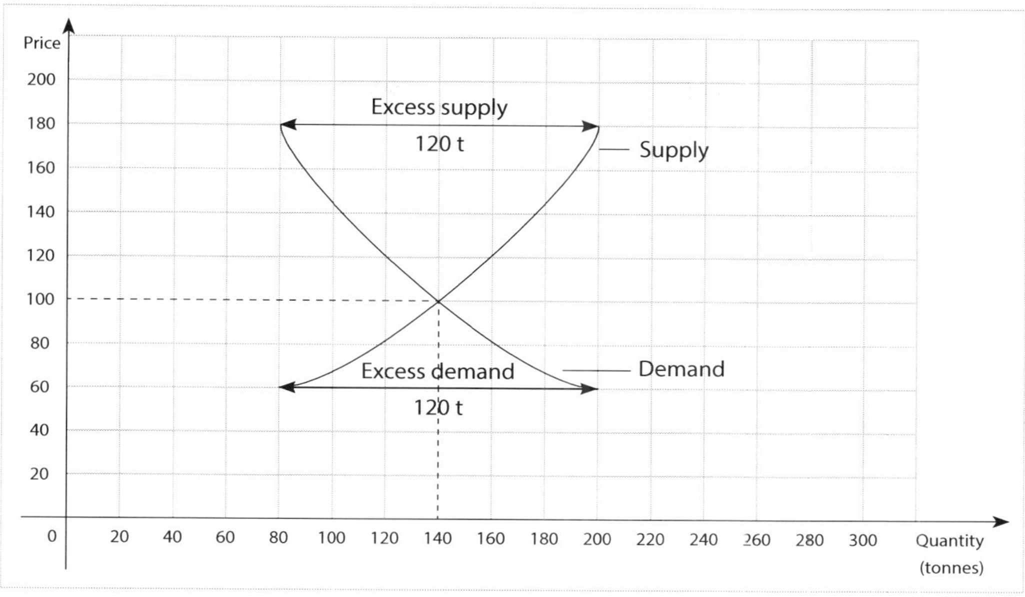

5.

Seller	Minimum price per tonne in €	Selling price per tonne in €	Additional profit per tonne in €
A	180	Sellers A and B cannot realise their selling plans since their minimum price is above the equilibrium price.	
B	120		
C	100	100	expectation and market price match
D	60	100	40

Buyer	Maximum price per tonne in €	Purchasing price per tonne in €	Savings per tonne in €
E	60	Buyer E cannot realise his buying plan since his maximum price is below the equilibrium price.	
F	100	100	expectation and market price match
G	120	100	20
H	180	100	80

6. Sales volume = traded quantity; in our case: 140 t.
Revenue = sold quantity · price per unit; in our case: 140 t · 100 €/t = 14,000 €.

Task 7 Price determination for shares at an exchange

1.

Price in €	Quantity supplied	Quantity demanded	Executable volume
154	130	10	10
153	130	10	10
152	110	50	50
151	**80**	**80**	**80**
150	10	100	10

- Equilibrium quantity: 80 shares
- Equilibrium price: €151

2. Market situation
   - at €150: excess demand / supply gap of 90 shares
   - at €153: excess supply / demand gap of 120 shares

3.

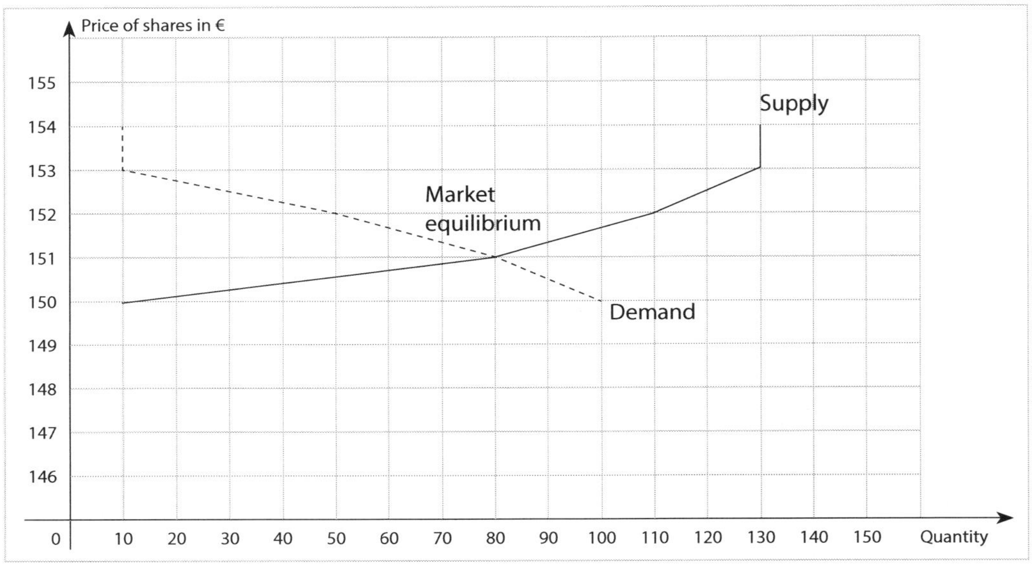

Equilibrium price = €151 Equilibrium quantity = 80 shares

4. The quantity demanded increases by 60 at any given price. The quantity supplied stays the same.

Price in €	Quantity supplied	Quantity demanded	Executable volume
154	130	70	70
153	130	70	70
152	110	110	110
151	80	140	80
150	10	160	10

- New equilibrium price: €152
- New equilibrium quantity: 110 shares
- The new market participant seems to be very willing to take risks since he does not limit his buying order (he doesn't set a maximum price). He runs the risk of paying a very high price in case the demand is very strong at that particular day.

Lernbereich B
Wirtschaftsordnung in der Bundesrepublik Deutschland

zu Kapitel 1 Leitbild der Sozialen Marktwirtschaft

ERARBEITUNGSAUFGABE

EA 1 Prioritätenbildung: Was kennzeichnet die Soziale Marktwirtschaft?

DIGITAL+

Spielbeschreibung und Spielunterlagen siehe das digitale Zusatzmaterial zum Lehrerhandbuch.

Lösungshinweis: Mehrere Aussagen sind deckungsgleich bzw. beinhalten sich gegenseitig. Bei den Schülerlösungen stehen häufig soziale Gesichtspunkte im Vordergrund. Wesentliches Ergebnis des Spiels muss aber die Erkenntnis sein, dass auch in einer sozialen Marktwirtschaft die Lenkung des Wirtschaftsprozesses durch Wettbewerbsmärkte erfolgen soll. Nur wenn die Marktergebnisse sozial unerwünscht sind oder als ungerecht empfunden werden, soll der Staat korrigierend eingreifen. Das bedeutet, dass u. a. folgende Aussagen zu den wichtigsten Merkmalen einer sozialen Marktwirtschaft gehören:

Preise bilden sich am Markt durch Angebot und Nachfrage, Recht auf Privateigentum, Staat muss für Wettbewerb unter den Unternehmen sorgen, **Staat muss bei sozial unerwünschten Marktergebnissen korrigierend eingreifen**, Löhne werden durch Tarifverhandlungen zwischen Arbeitgebern und Gewerkschaften ausgehandelt.

zu Kapitel 1 Leitbild der Sozialen Marktwirtschaft

ANWENDUNGS- UND ÜBUNGSAUFGABEN

Aufgabe 1 Abgrenzung: Soziale Marktwirtschaft und freie Marktwirtschaft

a) Rolle des Staates	Aktives Eingreifen des Staates in das Wirtschaftsgeschehen: Wettbewerbspolitik, Sozial- und Einkommenspolitik.
b) Eigentumsformen	Recht auf Privateigentum, aber mit Einschränkungen: Sozialbindung des Eigentums, Enteignung gegen Entschädigung, Staatseigentum ist möglich.
c) Wettbewerb und Preisbildung	Freier Wettbewerb, aber mit Einschränkungen: Staat kann in die Preisbildung eingreifen und selbst als Anbieter bzw. Nachfrager auf Märkten auftreten.
d) Verträge	Vertragsfreiheit, aber mit Einschränkungen: Verträge können nichtig sein, wenn z. B. ein Vertragspartner unangemessen benachteiligt wird.
e) Produktion/Handel	Produktions- und Gewerbefreiheit, aber mit Einschränkungen, wenn z. B. die Gesundheit oder die Sicherheit der Bevölkerung gefährdet sind.

f)	Außenhandel	Freihandel, aber mit Einschränkungen: Staatliche Genehmigungen für bestimmte Exportgüter, staatliche Auflagen und Zölle für bestimmte Importgüter.
g)	Konsum	Konsumfreiheit, aber mit Einschränkungen, wenn z. B. die Gesundheit einzelner oder der Bevölkerung gefährdet ist.
h)	Beruf/Arbeitsplatz	Freie Berufs- und Arbeitsplatzwahl, aber mit Einschränkungen: Staatliche Prüfungen für bestimmte Berufsgruppen und staatliche Zulassungen für Niederlassungen.
i)	Arbeitsmarkt	Koalitionsfreiheit und Tarifverhandlungen: Gewerkschaften und Arbeitgeberverbände handeln Löhne und Arbeitsbedingungen aus. Der Staat greift nicht in Tarifverhandlungen ein (Tarifautonomie).

Aufgabe 2 Ordnungsmerkmale der Sozialen Marktwirtschaft

1.

Fall	Begründung für staatlichen Eingriff	Welches Ordnungsmerkmal?
a) Bahnlinie	Interessen der Allgemeinheit werden höher bewertet als die individuellen Interessen der Anlieger.	Recht auf Privateigentum
b) Mindestlohn	Staat muss den Arbeitnehmern ein Einkommen zur Sicherung der Existenz sichern.	Vertragsfreiheit auf dem Arbeitsmarkt
c) Waffenexporte	Staat muss aus politischen Gründen Waffenexporte kontrollieren.	Vertragsfreiheit im Außenhandel

2.

Fall	Staatlicher Eingriff: Ja/Nein	Welches Ordnungsmerkmal?
a) Wohnungsnot	Ja, da eine Notlage ausgenutzt wird. Der Geschädigte muss vor Wucherpreisen *geschützt* werden.	Vertragsfreiheit
b) Kieswerk	Ja, da der Wettbewerb eingeschränkt wird.	Vertragsfreiheit; Wettbewerb und Preisbildung
c) Arbeitsvertrag	Ja, da der Lagerarbeiter vor ungerechtfertigter Kündigung *geschützt* werden muss.	Vertragsfreiheit auf dem Arbeitsmarkt
d) Buchhalter	Ja, da die Allgemeinheit vor nicht qualifizierten Ärzten *geschützt* werden muss.	Freie Berufswahl
e) Feuerwerkskörper	Ja, da Minderjährige *geschützt* werden müssen.	Konsumfreiheit
f) Zahlungsunfähigkeit	Nein, Bürger trägt Eigenverantwortung für seine Zahlungsunfähigkeit.	--

Aufgabe 3 Karikatur zur Sozialen Marktwirtschaft

Ein Lkw fährt mit einem Anhänger über einen Berg. Der Lkw mit der Aufschrift „Marktwirtschaft" ist über dem Berg, der Anhänger mit der Aufschrift („sozial") hat es noch nicht geschafft. Die

Karikatur könnte das Spannungsverhältnis zwischen der „marktwirtschaftlichen Ordnung" und der „sozialen Ausrichtung" aufzeigen. Die Soziale Marktwirtschaft wird behindert durch die „soziale Last", sie kommt nur schwer voran. Die marktwirtschaftliche Ausrichtung kann sich nicht entfalten. Es besteht die Notwendigkeit, dass die soziale Komponente reduziert werden muss.

Hinweis: Bei den beiden Fahrern handelt es sich offensichtlich um den ehemaligen Bundeskanzler Gerhard Schröder (Amtszeit von 1998 bis 2005) sowie den ehemaligen Finanzminister Hans Eichel (Amtszeit 1999 bis 2005).

Aufgabe 4 Regelung der Ladenöffnungszeiten

Einzelhandel und Gewerkschaften bzw. Kirchen stehen sich in diesem Streit gegenüber.

Argumente – Einzelhandel	Argumente – Gewerkschaften bzw. Kirchen
→ *Sichtweise: Unternehmen*	→ *Sichtweise: Arbeitgeber (Beschäftigte)*
▪ Unternehmen sollten frei über ihre Öffnungszeiten entscheiden dürfen. ▪ entspricht der marktwirtschaftlichen Ordnung; Staat sollte sich heraushalten. ▪ Unternehmen können ihren Mitarbeitern flexiblere Arbeitszeiten ermöglichen. ▪ bessere Versorgung der Bevölkerung, da Ladenöffnungszeiten entsprechend angepasst werden. ▪ höhere Umsätze sichern Arbeitsplätze.	▪ Unternehmen müssen in diesem Fall kontrolliert werden, um die Mitarbeiter zu schützen ▪ entspricht dem Anspruch der Sozialen Marktwirtschaft, einen „sozialen Ausgleich" zu schaffen. ▪ unregelmäßige Arbeitszeiten (abends/nachts, am Wochenende) beeinträchtigt die Teilnahme der Beschäftigten am sozialen Leben. Z. B. „Der Sonntag gehört der Familie!". ▪ Kunden kaufen wegen längeren Öffnungszeiten nicht mehr ein, da sich das Einkommen deswegen nicht erhöht; es werden somit keine zusätzlichen Arbeitsplätze geschaffen. ▪ Kostenbelastung der Unternehmen nimmt zu; dies führt zu einem Rationalisierungsdruck; somit eher Gefährdung von Arbeitsplätzen.

Aufgabe 5 Soziale Marktwirtschaft und Grundgesetz

Hinweis: Begründet sind auch abweichende Zuordnungen vertretbar.

Mit einer Zentralverwaltungswirtschaft unvereinbare Grundrechte:

Art. 2: Entfaltung der Persönlichkeit
Art. 9 (3): Koalitionsfreiheit
Art. 12 (1): Berufsfreiheit
Art. 14 (1): Recht auf Privateigentum

Es handelt sich um wirtschaftlich bedeutsame Freiheitsrechte, die in einer Zentralverwaltungswirtschaft nicht uneingeschränkt gelten.

Mit einer freien Marktwirtschaft unvereinbare Grundrechte:

Art. 14 (2): Sozialpflichtigkeit des Eigentums
Art. 14 (3): Enteignung zugunsten des Allgemeinwohls
Art. 15: Sozialisierung
Art. 20a: Umweltschutz

Es handelt sich bei Art. 14 (2), (3) sowie Art. 15 um Ergänzungen des Rechts auf Privateigentum, welche die Funktionsweise einer freien Marktwirtschaft wesentlich beschränken würden. Umweltschutz ist mit staatlichen Eingriffen verbunden und verträgt sich deswegen nicht mit der freien Marktwirtschaft.

Mit einer Zentralverwaltungswirtschaft und einer freien Marktwirtschaft unvereinbare Grundrechte:

Art. 20 (1): Sozialer Bundesstaat

Die soziale Verpflichtung in diesem Artikel spricht gegen die freie Marktwirtschaft, während die demokratische Ausrichtung, welche mit Freiheitsrechten verknüpft werden kann, die Zentralverwaltungswirtschaft nicht zulässt.

Mit einer Zentralverwaltungswirtschaft und einer freien Marktwirtschaft vereinbare Grundrechte:

Art. 5: Recht auf freie Meinungsäußerung

Es handelt sich um ein allgemeines Grundrecht, das in beiden Idealtypen gelten könnte. Die Wahrnehmung dieses Grundrechts durch die Bevölkerung könnte das Funktionieren beider Idealtypen unterstützen, aber auch gefährden.

Der Grundgesetzartikel ist ...	mit der freien Marktwirtschaft *vereinbar.*	mit der freien Marktwirtschaft *unvereinbar.*
mit der Zentralverwaltungswirtschaft *vereinbar.*	Art. 5	Art. 14 (2), 14 (3) Art. 15; Art. 20a
mit der Zentralverwaltungswirtschaft *unvereinbar.*	Art. 2, Art. 9 (3) Art. 12, Art. 14 (1)	Art. 20 (1)

Aufgabe 6 Materialien des Bundeskartellamtes zur Wettbewerbspolitik

DIGITAL+

Der nachfolgende Link des Bundeskartellamtes führt zur Gesamtübersicht:
http://www.bundeskartellamt.de/DE/UeberUns/Schulmaterial/Schulmaterial_Bundeskartellamt/schulmaterial_bundeskartellamt_node.html

Die Arbeits- und Aufgabenblätter im Überblick:		
Lehrerinformationen		
Wozu brauchen wir Wettbewerb?	Arbeitsblatt	Aufgabenblatt
▪ Praktische Übung zur Marktpreisbildung („Der Apfelmarkt")	Anleitung	
Braucht freier Wettbewerb Regeln?	Arbeitsblatt	Aufgabenblatt
Wie verfolgt das Bundeskartellamt Kartelle?	Arbeitsblatt	Aufgabenblatt
▪ Praktische Übung zur Kronzeugenregelung des Bundeskartellamtes	Anleitung	
Wieso kontrolliert das Bundeskartellamt Fusionen?	Arbeitsblatt	Aufgabenblatt
Was ist der Zweck der Missbrauchsaufsicht?	Arbeitsblatt	Aufgabenblatt
Schutz des Wettbewerbs in der Europäischen Union	Arbeitsblatt	Aufgabenblatt
Glossar	Glossar	
Komplette Mappe als Zip-Datei	Zip-Datei	

Hinweis:
Die einzelnen Aufgabenblätter beinhalten auch Lösungsvorschläge

Aufgabe 7 Vereinbarungen von Unternehmen auf dem Fliesenmarkt

Formen	Beurteilung aus der Sicht des Kartellamtes
a) Kartell, da Gewinnzuschläge abgesprochen werden. → Preiskartell	Nicht zulässig: Kartellverbot § 1 GWB Verbot wettbewerbsbeschränkender Vereinbarungen
b) Kartell, da die Fliesengrößen abgesprochen werden. → Normenkartell	Zulässig: Ausnahme des Kartellverbots § 2 GWB Freigestellte Vereinbarungen, da die Verbraucher von der Vereinbarung profitieren.
c) Weder ein Kartell noch eine Fusion. Es ist eine Arbeitsgemeinschaft, da die beiden Unternehmen im Rahmen eines Projektes befristet zusammenarbeiten.	Zulässig, da der Wettbewerb weder verhindert, eingeschränkt oder verfälscht wird.
d) Kartell, da Absatzgebiete aufgeteilt werden. → Gebietskartell	Nicht zulässig, da Kartellverbot § 1 GWB Verbot wettbewerbsbeschränkender Vereinbarungen
e) Fusion, da die beiden Unternehmen zu einem Unternehmen verschmelzen.	Fusion unterliegt der Fusionskontrolle durch das Bundeskartellamt. Das Bundeskartellamt prüft und bewertet die Auswirkungen, die diese Fusion für den Wettbewerb, die Arbeitnehmer und die Verbraucher haben wird.

Aufgabe 8 Notwendigkeit staatlicher Wettbewerbspolitik

Nach Adam Smith neigen Kaufleute dazu, den Wettbewerb einzuschränken. Ihr Ziel ist es, die Preise zu Lasten der Kunden über die „natürliche Spanne" hinaus zu erhöhen. Auch Walter Eucken schreibt, dass Unternehmen Konkurrenz vermeiden und stattdessen „monopolähnliche Stellungen" anstreben. Sie bevorzugen Absprachen und versuchen neue Mitbewerber vom Markt fernzuhalten.

In beiden Texten werden Gefahren beschrieben, welche das Funktionieren einer marktwirtschaftlichen Ordnung gefährden. Aus diesem Grund sollte der Staat als „Wettbewerbshüter" auftreten und durch eine aktive Wettbewerbspolitik Monopolbildungen und Wettbewerbsbeschränkungen verhindern.

Wettbewerb ist das Grundelement jeder Marktwirtschaft. Ohne Wettbewerb kann der Preis seine für die Steuerung und Koordination des Wirtschaftsprozesses unerlässlichen Funktionen nicht erfüllen. Die geschichtlichen Erfahrungen zeigen aber, dass in einer Marktwirtschaft Tendenzen zur Einschränkung des Wettbewerbs und damit zur Selbstauflösung dieser Wirtschaftsordnung bestehen, wenn der Wettbewerb nicht durch staatliche Maßnahmen gesichert wird. Unternehmen haben nämlich das Bestreben, sich den Zwängen und Kontrollen des Wettbewerbs zu entziehen und sich vor Konkurrenten zu schützen, indem sie z. B.

- untereinander wettbewerbsbeschränkende Vereinbarungen treffen (Kartell),
- ihre Marktmacht durch Unternehmenszusammenschlüsse erhöhen (Fusion),
- ihre Marktmacht dazu benutzen, andere Wettbewerber vom Markt auszuschließen (Missbrauch marktbeherrschender Stellung).

Unbegrenzte Vertragsfreiheit und weitgehender Verzicht auf Staatseingriffe sind Ursache für eine zunehmende Ausschaltung des Wettbewerbs durch Kartelle (= Kollektivmonopole) und eine wachsende Monopolisierung.

zu Kapitel 2 Arbeits- und Sozialordnung

ERARBEITUNGSAUFGABEN

EA 1 Koalitionsfreiheit – Tarifautonomie – Tarifvertrag – Streik

1. Haim hat Recht, da ein Tarifvertrag gem. § 3 TVG nur für die Mitglieder der Tarifvertragsparteien gilt:

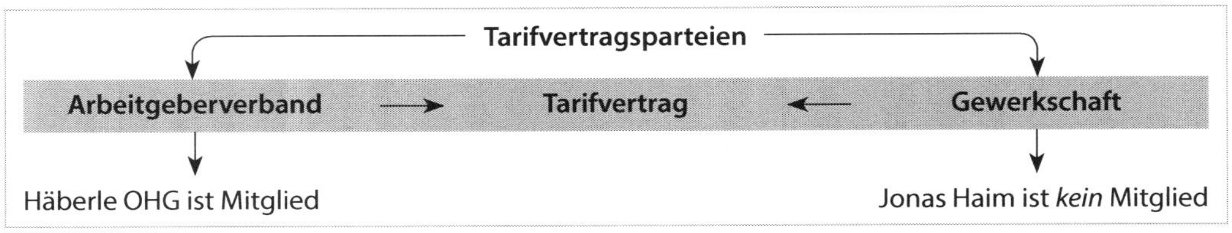

   Tarifverträge können aber nach § 5 TVG vom Bundesminister für Arbeit und Sozialordnung für allgemein verbindlich erklärt werden. In diesem Fall würde der Tarifvertrag dann auch für Haim gelten, obwohl er nicht Gewerkschaftsmitglied ist.

   In der Regel wenden die Arbeitgeber die tarifvertraglichen Regelungen jedoch auch auf Nichtmitglieder der Gewerkschaft an, um sie nicht zu einem Gewerkschaftsbeitritt zu veranlassen.

2. Zu dieser Entscheidung der Häberle OHG könnten folgende Überlegungen geführt haben:
   - Alle Beschäftigte mit jeweils vergleichbaren Tätigkeiten werden gleichbehandelt.
   - Es wird verhindert, dass Beschäftigte, die noch nicht in der Gewerkschaft sind, in die Gewerkschaft eintreten.
   - Jährlich wiederkehrende Lohnverhandlungen mit den Mitarbeitern entfallen, da die Beschäftigten gemäß den aktuellen Tariflöhnen bezahlt werden.
     → weniger Arbeit in der Personalabteilung, Kostenentlastung
   - Beschäftigte, die höhere Lohnforderungen haben, können mit dem Argument der Gleichbehandlung zurückgewiesen werden.
     → geringere Lohnkosten

   Folgende Nachteile sind dem gegenüberzustellen:
   - Leistungsstarke Beschäftigte, die über einen längeren Zeitraum keine höheren Löhne erhalten, kündigen und scheiden freiwillig aus dem Unternehmen aus.
   - Geeignete Bewerber sind erst gar nicht bereit, beim Unternehmen zu arbeiten.
   - Die Gleichbehandlung übt auf die Beschäftigten geringe Leistungsanreize aus. Eine insgesamt gering motivierte Belegschaft gefährdet auf längere Sicht den Bestand des Unternehmens.

3. Die Regelungen des Tarifvertrags gelten als Mindestarbeitsbedingungen. Abweichungen in Einzelarbeitsverträgen sind gem. § 4 Abs. 3 TVG nur zugunsten des Arbeitnehmers erlaubt. Dieser Grundsatz wird als „Günstigkeitsprinzip" bezeichnet.

   Haim kann deshalb auf der Grundlage des Tarifvertrags 4.000 EUR Gehalt und aus dem Einzelarbeitsvertrag 28 Tage Urlaub beanspruchen.

4. Gründe für den Eintritt in eine Gewerkschaft:
   - Solidarisches Verhalten, da er mit seinem Beitrag eine Interessenvertretung der Beschäftigten finanziell unterstützt. Der Vorwurf, als Trittbrettfahrer von den Tarifvertragsergebnissen zu profitieren, kann nicht erhoben werden.
   - Gewerkschaftsmitglieder erhalten von der Gewerkschaft bei Streik eine Unterstützung (Streikgeld).
   - Bei arbeitsrechtlichen Fragen stehen die Gewerkschaften als beratende Stelle zur Verfügung. Die Gewerkschaften informieren ihre Mitglieder über allgemeine Entwicklungen.
   - Hohe Mitgliederzahlen stärken die Position der Gewerkschaften gegenüber den Arbeitgeberverbänden.

   Gründe gegen den Eintritt in eine Gewerkschaft:
   - Die Zahlung eines monatlichen Mitgliedsbeitrags
   - Eine kritische Haltung gegenüber der Arbeit der Gewerkschaften
   - Ein bestehender Interessenskonflikt zwischen der eigenen betrieblichen Tätigkeit und den Interessen der Gewerkschaft
   - Eine hohe Zufriedenheit mit der Personalpolitik und den Arbeitsbedingungen im Unternehmen

5. Arbeitgeberverband: Geringe Lohnzuwächse ...
   - entlasten in der aktuellen wirtschaftlichen Situation die Unternehmen.
   - sichern die Wettbewerbsfähigkeit der Unternehmen und somit Arbeitsplätze.
   - geben den Unternehmen finanzielle Spielräume für erforderliche Investitionen.

   Gewerkschaft: Hohe Lohnzuwächse ...
   - gleichen die allgemeinen Preissteigerungen (Inflation) aus.
   - korrigieren die ungleiche Einkommensverteilung („von oben nach unten").
   - beteiligen die Beschäftigte angemessen an den Unternehmensgewinnen
   - sind in der guten wirtschaftlichen Lage vertretbar
   - da die Lohnerhöhungen in den letzten Jahren gering waren

6. a) Nein, ein rechtmäßiger Streik ist kein zulässiger Kündigungsgrund.
   b) Bei einem Streik ruht das Arbeitsverhältnis. Da die Mitarbeiter keine Arbeitsleistung erbringen, müssen die Unternehmen umgekehrt auch keine Vergütung zahlen.
   c) Wenn eine Beschäftigung in einem Unternehmen aufgrund des Streikes nicht möglich ist, muss das Unternehmen auch Arbeitswilligen keinen Lohn bezahlen. Arbeitswillige tragen in diesem Fall das Streikrisiko, profitieren aber auch von den Ergebnissen der Tarifverhandlungen (z. B. höhere Löhne).
   d) Nein, eine Zwangsschlichtung durch den Staat ist nicht zulässig. Gemäß Art. 9 Grundgesetz besteht Tarifautonomie, d. h. der Staat darf nicht in Tarifvertragsverhandlungen eingreifen.

7. Die vorgeschlagene Regelung ist unzulässig. Sie verstößt gegen Art. 9 Abs. 3 des Grundgesetzes, der garantiert, dass sich Arbeitnehmer zu Gewerkschaften und Arbeitgeber in Arbeitgeberverbänden frei zusammenschließen können (Koalitionsfreiheit). Die Koalitionsfreiheit schließt auch das Recht ein, sich nicht zu organisieren („negative" Koalitionsfreiheit). Niemand darf gezwungen werden, einer Gewerkschaft beizutreten. Wenn in einem Tarifvertrag vereinbart wäre, bestimmte Vergünstigungen nur den Gewerkschaftsmitgliedern zu gewähren, würde dadurch (nach herrschender Meinung der Rechtsprechung) ein unzulässiger Druck ausgeübt.

EA 2 Beiträge zur Sozialversicherung – Ausbildungsvergütung

1.

	Überweisungsbetrag	858,40 EUR	(Nettolohn)
	Sozialabgaben	211,60 EUR	
	Steuern	0,00 EUR	

2.

	Monatsgehalt brutto	1.070,00 EUR	
–	Lohnsteuer	0,00 EUR	
–	Solidaritätszuschlag	0,00 EUR	
–	Kirchensteuer	0,00 EUR	
=	Zwischensumme	1.070,00 EUR	
–	Rentenversicherung	99,51 EUR	ArbG + ArbN je 9,30 % von 1.070,00 EUR
–	Krankenversicherung	82,93 EUR	ArbG + ArbN je 7,30 % ArbG + ArbN je 0,45 %
–	Pflegeversicherung	16,32 EUR	ArbG + ArbN je 1,525 %
–	Arbeitslosenversicherung	12,84 EUR	ArbG + ArbN je 1,20 %
=	Nettogehalt	858,40 EUR	

3. Die Höhe der Ausbildungsvergütungen wird von den Tarifparteien festgelegt. Die zuständigen Arbeitgeberverbände und Gewerkschaften orientieren sich dabei an den Besonderheiten der jeweiligen Branche; z. B. Gehalts- bzw. Lohngefüge, allgemeine wirtschaftliche Entwicklung, Ausbildungssituation.

4. Sophia muss keine Steuern bezahlen, da sie bei Anrechnung von Freibeträgen mit ihrer Ausbildungsvergütung unter dem steuerfreien Existenzminium (Grundfreibetrag) liegt. Das Existenzminimum ist der Betrag, den Menschen brauchen, um den grundlegenden Lebensunterhalt bestreiten zu können.

5. Sophia kann sich nicht von der Sozialversicherung befreien lassen, da es sich dabei um eine gesetzliche Pflichtversicherung handelt. Sophia schätzt offensichtlich die Tragweite ihres Vorschlags, jedes Risiko zu übernehmen, nicht umfassend ein. Sollte sie beispielsweise nach ihrer Befreiung eine schwere Krankheit erleiden, wären ihre finanziellen Mittel vermutlich schnell aufgebraucht und sie müsste von der Fürsorge oder anderen Formen der staatlichen Grundsicherung unterstützt werden.

   Die Sozialversicherung deckt nach dem Solidaritätsprinzip („Einer für alle, alle für einen.") Lebensrisiken, wie z. B. Krankheit, Unfall, Alter oder Tod eines Familienangehörigen sowie Beschäftigungsrisiken, wie z. B. Arbeitslosigkeit oder Arbeitsunfall ab. Grundgedanke der gesetzlichen Sozialversicherung ist, Beschäftigte, die nicht in der Lage, sind besondere finanzielle Notlagen aus eigener Kraft zu bewältigen, eine Vorsorge durch eine staatliche Pflichtversicherung zu bieten. Aus diesem Grund besteht in allen Versicherungszweigen grundsätzlich Versicherungszwang.

zu Kapitel 2 Arbeits- und Sozialordnung

ANWENDUNGS- UND ÜBUNGSAUFGABEN

Aufgabe 1 Ablauf von Tarifverhandlungen

schülerindividuelle Textbeiträge; Beispiel für eine Schülerantwort:

Tarifverträge werden zwischen **Gewerkschaften** und **Arbeitgeberverbänden** abgeschlossen. Während dieser Zeit herrscht **Friedenspflicht**, d. h. es darf z. B. nicht gestreikt werden. Läuft ein Tarifvertrag aus oder wird der Tarifvertrag von einer der Tarifvertragsparteien **gekündigt**, finden neue Tarifverhandlungen statt. In diesen Verhandlungen muss ein Kompromiss zwischen den meist gegensätzlichen Gewerkschafts- und Arbeitgeberpositionen gefunden werden.

Einigen sich die Tarifvertragsparteien nicht, wird ein Schlichtungsverfahren eingeleitet. Scheitert auch das **Schlichtungsverfahren**, kann es zum **Streik** kommen, bei dem gewerkschaftlich organisierte Arbeitnehmer ihre Arbeit gemeinsam und planmäßig niederlegen. Voraussetzung für einen Streik ist, dass 75 Prozent der betroffenen Gewerkschaftsmitglieder im Rahmen einer **Urabstimmung** für Streik stimmen. Die Arbeitgeber können mit **Aussperrung** reagieren, d. h. sie verweigern allen Arbeitnehmern des Unternehmens die Möglichkeit zu arbeiten. Nach den **Arbeitskampf**maßnahmen kommt es zu weiteren Tarifverhandlungen bis ein neuer Tarifvertrag abgeschlossen wird. Der Streik wird beendet, wenn in einer weiteren Urabstimmung mindestens 25 Prozent der betroffenen Gewerkschaftsmitglieder dem Verhandlungsergebnis zustimmen.

Die aus Art. 9 Grundgesetz abgeleitete **Tarifautonomie** bedeutet, dass der Staat nicht in die Tarifvertragsverhandlungen der Gewerkschaften und Arbeitgeberverbände eingreifen darf.

Aufgabe 2 Artikel zur aktuellen Entwicklung von Tarifverträgen

1. Die acht Mitgliedsgewerkschaften des Deutschen Gewerkschaftsbundes verhandeln mit den Arbeitgebern über tarifpolitische Verbesserungen und vertreten ihre Mitglieder in den Betrieben.

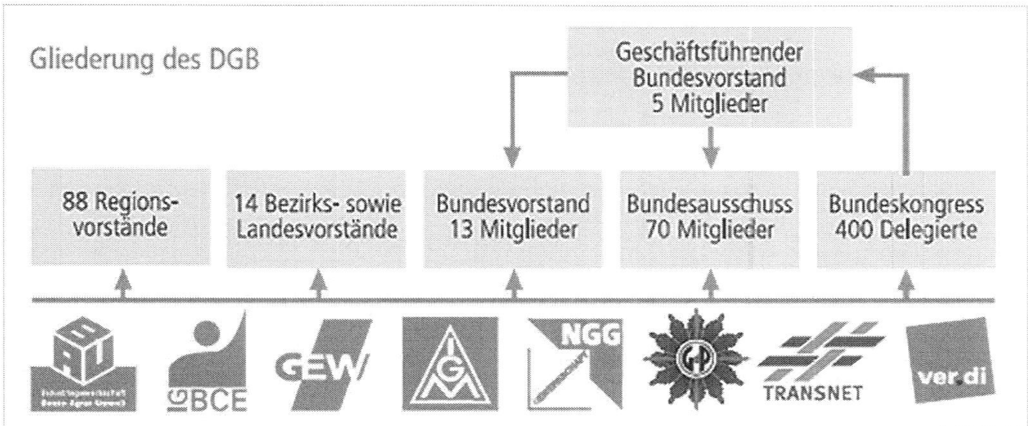

Die Mitgliedsgewerkschaften gewähren ihren Mitgliedern Rechtsschutz bei arbeits- und sozialrechtlichen Streitigkeiten. Sie unterstützen ihre organisierten Mitglieder bei Streik, Aussperrung und Maßregelung, bieten Qualifizierung und Weiterbildung, beraten und unterstützen. Zum Beispiel bei arbeitsvertraglichen Fragen, zum Beispiel bei Betriebsratswahlen.

Quelle: https://www.dgb.de/uber-uns; Abruf: 03.06.2020

2. Bei Tarifverträgen sind die beiden Voraussetzungen für öffentliche Güter gegeben: ① **Nicht-Ausschließbarkeit:** Jeder Beschäftigte kann unabhängig von einer Mitgliedschaft in einer Gewerkschaft von Tarifverträgen profitieren, wenn die Unternehmen den Tarifvertrag freiwillig für alle Beschäftigte anwenden oder wenn der Tarifvertrag für allgemeinverbindlich erklärt wird. ② **Nicht-Konsumrivalität:** Alle Beschäftigten profitieren gleichzeitig von den Regelungen in den Tarifverträgen. Hieraus lässt sich auch das „Trittbrettfahrerproblem" ableiten, d.h. eine Leistung nutzen, ohne selbst eine Gegenleistung zu erbringen.

3. Die Arbeitgeber drücken sich aus unterschiedlichen Gründen vor neuen Tarifverträgen:
   - Einsparung von Personalkosten; eher „Wettbewerb über Lohndumping"
   - Unabhängige, flexible Gestaltung der arbeitsrechtlichen Regelungen; z.B. Arbeitszeit, Vorruhestandsregelung, Tariflöhne.
   - Vermeidung von „schädlichen" Arbeitskampfmaßnahmen (Streik, Aussperrung)
   - Abnehmende Mitgliederzahlen der Gewerkschaften: z.B. Beschäftigte sind nicht bereit, Mitgliedsbeiträge für Gewerkschaften zu bezahlen; Beschäftigte schätzen die Arbeit der Gewerkschaften als weniger wichtig ein.

     → Die Gewerkschaften verlieren an Bedeutung.

4. - Arbeitgeber sollten stärker über die Vorteilhaftigkeit von Tarifverträgen informiert werden. Siehe Text „Mehr Tarifverträge braucht das Land": Sichert den sozialen Frieden, erleichtert Suche nach Fachkräften.
   - Notwendigkeit von Tarifverträgen in der Öffentlichkeit deutlich machen
   - geleistete Arbeit der Gewerkschaften stärker ins Bewusstsein rufen
   - Mitgliedsbeiträge senken, um Mitgliederzahl zu erhöhen

Aufgabe 3 Rechte des Betriebsrates

a) Es handelt sich um eine *soziale* Angelegenheit, da dies alle Beschäftigte betrifft.
Gemäß § 87 (1), Nr. 1 BetrVG hat der Betriebsrat Mitbestimmungsrechte.
Die Betriebsleitung benötigt die Zustimmung des Betriebsrates.

b) Es handelt sich um eine *personelle Angelegenheit,* da dies nur einen Beschäftigten betrifft.
Gemäß § 102 (1) BetrVG hat der Betriebsrat Mitbestimmungsrechte. Die Personalabteilung muss den Betriebsrat die Gründe für die Kündigung mitteilen und hat den Betriebsrat zu hören.

c) Es handelt sich um eine *wirtschaftliche Angelegenheit.* Die Maßnahme wird in § 106 (3) BetrVG aufgeführt. Wenn das Unternehmen mehr als einhundert Arbeitnehmer beschäftigt, ist ein Wirtschaftsausschuss zu bilden. Gemäß § 106 (3), Nr. 7 BetrVG hat der Wirtschaftsausschuss Informationsrechte. Die Geschäftsleitung muss den Wirtschaftsausschuss rechtzeitig und umfassend unterrichten.

d) Es handelt sich um eine *personelle Angelegenheit,* da dies nur einen Beschäftigten betrifft.
Gemäß § 99 (1) BetrVG hat der Betriebsrat bei personellen Einzelmaßnahmen ein Mitbestimmungsrecht. Die Personalabteilung muss den Betriebsrat unterrichten; der Betriebsrat kann seine Zustimmung unter bestimmten Voraussetzungen verweigern.

e) Es handelt sich um eine *soziale Angelegenheit,* da dies alle Beschäftigte betrifft.
Gemäß § 87 (1), Nr. 6 BetrVG hat der Betriebsrat Mitbestimmungsrechte.
Die Geschäftsleitung benötigt die Zustimmung des Betriebsrates.

f) Es handelt sich gemäß § 106 (3), Nr. 3 BetrVG um eine *wirtschaftliche Angelegenheit*. Der zu bildende Wirtschaftsausschuss hat Informationsrechte. Der Verkaufsleiter muss den Wirtschaftsausschuss rechtzeitig und umfassend unterrichten.

Aufgabe 4 Teste dein Wissen zur Sozialpolitik!

Schülerindividuelles Arbeiten

Aufgabe 5 Grafik zum Sozialen Netz

1. Das soziale Netz beinhaltet sehr viele Sozialleistungen. Diese werden den Bürgerinnen und Bürgern in bestimmten Lebenssituationen und unter bestimmten Voraussetzungen gewährt. Das Bild „Netz" soll zum Ausdruck bringen, dass jeder bei Bedürftigkeit durch eine dafür vorgesehene staatliche Leistung aufgefangen wird, also nicht durch die Maschen des engen Netzes fällt.

2.

Rentenversicherung	330,2 Mrd. EUR
Krankenversicherung	250,1 Mrd. EUR
Arbeitslosenversicherung	28,2 Mrd. EUR
Gesetzliche Pflegeversicherung	42,4 Mrd. EUR
Unfallversicherung	14,2 Mrd. EUR
Gesetzliche Sozialversicherung	665,1 Mrd. EUR

3. **Wohngeld** ist ein staatlicher Zuschuss zur Miete, der vielen Bürgerinnen und Bürgern mit geringem Einkommen hilft, die Wohnkosten für angemessenen und familiengerechten Wohnraum zu tragen. In Deutschland bezogen im Dezember 2019 ca. 600.000 Haushalte Wohngeld (destatis).

   Informationen zum Wohngeld: Bundesministerium des Innern, für Bau und Heimat (inkl. Broschüre im Downloadbereich)

   Die **Ausbildungsförderung** ist ein staatlicher Zuschuss, der es Jugendlichen und jungen Erwachsenen ermöglicht, eine ihrer Eignung und Neigung entsprechende Ausbildung zu absolvieren. Schüler*Innen müssen den Zuschuss nicht zurückzahlen. Studierende müssen nur die Hälfte des BAföG-Geldes zurückzahlen, die andere Hälfte schenkt ihnen der Staat. Für die Rückzahlung des zinslosen Darlehens gibt es Regelungen, die die individuelle berufliche und finanzielle Situation berücksichtigen. Im Jahr 2018 erhielten in Deutschland 727.000 Personen Leistungen nach dem Bundesausbildungsförderungsgesetz (destatis).

   Informationen zur Ausbildungsförderung: Bundesministerium für Bildung und Forschung (inkl. Broschüre im Downloadbereich)

   Elterngeld schafft einen finanziellen Ausgleich, falls die Eltern weniger Einkommen haben, weil sie nach der Geburt zeitweise weniger oder gar nicht mehr arbeiten. Dadurch hilft das Elterngeld, die finanzielle Lebensgrundlage der Familien zu sichern. Elterngeld gibt es auch für Eltern, die vor der Geburt gar kein Einkommen hatten. Im Jahr 2018 haben 1,4 Millionen Mütter und 433.000 Väter Elterngeld bezogen (destatis).

   Informationen zum Erziehungs- und Elterngeld: Bundesministerium für Familie, Senioren, Frauen und Jugend (inkl. Broschüre im Downloadbereich)

   Wohngeld, Ausbildungsförderung und Elterngeld helfen zeitlich befristet über 3 Millionen Bürgerinnen und Bürger in bestimmten Lebenssituationen. Die Gewährung dieser Sozialleistungen entspricht dem Leitbild der Sozialen Marktwirtschaft.

4. Beim **Versicherungsprinzip** werden im Rahmen der gesetzlichen Sozialversicherung staatliche Leistungen den Mitgliedern einer Solidargemeinschaft gewährt; z. B. Renten- und Arbeitslosenversicherung. Die Finanzierung der Versicherungsleistungen wird von den Versicherten selbst übernommen, die meist monatlich Beiträge in einen gemeinsamen Topf einzahlen. Beim Versicherungsprinzip findet innerhalb den Mitgliedern, die von gleichartigen Gefahren (z. B. Krankheit) bedroht sind, ein Risikoausgleich statt.

   Beim **Fürsorgeprinzip** werden staatliche Leistungen Menschen in individuellen Notlagen gewährt; z. B. bei Arbeitslosengeld II, Sozialhilfe und Wohngeld. Die Finanzierung der Fürsorgeleistungen wird von der Allgemeinheit übernommen, also z. B. Steuerzahlungen der Bürger*Innen. Nach dem Fürsorgeprinzip werden Menschen, welche keine Möglichkeit haben sich selbst zu helfen, unterstützt; im Gegensatz zum Versicherungsprinzip setzt das Fürsorgeprinzip keine Gegenleistungen voraus.

5. schülerindividuelle Antworten

zu Kapitel 3 Leistungserstellung und Leistungsverwendung in der Bundesrepublik Deutschland

ERARBEITUNGSAUFGABEN

EA 1 Grafische Darstellung des Wirtschaftskreislaufs

1.

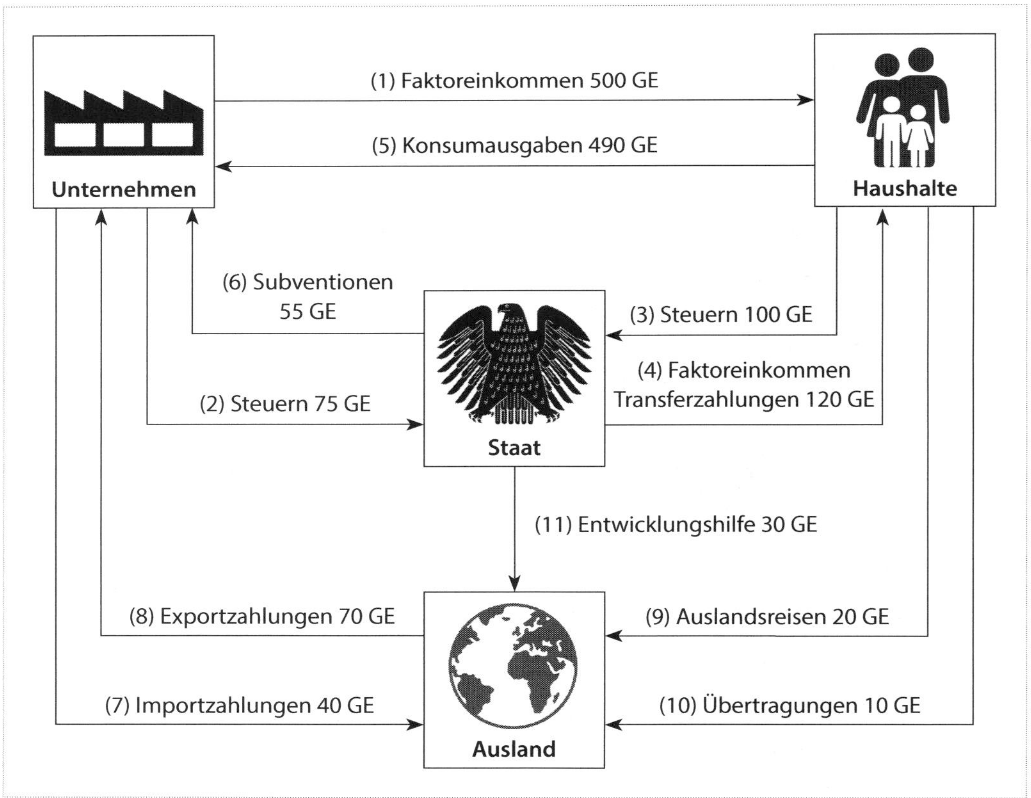

EA 2 Messgrößen der volkswirtschaftlichen Gesamtrechnung

1.

Brutto-Wertschöpfung		Rang	Erläuterung
Landwirt	**10.000 €**	③	Wertschöpfung berücksichtigt die Vorleistungen → *Geeigneter Vergleich*
Mühle	**14.000 €**	②	
Bäckerei	**16.000 €**	①	

Netto-Wertschöpfung		Rang	Erläuterung
Landwirt	**7.000 €**	③	zusätzlich wird auch der Werteverlust (= Abschreibungen) berücksichtigt → *Geeigneter Vergleich*
Mühle	**13.000 €**	①	
Bäckerei	**10.000 €**	②	

Hinweis: Alternativ könnte auch die Brutto-Wertschöpfung je Mitarbeiter zugrunde gelegt werden. Üblicherweise wird die Brutto-Wertschöpfung verwendet, da es auch eine Leistung der Unternehmen darstellt, den Werteverzehr auszugleichen.

2. Δ BIP = 40.000 € → Verwendungsrechnung

oder

Δ BIP = 10.000 € + 14.000 € + 16.000 € = 40.000 € → Entstehungsrechnung *(Summe der Bruttowertschöpfung)*

Δ Volkseinkommen = 7.000 € + 13.000 € + 10.000 € = 30.000 € → Verteilungsrechnung

Fachlicher Hinweis: Bruttoinlandsprodukt und Volkseinkommen stimmen nicht überein, da die verrechneten Abschreibungen in Höhe von 10.000 € die Gewinne der Unternehmerhaushalte verringern, also wie eine Ausschüttungssperre wirken.

zu Kapitel 3 Leistungserstellung und Leistungsverwendung in der Bundesrepublik Deutschland

ANWENDUNGS- UND ÜBUNGSAUFGABEN

Aufgabe 1 Bedeutung der Wirtschaftssektoren

Ausgewählte Geldströme

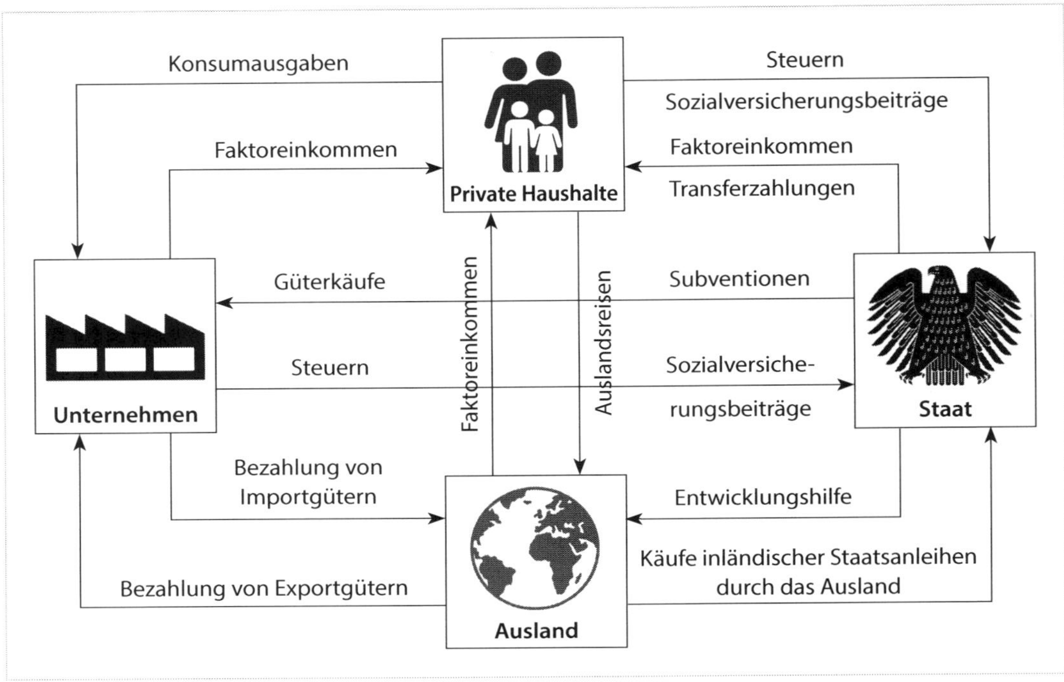

Unternehmen produzieren Güter und schaffen Arbeitsplätze für die privaten Haushalte. Sie gelten als Motor der Wirtschaft, weil sie mit ihren Innovationen entscheidend sind für Wachstum und Wohlstand und mit ihren Investitionen die internationale Wettbewerbsfähigkeit von Deutschland prägen.

Private Haushalte haben aufgrund ihrer Beteiligung an den Produktionsprozessen in den Unternehmen sowie ihres Konsums eine sehr hohe Bedeutung für die deutsche Wirtschaft.

Das **Ausland** hat aufgrund der hohen Exporte und Importe eine sehr große Bedeutung für die deutsche Volkswirtschaft

Dem **Staat** kommt in einer Volkswirtschaft eine besondere Rolle zu, da er das Wirtschaftsgeschehen aufgrund seiner Einnahmen- und Ausgabenpolitik maßgeblich beeinflussen kann.

Zusammenfassend lässt sich feststellen, dass alle vier Wirtschaftssektoren einen bedeutsamen Anteil an der Leistungserstellung und der Leistungsverwendung haben; alle vier Sektoren sind „Geber" und „Nehmer". Sollte auch nur ein Sektor „ausfallen", hätte dies negative Folgen für das gesamte Wirtschaftssystem.

Aufgabe 2 Bruttoinlandsprodukt und gesamtwirtschaftliches Produktionskonto

Gesamtwirtschaftliches Produktionskonto

Abschreibungen	700	Bruttoinvestitionen	1.200
Produktionsabgaben – Subventionen	300	Privater Konsum	3.000
Löhne, Gehälter	2.900	Staatlicher Konsum	1.000
Pachten, Zinsen	600	Außenbeitrag (Export – Import)	400
Gewinne	1.100		
Summe	5.600	Summe	5.600

→ Bruttoinlandsprodukt = **5.600**

Aufgabe 3 Entstehungs-, Verwendungs- und Verteilungsrechnung

1./ 2.

③ Pachten, Zinsen und Gewinne	=	4.600 – 2.900 = 1.700	→ 1,7 Mio. €
④ Bruttoinlandsprodukt	=	4.600 + 300 + 700 = 5.600	→ 5,6 Mio. €
① Produzierendes Gewerbe	=	5.600 – (200 + 800 + 1.100 + 600 + 500 + 600 + 300)	
	=	1.500	→ 1,5 Mio. €
② Außenbeitrag	=	5.600 – (3.000 + 1.000 + 1.200)	→ 0,4 Mio. €
	=	400	
Lohnquote	=	(2.900 / 4.600) · 100	= 51,8 %

51,5 % des Volkseinkommens wurde an die Arbeitnehmer in Form von Löhnen und Gehältern (= Arbeitnehmerentgelt) ausbezahlt.

Aufgabe 4 Lohn- und Gewinnquote

2015		
	Löhne/Gehälter	Unternehmens-/ Vermögens-einkommen
	50.000	5.000 60.000 5.000
Summe	50.000	70.000
Summe	120.000	
in %	**41,7**	**58,3**
	Lohnquote	**Gewinnquote**

2020		
	Löhne/Gehälter	Unternehmens-/ Vermögens-einkommen
	58.000	18.000 3.000 70.000 1.000
Summe	58.000	92.000
Summe	150.000	
in %	**38,7**	**61,3**
	Lohnquote	**Gewinnquote**

Die Lohnquote hat sich verringert. Da Rune Einkommen aus unselbstständiger Tätigkeit bezieht, könnte dies auf eine Verschlechterung hinweisen. Allerdings hat sich sein Buchhaltergehalt erhöht, zudem erzielt er Vermögenseinkommen. Die Einkommenssituation von Rune hat sich nicht verschlechtert.

Aufgabe 5 Nominales und reales Bruttoinlandsprodukt

1. ① = (1.200 – 1.150) / 1.150 · 100 = 4,3 %
   ② = (1.200 / 115) · 100 = 1.043,5 Mrd. EUR
   ③ = (1.043,5 / 1.000) · 100 = 104,3
   ④ = (1.043,5 – 1.008,8) / 1.008,8 · 100 = 3,4 %
   ⑤ = (1.150 / 1.008,8) · 100 = 114,0

Jahr	Nominales BIP in jeweiligen Preisen		Reales BIP in Preisen des Jahres 1			Preisindex (Deflator)
	Mrd. EUR	Veränderung in %	Mrd. EUR	Indexzahl	Veränderung in %	
1	1.000,0	–	1.000,0	100,0	–	100,0
2	1.050,0	5,0	1.009,6	101,0	1,0	104,0
3	1.100,0	4,8	1.000,0	100,0	– 1,0	110,0
4	1.150,0	4,5	1.008,9	100,9	0,9	**114,0**
5	1.200,0	**4,3**	**1.043,5**	**104,3**	**3,4**	115,0

2. Unter der Voraussetzung, dass die Volkswirtschaft möglichst stark wachsen soll, war Jahr 5 das beste Jahr. In diesem Jahr ist die Wirtschaft real – also preisbereinigt – um 3,4 % gewachsen. Jahr 3 war das schlechteste Jahr, weil das reale BIP um 1,0 % geschrumpft ist.

Aufgabe 6 Bruttoinlandsprodukt als Wohlstandsindikator (I)

Pro-Argumente	Kontra-Argumente
▪ je mehr Güter hergestellt werden , desto mehr Güter können der Bevölkerung zugeteilt werden. ▪ materieller Wohlstand ist eine bedeutende Grundlage für die Zufriedenheit der Bevölkerung. ▪ es gibt keinen besseren Indikator, um die wirtschaftliche Leistung eines Landes auszudrücken. (Produktionsindikator)	▪ materieller Wohlstand ist allein nicht ausschlaggebend für die Zufriedenheit der Bevölkerung. ▪ es gibt viele „weiche" Glücksfaktoren, die berücksichtigt werden müssen. ▪ die Ermittlung des Bruttoinlandsprodukts ist mit Erfassungs-, Bewertungs- und Zurechnungsproblemen verbunden. ▪ das BIP ist als Größe höchst problematisch; erfasst nur zahlenmäßig, welche Güter hergestellt wurden.

Didaktische Hinweise: Die Diskussion könnte mit folgendem Text eröffnet werden:

„**Ein gigantischer Filter** – Die größte Schwäche des BIP ist zugleich seine größte Stärke: Wie ein gigantischer Filter fasst es Unmengen von Daten über den Wert von Waren und Dienstleistungen zu einer einzigen Zahl zusammen, welche die Wirtschaftskraft eines Landes misst. Das Verfahren zur Berechnung, die sogenannte Volkswirtschaftliche Gesamtrechnung, ist international standardisiert, so dass die Werte einzelner Länder gut miteinander verglichen werden können. Weil das BIP so stark vereinfacht, kann es aber viele Entwicklungen nicht abbilden. Negative Einflüsse wie Umweltverschmutzung werden ebenso wenig berücksichtigt wie unbezahlte Leistungen, etwa Hausarbeit. Die Suche nach BIP Alternativen läuft deshalb schon länger."

http://www.spiegel.de/wirtschaft/soziales/wie-misst-man-wohlstand-kritik-am-bruttoinlandsproduktbip-a-824877.html

Aufgabe 7 Bruttoinlandsprodukt als Wohlstandsindikator (II)

Fall	Wird der Vorgang im BIP berücksichtigt?	Müsste das BIP korrigiert werden?	Bemerkungen
a)	Ja, Fahrradverkauf wird in der amtlichen Statistik erfasst.	Nein	Zählt zum Konsum der privaten Haushalte.
b)	„Werbeprospekt“: Ja (wenn angemeldete Tätigkeit) „Nachhilfeeinnahmen“: Nein	Nein Ja, Erhöhung	Personalkosten (Volkseinkommen) finden in den Güterpreisen entsprechende Berücksichtigung. Dies wird gewöhnlich nicht in der amtlichen Statistik erfasst.
c)	Nein	Ja, Erhöhung	Freiwillige Tätigkeit erhöht den Wohlstand.
d)	Ja, im Falle der Arztkosten und der Fahrradreparatur. Nein, im Falle der Krankheit.	Ja, Kürzung Ja, Kürzung	Beseitigung des Unfallschadens stellt keine Wohlstandsmehrung dar.
e)	Ja	Nein	Unterricht wird als staatlicher Konsum erfasst.
f)	Nein	Ja, Kürzung	Luftverschmutzung verringert den Wohlstand
g)	Nein	Ja, Erhöhung	Freizeitaktivitäten wie „Waldspaziergänge“ erhöhen den Wohlstand.

Aufgabe 8 Alternative Wohlstandsindikatoren

Schülerindividuelle Antworten

Alternative Wohlstandsindikatoren – Gesamtüberblick

http://www.laenderdaten.de/glossar/wohlstandsindikatoren.aspx

Ein Wohlstandsindikator ist ein Maß für den Wohlstand eines Landes. Weil das BIP so stark vereinfacht, kann es viele Entwicklungen nicht abbilden.

Kritik am Bruttoinlandsprodukt → Alternative Ansätze zur Wohlstandsmessung

Bruttonationaleinkommen	Gesamtes Einkommen, das von der Bevölkerung eines Landes oder Gebietes in einem bestimmten Zeitraum erzielt wurde.
Pro-Kopf-Einkommen	Ergibt sich aus dem Volkseinkommen dividiert durch die Bevölkerungszahl und gibt das Einkommen wieder, das eine einzelne Person durchschnittlich in einem bestimmten Zeitraum erzielt.

Es handelt sich um Durchschnittsgrößen (quantitativ); keine Aussagen über die Einkommensverteilung

↓

Human Development Index deutsch: „Index für humane Entwicklung“	Ansatz mit umfassenderen Kriterien. Neben dem BIP pro Kopf, ausgedrückt in Kaufkraftparität, werden auch die Lebenserwartung und der Bildungsgrad berücksichtigt.
Index of Sustainable Economic Welfare	Berücksichtigt über das BIP hinaus Faktoren wie Einkommensverteilung, unbezahlte Hausarbeit, öffentliche Ausgaben für das Gesundheitswesen, Bildung, Umweltverschmutzung, Ressourcenverbrauch und Kosten des Klimawandels.

Big-Mac-Index	Gibt an, wie lange man in einem Land oder in einer Stadt durchschnittlich arbeiten muss, um einen Big-Mac kaufen zu können.
Happy Planet Index deutsch „Index des glücklichen Planeten"	Maß für die ökologische Effizienz der Erzeugung von Zufriedenheit unter Einbeziehung von Lebenszufriedenheit, Lebenserwartung und ökologischem Fußabdruck/span.
W3-Indikatoren	Ein aus zehn Variablen bestehender Indikatorensatz der Enquete-Kommission Wachstum, Wohlstand, Lebensqualität – Wege zu nachhaltigem Wirtschaften und gesellschaftlichem Fortschritt in der Sozialen Marktwirtschaft.

Human Development Index (HDI)

- deutsch „Index für humane Entwicklung"
- **Wohlstandsindikator** der Vereinten Nationen; wird seit 1990 im jährlich erscheinenden Human Development Report Report der Vereinten Nationen veröffentlicht; wurde von dem pakistanischen Ökonomen Mahbub ul Haq entworfen.
- Messzahl für den Entwicklungsstand eines Landes; setzt sich aus drei Komponenten zusammen:

Lebenserwartung	Ausbildung	Kaufkraft
Sterbetafeln, ...	Anzahl an Schuljahren eines 25-jährigen;	Bruttonationaleinkommen pro Kopf

- Top Ten Länder (2013): Norwegen, Australien, Schweiz, Niederlande, USA, Deutschland, Neuseeland, Kanada, Singapur, Dänemark
- Kritik am HDI: *nicht berücksichtigt* werden ...
  ... soziale Verschiedenheiten und Einkommensunterschiede sowie
  ... Unterschiede zwischen Städten und ländlichen Gebieten und
  ... Fragestellungen zur Natur, wie z.B. Umweltverschmutzung

Happy Planet Index (HPI)

- deutsch „Index des glücklichen Planeten"
- **Wohlstandsindikator** der britischen Denkfabrik „new economics foundation"; wurde 2006 als Alternative zum BIP entwickelt; beinhaltet drei Komponenten:

Subjektives Wohlbefinden	Lebenserwartung	Ökologischer Fußabdruck

- Leitfrage: → *Welche Länder ermöglichen der Bevölkerung ein gutes (glückliches) Leben, ohne dabei die Natur stark zu belasten?*
- Wohlbefinden und die Lebenserwartung der Bürgerinnen und Bürger wird den Umweltbelastungen bzw. dem Ressourcenverbrauch einer Nation gegenübergestellt.
- Formel zur HPI - Berechnung: $\frac{\text{Subjektives Wohlbefinden} \cdot \text{Lebenserwartung}}{\text{Ökologischer Fußabdruck}}$
- Top Länder (2012): Botsuana, Tschad, Katar,
  Europäische Länder: Albanien (18.), Norwegen (29.), Schweiz (34.), Niederlande (67.), Deutschland (46.), Dänemark (110.)
- Kritik am HPI: Wegen der Division mit dem „ökologischen Fußabdruck" ist der HPI nicht als Indikator für den Wohlstand oder die Lebensqualität in einem Land geeignet.

zu Kapitel 4 Abgrenzung der Aufgabenbereiche von Volks- und Betriebswirtschaftslehre anhand des Wirtschaftskreislaufes

ANWENDUNGS- UND ÜBUNGSAUFGABEN

Aufgabe 4.1 Betriebswirtschaftslehre – Volkswirtschaftslehre

a) BWL und VWL (Kosten, Nachfrage, Angebot)
b) BWL (Kosten, Outsourcing)
c) VWL (Einkommensverteilung)
d) VWL (Arbeitsmarkt)
e) VWL (Außenwirtschaft)
f) BWL (Finanzierungsentscheidung)
g) VWL (Volkswirtschaftliche Gesamtrechnung)
h) BWL (Rechtsformen der Unternehmung)
i) BWL (Materialwirtschaft)
j) VWL (Wirtschaftsordnung)

Lernbereich C
Rechtliche Grundlagen des Handelns privater Haushalte

zu Kapitel 1 Rechtliche Grundlagen

zu Kapitel 1.1 Rechtsfähigkeit

ERARBEITUNGSAUFGABE

EA 1 Rechtsfähigkeit von Personen

1. Ja. Ellen Beral erlangt als **natürliche Person** gem. § 1 BGB mit ihrer Geburt die Rechtsfähigkeit. Demnach kann sie auch Eigentümerin des Sparbuches sein. Sie ist aber nicht geschäftsfähig und ist daher im rechtlichen Sinne nicht handlungsfähig.
2. Ein Verein erlangt als **juristische Perso**n seine Rechtsfähigkeit mit der Eintragung ins Vereinsregister. Der Rosenheimer Schäferhundeverein e.V. kann damit als Eigentümer in einem Sparbuch eingetragen werden.
3. Eine GmbH ist eine juristische Person (§ 13 GmbHG). Da eine juristische Person eine eigene Rechtspersönlichkeit besitzt, kann sie auch verklagt werden. Somit kann Frau Mieth den Baumarkt auf Schmerzensgeld verklagen.

zu Kapitel 1.1 Rechtsfähigkeit

ANWENDUNGS- UND ÜBUNGSAUFGABEN

Aufgabe 1 Rechtsfähigkeit von Personen und Institutionen

1., 2., 5., 7.
Anmerkung: Eine OHG ist eine rechtsfähige Personengesellschaft (§ 14 (1) BGB), aber keine juristische Person.

Aufgabe 2 Rechtsfähigkeit eines ungeborenen Kindes – Internetrecherche

Nach der Definition des § 1 BGB ist die Aussage zutreffend. Dennoch wird ein ungeborenes Kind durch eine Reihe von Sondervorschriften geschützt:

Das ungeborene Kind
- ist erbfähig (§ 1923 (2) BGB)
- kann durch einen Vertrag zu Gunsten Dritter begünstigt werden (§ 331 (2) BGB)
- steht unter dem Schutz der Verfassung (vgl. Abtreibungsproblematik)

Ergebnis: Die Rechtsordnung erkennt dem ungeborenen Kind damit eine beschränkte Rechtsfähigkeit zu.

Aufgabe 3 Wirksamkeit eines Testaments

in den Fällen 1., 2., 3., 4. und 6. ist eine Vererbung möglich, da Rechtsfähigkeit vorliegt.

Hinweis: Grundsätzlich beginnt die Rechtsfähigkeit nach § 1 BGB mit der Vollendung der Geburt. Für das Erbrecht ist aber die Rechtsfähigkeit gem. § 1923 (2) BGB vorverlagert: Wer zum Zeitpunkt des Erbfalls zwar noch nicht geboren, aber bereits gezeugt worden ist, gilt als vor dem Erbfall geboren.

zu Kapitel 1.2 Geschäftsfähigkeit

ANWENDUNGS- UND ÜBUNGSAUFGABEN

Aufgabe 1 Verträge mit geschäftsunfähigen und beschränkt geschäftsfähigen Personen

1. und 2.

	Stufe der Geschäftsfähigkeit	zu 1. Schenkungsvertrag	zu 2. Kaufvertrag
Peter	geschäftsunfähig (§ 104 BGB)	ungültig, da ein Geschäftsunfähiger keine rechtswirksame Willenserklärung abgeben kann (§ 105 (1) BGB)	nichtig
Paul	beschränkt geschäftsfähig (§ 106 BGB)	Gültig, da rechtlicher Vorteil eines Minderjährigen (§ 107 BGB)	Großmutter hat zwar Mittel zur freien Verfügung gestellt, Eltern stimmen aber dem Kauf nicht zu; Zunächst: schwebend unwirksam; da Eltern nicht genehmigen: von Anfang an unwirksam
Bernd	geschäftsfähig	Gültig, da voll geschäftsfähig	Von Anfang an wirksam

Aufgabe 2 Kaufvertrag mit einem Auszubildenden

1. Der Abschluss eines Ratenkaufs ist für einen beschränkt Geschäftsfähigen nicht möglich. Der „Taschengeldparagraf" geht davon aus, dass die zu erbringende Leistung aus „überlassenen Mitteln" bewirkt wird und nicht aus zukünftigen. Ein Ratenkauf stellt eine Kreditgewährung des Verkäufers dar. Beschränkt geschäftsfähige Minderjährige bedürfen zum Abschluss von Kreditverträgen der Zustimmung des gesetzlichen Vertreters (Eltern, Vormund). Die Zustimmung des Familiengerichts ist bei Ratenzahlungskäufen nicht erforderlich. Der Vater kann die Herausgabe des Smartphones zu Recht verlangen.
2. Der Vertrag wäre gültig. Der Vater könnte die Herausgabe nicht verlangen. Hier wäre die Bestimmung des „Taschengeldparagrafen" erfüllt, denn
   - die Mittel waren zur freien Verfügung überlassen und
   - die vertragsmäßige Leistung ist mit der Zahlung „bewirkt".

Aufgabe 3 Arbeitsvertrag mit einem Schüler

1. Oscar Klein erlangt lediglich **einen wirtschaftlichen Vorteil** jedoch keinen rechtlichen, da er aus dem Arbeitsverhältnis Pflichten übernehmen würde. Der Vertrag ist demnach zunächst **schwebend unwirksam**.
2. Nein, weil die Einwilligung bereits vorliegt.

3. Zahlungsdienstleisterrahmenvertrag (Girovertrag) ist gültig, da der Minderjährige zur Eingehung des Arbeitsverhältnisses vom gesetzlichen Vertreter ermächtigt war; Kontoeröffnung ist eine Nebenpflicht aus dem Arbeitsverhältnis und daher ohne Zustimmung des gesetzlichen Vertreters möglich (§ 113 (1) S. 1 BGB).
   anders: bei Ausbildungsvertrag, da Ausbildungsvertrag kein Arbeitsvertrag

Aufgabe 4 Rechtshandlungen eines 5-jährigen Kindes

Beim Kauf des Rasierwassers handelt das 5-jährige Kind als Bote. Deshalb ist der Kaufvertrag zwischen der Drogerie und Herrn Broßmer zustande gekommen. Der Kauf des Müsli-Riegels ist hingegen nicht gültig, weil der geschäftsunfähige Lennox keine rechtswirksame Willenserklärung abgeben kann. Deshalb kann Herr Broßmer gegen Rückgabe der Ware, falls diese noch nicht verzehrt wurde (andernfalls auch ohne Rückgabe) den Kaufpreis (1 EUR) zurückverlangen.

Hinweis: Da beide (Verkäufer und Käufer) Leistungen ohne Rechtsgrund (gültiger Kaufvertrag) erlangt haben, handelt es sich um eine ungerechtfertigte Bereicherung (§ 812 (1) BGB).

Aufgabe 5 Rechtsgeschäfte mit Taschengeld und Losgewinn

1. Ja. Florian ist beschränkt geschäftsfähig (16 Jahre), dennoch ist der Vertrag gültig, weil er von Florian Bachmann mit Mitteln bewirkt wurde, die ihm der gesetzliche Vertreter zu diesem Zweck überlassen hat (§ 110 BGB).
2. Ja. Florian Bachmann darf über Vermögensgegenstände, die er mit Taschengeld erworben hat, weiter verfügen.
3. Nein. Florian Bachmann will den Kauf mit Mitteln tätigen, die ihm vom gesetzlichen Vertreter für den vorgesehenen Zweck nicht zur Verfügung gestellt wurden (§ 110 BGB).

Aufgabe 6 Vertragsschluss ohne Einwilligung

1. Der Kaufvertrag ist nicht zustande gekommen, weil der gesetzliche Vertreter nach Aufforderung durch den Verkäufer den Vertrag nicht innerhalb von zwei Wochen (§ 108 (2) S. 2 BGB) genehmigt hat. Da die Eltern erst nach einem Monat zugestimmt haben, gilt die Genehmigung als verweigert.
2. In diesem Fall tritt die Genehmigung des nunmehr volljährigen Jörg Kleinschmidt an die Stelle der Genehmigung des Vertreters (§ 108 (3) BGB). Der Vertrag wird daher gültig.

zu Kapitel 1.3 Willenserklärungen

ANWENDUNGS- UND ÜBUNGSAUFGABEN

Aufgabe 1 Willenserklärungen

		Willens-erklärung	Art, Begründung
1.	Ulf Seeber bietet einem Studenten auf der Straße seine Armbanduhr zum Kauf für 10 EUR an.	Ja	Mündliche Erklärung; Rechtsfolge (Kauf) soll herbeigeführt werden.
2.	Fußballspieler Mario Neumann gibt einem Fußballfan ein Autogramm.	Nein	Keine Rechtsfolge beabsichtigt.

		Willens-erklärung	Art, Begründung
3.	Helena Fässler informiert sich im Internet über den Preis des Kosmetikartikels „Reinwasch“.	Nein	Keine Rechtsfolge beabsichtigt.
4.	Volksmusikant Brohmer sagt telefonisch zu, bei einer Eröffnungsveranstaltung des Möbelhauses Kern einige Lieder zu singen (Honorar: 800 EUR).	Ja	Mündliche Erklärung; Rechtsfolge (Gesang gegen Entgelt) soll herbeigeführt werden.
5.	Zu fortgeschrittener Stunde (vgl. Fall 4) bittet eine Zuhörerin den Musiker Brohmer, mit ihr zusammen in privater Runde einige Volkslieder zu singen. Brohmer sagt zu.	Nein	Brohmer hat zwar zugesagt, er wollte sich rechtlich jedoch nicht binden (keine Bindungsabsicht).
6.	Helmut Dorsch hebt bei einer Teppichversteigerung die rechte Hand, um den Zuschlag (Gebot: 1.500 EUR) zu erhalten.	Ja	Schlüssiges Handeln: Bindungsabsicht, weil Dorsch den Teppich für 1.500 EUR ersteigern will.
7.	Kuno Käfer bestellt über das Internet das Buch „Stressfrei durchs Leben“.	Ja	Elektronische Willenserklärung; Bindungsabsicht ist gegeben.
8.	Luise Volk beabsichtigt, eine private Rentenversicherung abzuschließen. Über das Internet hat sie eine Verbindung zu einer Versicherungsgesellschaft erstellt. Über die Tastatur gibt sie nach entsprechender Aufforderung ihre persönlichen Daten ein. Daraufhin erhält sie von der Versicherungsgesellschaft ein Angebot für den Abschluss eines Rentenversicherungsvertrages.	WE Luise Volk: nein WE Vers. Gesellschaft: Ja	WE Luise Volks: Anfrage ohne Bindungsabsicht. WE Versicherungsgesellschaft: Automatisierte Willenserklärung, da Bindungsabsicht hinsichtlich des Abschlusses eines Rentenversicherungsvertrages.
9.	Der Computer eines Online-Händlers über Autozubehör schickt automatisch eine Auftragsbestätigung an Bernd Kitschke.	Ja	Computererklärung bringt Bindungsabsicht des Online-Händlers zum Ausdruck (Wille, zu liefern).

Aufgabe 2 Rechtswirksamkeit von Willenserklärungen

1. Keine Willenserklärung, da unverbindliche Anfrage
2. Willenserklärung, da Bestellung
3. Keine Willenserklärung, sondern Absichtserklärung (rechtlich unbedeutend)
4. Willenserklärung durch schlüssiges Handel; Antrag zum Abschluss eines Kaufvertrags
5. Keine Willenserklärung
6. Keine Willenserklärung (es besteht keine Bindungsabsicht; Ömer Demirci wollte sich rechtlich nicht binden; d. h. er wollte sich nicht in der Weise verpflichten, dass z. B. ein Anspruch auf Schadenersatz gegen ihn entsteht, wenn er den Termin nicht einhalten kann oder will).

zu Kapitel 1.4 Arten und Zustandekommen von Rechtsgeschäften

ANWENDUNGS- UND ÜBUNGSAUFGABEN

Aufgabe 1 Arten von Rechtsgeschäften

1. Testament: einseitiges Rechtsgeschäft; Abgabe einer einzigen, nicht empfangsbedürftigen Willenserklärung genügt

2. Kündigung: einseitiges Rechtsgeschäft; empfangsbedürftige Willenserklärung; Kündigung ist wirksam, da sie Frau Seeger am 13.05. zugegangen ist.

   Hinweis: Die Kündigung in einem Brief wird regelmäßig mit der Übergabe an den anwesenden Empfänger und bei der Übersendung dann wirksam, wenn die Erklärung in den Bereich des Empfängers gelangt ist und mit der Möglichkeit der Kenntnisnahme unter normalen Umständen gerechnet werden kann. Der Zugang kann auch unter Inanspruchnahme eines Empfangsboten erfolgen. In diesem Fall wird die Kündigungserklärung wirksam in dem Augenblick, da sie dem Empfangsboten ausgehändigt wird.

   Eine Kündigung durch Einschreibebrief mag für einen später erforderlich werdenden Nachweis empfehlenswert sein; jedoch ist diese Art der Kündigung für den Kündigenden nachteilig, wenn die Post heute einen Benachrichtigungszettel beim Empfänger hinterlässt, der Brief aber erst einen Tag später dem Empfänger von der Post ausgehändigt wird und inzwischen die Kündigungsfrist verstrichen ist. Holt der Arbeitnehmer den Brief nicht ab, ist ihm die Kündigung nicht zugegangen; musste er allerdings mit einer Kündigung rechnen, liegt eine Zugangsvereitelung vor. Ein an die Heimatanschrift gerichtetes Kündigungsschreiben geht dem in Urlaub befindlichen Arbeitnehmer grundsätzlich mit Einwurf in den Hausbriefkasten zu.

   (Vgl. Brox/Rüthers: Arbeitsrecht, 15. Auflage 2002, S. 139 f.)

3. zweiseitiges Rechtsgeschäft (Erfüllungsgeschäft), da zwei inhaltlich übereinstimmende Willenserklärungen (Einigung) über den Eigentumsübergang vorliegen; sachenrechtlicher Vertrag

4. zweiseitiges Rechtsgeschäft (einseitig verpflichtender Vertrag: Gegenleistung nicht erforderlich), da zwei inhaltlich übereinstimmende Willenserklärungen vorliegen

5. Kaufvertrag; zweiseitiges Rechtsgeschäft (Verpflichtungsgeschäft), da zwei inhaltlich übereinstimmende Willenserklärungen vorliegen.

6. zweiseitiges Rechtsgeschäft (Verpflichtungsgeschäft), da zwei inhaltlich übereinstimmende Willenserklärungen vorliegen; Erbvertrag

7. einseitiges Rechtsgeschäft durch ausdrückliche Willenserklärung (Finderlohn in Höhe von 200 EUR).

Aufgabe 2 Einseitige und mehrseitige Rechtsgeschäfte

	Einseitige Rechtsgeschäfte		Mehrseitige Rechtsgeschäfte (= Verträge)
	Empfangsbedürftige Willenserklärung	Nicht empfangsbedürftige Willenserklärung	
1. Kündigung	x		
2. Mietvertrag			x
3. Bestellung	1)		
4. Schenkungsvertrag			x
5. Testament		x	

1) Eine Bestellung (= Antrag) ist **kein** einseitiges Rechtsgeschäft, sondern soll Teil des zweiseitigen Rechtsgeschäfts „Vertrag" werden.

Aufgabe 3 Zugang eines Kündigungsschreibens

Eine Kündigung ist eine einseitige, empfangsbedürftige Willenserklärung. Durch Nichtöffnen des Briefkastens oder durch Verreisen kann der Empfang nicht umgangen werden; es reicht, wenn der Brief in den Verfügungsbereich des Empfängers gelangt.
Ergebnis: Kündigung ist rechtzeitig zugegangen (aber: Unternehmen muss den Zugang beweisen können – siehe Hinweis bei Aufgabe 1 Nr. 2).

Aufgabe 4 Verpflichtungs- und Erfüllungsgeschäft

	Verpflichtungsgeschäft	Erfüllungsgeschäft
1.	z. B. mündlich: „Ich möchte ein Brötchen kaufen". – Der Verkäufer holt ein Brötchen.	Übergabe des Brötchens Bezahlung des Kaufpreises
2.	Mündliche Vereinbarung im Geschäft	Lieferung des Sofas Begleichung der Rechnung per Überweisung
3.	Abschluss des Ausbildungsvertrages (mündlich oder schriftlich)	Ausbildungsbetrieb: u. a. ordnungsgemäß durchführen, Zahlung der vereinbarten Vergütung Auszubildende: u. a. Lernbereitschaft

zu Kapitel 1.5 Vertragsfreiheit und Vertragsbindung

ANWENDUNGS- UND ÜBUNGSAUFGABEN

Aufgabe 1 Vertragsfreiheit – Kontrahierungszwang

1. Sylvia Winterhalter ist nicht verpflichtet, mit Erwin Kramer einen Vertrag zu schließen. Sie kann selbst entscheiden, ob und mit wem sie einen Vertrag schließen will (Vertragsfreiheit i. S. v. Abschlussfreiheit).

   Außerdem handelt es sich bei dem im Aushang angebotenen Tagesessen nicht um einen Antrag im rechtlichen Sinne, sodass die Bestellung eines Gastes kein Vertragsverhältnis begründet.

2. Die Stadtwerke unterliegen dem Kontrahierungszwang, da ihnen eine öffentliche Versorgungsaufgabe zukommt. Demnach besteht unter den gegebenen Bedingungen eine Verpflichtung zum Vertragsschluss.

   Hinweis: Falls der Stadtwerke Heilbronn durch das Verhalten des Mitarbeiters Kiel ein Schaden entsteht, wäre Kiel zum Ersatz verpflichtet. Schon allein aus der Treuepflicht zu seinem Arbeitgeber ist Kiel verpflichtet, den Vertragsabschluss herbeizuführen.

3. Ja. Banken dürfen niemandem verwehren, ein Konto zu eröffnen. Auch Wohnungslose, Asylsuchende und Personen ohne Aufenthaltsstatus, die aus rechtlichen oder tatsächlichen Gründen nicht abgeschoben werden dürfen (sogenannte Geduldete), haben Anspruch darauf. Allerdings muss der Kunde geschäftsfähig sein, also mindestens 18 Jahre alt sein.

   Hinweis:
   Beim „Basiskonto" handelt es sich grundsätzlich um ein Konto auf Guthabenbasis. Der Kunde erhält in der Regel kein Recht, Schulden zu machen – also keinen Überziehungsrahmen. Inhaber eines Basiskontos erhalten – im Vergleich zu sonstigen Zahlungskonten – besonderen Schutz: Banken dürfen nur angemessene Entgelte erheben und die Kündigungsmöglichkeiten des Kreditinstituts sind deutlich eingeschränkt.

   Ein Wechsel zu einem anderen, eventuell kostengünstigeren Institut ist problemlos möglich. Das neue Finanzinstitut muss die ein- und ausgehenden Überweisungen und Lastschriften des alten Kontos übernehmen. Das gilt auch bei grenzüberschreitenden Kontowechseln. Dazu hat die bisherige der neuen Bank und dem Verbraucher unter anderem eine Liste der bestehenden und zu übertragenden Daueraufträge und Lastschriften zu übermitteln.

   Damit Kontoinhaber wissen, was das Konto kostet, müssen die Banken sowohl vor Vertragsschluss als auch während der Vertragslaufzeit über alle Gebühren transparent informieren. Den besten Überblick für Verbraucher sollen künftig Vergleichs-Webseiten geben. Und: Gibt es einmal Streit mit dem Finanzinstitut um eine Finanzanlage, ein Darlehen oder ein Konto, gibt es auch hier künftig die Möglichkeit der außergerichtlichen Streitbeilegung. Damit will die Bundesregierung dem Verbraucher zu seinem Recht verhelfen. Gerichtliche Verfahren sind eher langwierig, teuer und mühsam, was viele davon abhält, ihr Anliegen gegebenenfalls vor Gericht zu bringen.

   Ein Guthaben auf einem Jedermann-Konto ist in gleicher Weise wie auf einem anderen Konto pfändbar. Um eine Pfändung (zumindest teilweise) zu vermeiden, kann dieses wie auch jedes andere Girokonto gegebenenfalls auf ein Pfändungsschutzkonto (kurz: P-Konto) umgestellt werden. Das Pfändungsschutzkonto ist ein Guthabenkonto mit dem Zusatzvermerk „P-Konto". Weist es ein Guthaben auf, das unter dem monatlich pfändbaren Betrag gem. § 850c ZPO liegt, so kann dieses Guthaben von einem Gläubiger nicht gepfändet werden. Die Möglichkeit zur Einrichtung eines Pfändungsschutzkontos besteht seit 1. Juli 2010.

Aufgabe 2 Vertragsfreiheit

1. Bei einer Zeitungsanzeige handelt es sich um eine Anpreisung und demnach nicht um einen Antrag i. S. d. § 145 BGB; Hundehändler Binz macht einen Antrag, den Zec aber nicht annehmen muss (Vertragsfreiheit).

2. Zec muss keinen Kostenersatz leisten, da er keinerlei rechtliche Verpflichtungen übernommen hat (kein Vertragsverhältnis).

zu Kapitel 1.6 Formvorschriften

ANWENDUNGS- UND ÜBUNGSAUFGABEN

Aufgabe 1 Unterschiedliche Formvorschriften

1. Für Kündigung ist Schriftform vorgeschrieben (BGB § 623).
2. Für Eintragungen ins Vereinsregister ist öffentliche (notarielle) Beglaubigung vorgeschrieben (BGB § 77).
3. Neben dem Namen von Carola Fliehler muss das elektronische Dokument mit einer elektronischen Signatur (BGB § 126a) versehen werden (= Elektronische Form).
4. Formfreiheit (mündliche Form genügt)
5. Notarielle Beurkundung des Grundstückskaufvertrages erforderlich (BGB § 311b)

Aufgabe 2 Formvorschriften für bestimmte Rechtsgeschäfte

1. Normaler Kaufvertrag, bedarf keiner besonderen Form
2. Kaufvertrag über ein Grundstück bedarf der notariellen Beurkundung; § 311b BGB
3. Ein Schuldanerkenntnis in elektronischer Form hat keine Gültigkeit; § 781 BGB

Hintergrundinformation: Unterscheidung zwischen Rücktritt, Widerruf und Kündigung

Gestaltungserklärungen geben dem Erklärenden die Befugnis, ein Schuldverhältnis einseitig zu gestalten, d. h. es aufzuheben oder inhaltlich zu verändern.

Gestaltungserklärungen im Überblick		
Rücktritt	**Widerruf**	**Kündigung**
■ Bedeutet die **Rückgängigmachung** eines Schuldverhältnisses durch eine empfangsbedürftige Willenserklärung ■ Rücktritt verwandelt Vertrag in ein **Rückgewährschuldverhältnis** (§ 346 BGB)	■ Empfangsbedürftige Willenserklärung, durch die der Kunde (Käufer) in bestimmten Fällen das Wirksamwerden seiner Willenserklärung und damit den Vertragsschluss verhindern kann ■ Beispiel: Haustürwiderruf, Fernabsatzvertrag (§§ 312–312a BGB)	■ Empfangsbedürftige Willenserklärung, die das Schuldverhältnis für die Zukunft auflöst. ■ Im Gegensatz zum Rücktritt keine Rückabwicklung ■ Bei Dauerschuldverhältnissen tritt die Kündigung an die Stelle des Rücktritts, weil die Rückabwicklung der gegenseitigen Leistungen schwer durchführbar ist.

zu Kapitel 1.7 Eigentum und Eigentumsübertragung

ERARBEITUNGSAUFGABE

EA 1 Eigentum und Besitz eines geliehenen Buches

Lehrer/Lehrerin ist Besitzer*in, da er/sie die tatsächliche Herrschaft über das Buch hat.
Schulträger (Stadt Freiburg) ist Eigentümer.
Da Schüler bereits Besitzer des Buchs ist, erfolgt die Eigentumsübertragung durch bloße Einigung.

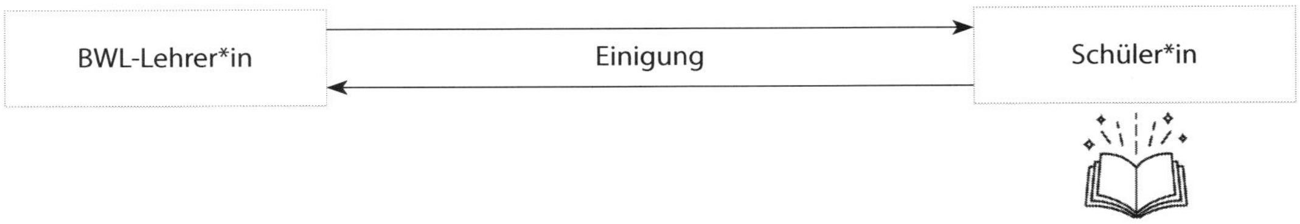

zu Kapitel 1.7 Eigentum und Eigentumsübertragung

ANWENDUNGS- UND ÜBUNGSAUFGABEN

Aufgabe 1 Eigentum und Besitz bei gestohlenen Sachen

1. Besitzer des Computers ist Franz Stoll.
   Eigentümer des Computers ist das Unternehmen.
   Begründung: bei **gestohlenen Sachen** ist gutgläubiger Eigentumserwerb nicht möglich; § 935 (1) BGB.
2. Eigentümer des Farbdruckers ist der Dieb. Begründung: Farbdrucker wurde nicht gestohlen, daher Eigentumserwerb durch Einigung und Übergabe (§ 929 (1) BGB).
3. Eigentümer des Geldes ist der Verkäufer des Farbdruckers.
   Begründung: gutgläubiger Eigentumserwerb bei gestohlenem **Geld** ist möglich; § 935 (2) BGB.

Aufgabe 2 Eigentum und Besitz bei verlorenen Sachen

1. Besitzer der Handschuhe ist Lucas Maßen, da er die tatsächliche Herrschaft über die Handschuhe hat.
2. Eigentümer der Handschuhe ist Michael Mai.
   Begründung: gutgläubiger Eigentumserwerb ist bei **verlorenen Sachen** nicht möglich; § 935 (1) BGB.
3. In beiden Fällen gibt es zwei Benachteiligte: den ursprünglichen Eigentümer sowie den „gutgläubigen Erwerber". Die Frage lautet: „Wer ist schutzbedürftiger?". Im Falle von verlorenen Sachen hat sich der Gesetzgeber für den ursprünglichen Eigentümer entschieden. Das Recht auf Privateigentum soll geschützt werden. Im Falle von verlorenem Geld kann dies nicht beibehalten werden, da ansonsten die allgemeine Rechtsunsicherheit zu groß wäre.

Hintergrundinformation

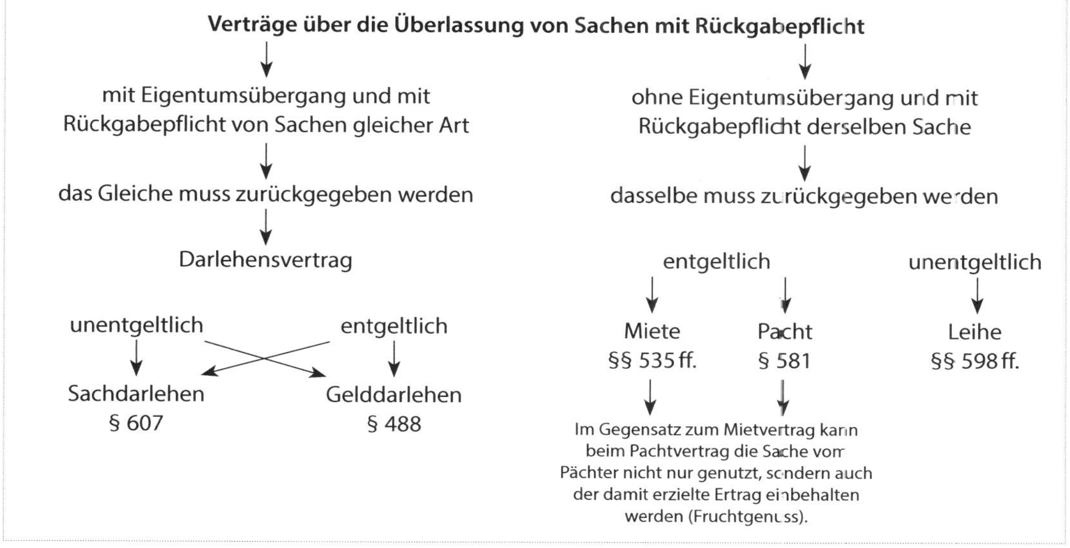

zu Kapitel 1.8 Störungen beim Abschluss des Kaufvertrages: Nichtigkeit und Anfechtbarkeit von Rechtsgeschäften und Willenserklärungen

ERARBEITUNGSAUFGABE

EA1 Zustandekommen von Verträgen – Nichtigkeit und Anfechtbarkeit

1. Sie standen zum Zeitpunkt des Vertragsabschlusses unter Schock und befanden sich somit im Zustand der Bewusstlosigkeit[1] nach § 105 (2) BGB. Ein unter dieser Bedingung geschlossener Kaufvertrag ist nichtig.
2. Hierbei handelt es sich um einen Motivirrtum. Es liegt kein gesetzlicher Anfechtungsgrund vor und somit ist der Kaufvertrag wirksam; sie müssen die 5. Auflage des Wirtschaftslexikons behalten.
3. Es liegt eine nicht ernstlich gemeinte Willenserklärung vor. Die Lehrkraft wollte lediglich einen Sachverhalt verdeutlichen und dies war unverkennbar. Der „Kaufvertrag" ist in diesem Fall nach § 118 BGB nichtig (Scherzgeschäft).
4. Bei diesem Rechtsgeschäft wird gegen ein gesetzliches Verbot verstoßen (§ 134 BGB); somit ist der Kaufvertrag nichtig.

1 Bewusstlosigkeit bedeutet nicht völliges Fehlen des Bewusstseins (dann würde gar keine Willenserklärung vorliegen). Es genügt eine hochgradige Bewusstseinstrübung, die das Erkennen von Inhalt und Wesen der Handlung ganz oder z. T. ausschließt.

zu Kapitel 1.8 Störungen beim Abschluss des Kaufvertrages: Nichtigkeit und Anfechtbarkeit von Rechtsgeschäften und Willenserklärungen

ANWENDUNGS- UND ÜBUNGSAUFGABEN

Aufgabe 1 Nichtigkeit und Anfechtbarkeit von Verträgen

Fall	Wirkung	Begründung
1.	Anfechtbar	Irrtum über wesentliche Eigenschaft einer Person nach § 119 (2) BGB
2.	Gültige Schenkung	Mirco Steiner überlässt seinem Enkel ohne ein vorhergehendes Schenkungsversprechen das Saxophon (= **Handschenkung**). Dem Beschenkten Karl-Friedrich wird also die Sache sofort übereignet (§ 516 BGB). Eine solche Handschenkung bedarf keiner besonderen Form, um gültig zu sein. Deshalb muss Mirco Steiner das Saxophon nicht mehr zurückgeben. *Hinweis: Bei der* ***Handschenkung*** *enthält der Schenkungsvertrag keinerlei Verpflichtung, sondern nur einen „nackten" Rechtsgrund. § 518 BGB ist daher auf die Handschenkung nicht anwendbar.*
3.	Nichtig Gültiger Vertrag	■ **Grundbucheintragung ist bislang nicht erfolgt:** Der Grundstückskaufvertrag ist wegen eines Formmangels (notarielle Beurkundung) **nichtig** (§ 311b i. V. m. § 125 BGB). Sara Veliç braucht nicht zu zahlen (auch nicht den geringeren Betrag von 100.000 EUR). ■ **Grundbucheintragung ist erfolgt:** Das im Vertrag vom 15. April nicht beachtete Formerfordernis (notarielle Beurkundung gem. § 311b (1) BGB) wird durch die Eintragung ins Grundbuch am 20. Mai d. J. **geheilt**. Bei dem vor dem Notar geschlossenen Vertrag (Kaufpreisvereinbarung 100.000 EUR) handelt es sich um ein Scheingeschäft (§ 117 (1) BGB), durch welches ein anderes Rechtsgeschäft (Kaufpreisvereinbarung 120.000 EUR) verdeckt wird. Gem. § 117 (2) BGB finden damit die Vorschriften über das verdeckte Rechtsgeschäft Anwendung. Der Mangel der Form (notarielle Beurkundung) des gewollten (= verdeckten) Rechtsgeschäfts wird durch die Eintragung geheilt (§ 311b (1) S. 2 BGB). Deshalb muss Sara Veliç den Betrag von 120.000 EUR bezahlen.
4.	Anfechtbar	Widerrechtliche Drohung nach § 123 (1) BGB
5.	Anfechtbar	Erklärungsirrtum, da Schreibfehler (§ 119 (1))
6.	Nichtig	Wuchergeschäft nach § 138 (2) BGB
7.	Wirksam	Wirtschaftliches Unternehmensrisiko – Motivirrtum

zu Kapitel 2 Zustandekommen und Erfüllung von Verträgen

Themenbereich: Zustandekommen eines Kaufvertrages

Durch Bestätigungsmail kommt noch kein Vertrag zustande

Die Bestätigungsmail nach einer Bestellung begründet noch keinen Vertrag, sondern dokumentiert nur den Eingang der Bestellung. Sie sagt nichts darüber aus, ob die Bestellung selbst angenommen wird – wichtig bei irrtümlichen Preisauszeichnungen.

Amtsgericht München (AZ: 281 C 27753/09)

zu Kapitel 2.1 Zustandekommen des Kaufvertrages

ERARBEITUNGSAUFGABE

EA 1 Zulässigkeit von Vereinbarungen in AGB

1. Die Allgemeinen Geschäftsbedingungen sind Vertragsbestandteil, weil ein deutlich sichtbarer Aushang am Ort des Vertragsschlusses vorhanden ist , Helena Schuler in zumutbarer Weise von den AGB Kenntnis nehmen konnte und sie sich mit dem Kauf des Mediacomputers mit den AGB einverstanden erklärt. (§ 305 (2) BGB).
2. § 6 Lehrgangsservice: Wer einen PC kauft, muss nicht damit rechnen, dass gleichzeitig ein Fort- und Weiterbildungslehrgang gebucht wird. Dies ist nach § 305c BGB eine überraschende Klausel und wird nicht Vertragsbestandteil.

   § 7 Rücktritt: Die Vereinbarung eines Rechts des Verwenders (hier: MediaPlus GmbH), ohne Angabe eines sachlichen Grundes vom Vertrag zurückzutreten, ist unwirksam (§ 308 Nr. 3 BGB). Auch diese Klausel wird nicht Vertragsbestandteil.

   § 8 Mangelansprüche: Gemäß § 309 Nr. 8 b) cc) BGB kann der Verwender im Falle einer Nacherfüllung bei Schlechtleistung den Käufer nicht verpflichten, die erforderlichen Aufwendungen, insb. Transport- und Materialkosten zu übernehmen. Diese Klausel wird nicht Vertragsbestandteil. Eine Vereinbarung, nach der die Mängelanzeige innerhalb eines Jahres erfolgen muss, ist zulässig (§ 309 Nr. 8b), ee) und ff) BGB).
3. Die Lehrgangsgebühr in Höhe von 200 EUR muss Helena Schuler nicht überweisen, diese Klausel in den AGB unzulässig und somit nicht Vertragsbestandteil geworden ist (§ 305c BGB).

zu Kapitel 2.1 Zustandekommen des Kaufvertrages

ANWENDUNGS- UND ÜBUNGSAUFGABEN

Aufgabe 1 Bindung an ein Angebot

1. Solange die Uhrenfabrik unter regelmäßigen Umständen den Eingang der Antwort erwarten durfte (E-Mail + Bearbeitungszeit), bis ca. 21.10. d. J.
2. Durch die Bestellung kommt kein Vertrag zustande, da der Antrag abgeändert angenommen wurde (= neuer Antrag – § 150 (1) BGB).
3. a) „gilt bis 19.11..." (befristetes Angebot gem. § 148 BGB)

   b) „so lange Vorrat reicht",„unverbindlich",„freibleibend" (freibleibendes Angebot gem. § 145 BGB)

Aufgabe 2 Rechtliche Bedeutung eines Inserats – Zustandekommen eines Kaufvertrages

1. Ohne rechtliche Wirkung, da nur an die Allgemeinheit gerichtet (Anpreisung).
2. Angebot von Braun = erster Antrag zum Stückpreis von 160 EUR
   Bestellung von Steiner = Ablehnung und neuer Antrag zum Stückpreis von 150 EUR
   Schweigen und Lieferung durch Braun = Annahme des Antrags zum Stückpreis von 150 EUR
3. Rechnungsbetrag = 150 EUR

Aufgabe 3 Verpflichtungen aus der Bestellung eines kostenlosen Posters

1. - Anfrage des Schülers = Antrag zu einem Schenkungsvertrag
   - Päckchen mit Rechnung = neuer Antrag zum Abschluss eines Kaufvertrages
   - Ergebnis: Es wurde kein Kaufvertrag abgeschlossen, da nicht zwei übereinstimmende Willenserklärungen vorliegen.
2. Der Berufsschüler ist nicht verpflichtet, die Ware zurückzuschicken. Er muss dem Fanbüro die unbestellte Ware lediglich zur Verfügung stellen (§ 241a (1) BGB).

Aufgabe 4 Kaufvertrag über Gartenmöbel

1. Alle im Zusammenhang mit der Auslieferung anfallenden Kosten muss das Möbelhaus Schmidt GmbH tragen, weil Lieferung frei Haus vereinbart wurde.
2. Enthält der Kaufvertrag zu den Kosten der Auslieferung keine Vereinbarungen, so muss Karl Sonne diese Kosten übernehmen (Warenschulden = Holschulden gem. § 448 BGB). Die Kosten der Übergabe (z. B. Messen, Zählen, Wiegen) trägt hingegen der Verkäufer (Möbelhaus Schmid GmbH).

   Hinweis: Falls kein Versendungsverlangen des Käufers vorliegt, der Verkäufer also ohne entsprechende Regelung eine Versendung zum Käufer am Erfüllungsort vornimmt, so muss der Verkäufer auch die entstehenden Transportkosten übernehmen. Das Verlangen muss nicht vom Käufer ausgehen. Es kann auch schon im Angebot des Verkäufers enthalten sein.

Aufgabe 5 Vereinbarung von Preiserhöhungen im Rahmen von AGB

Hinweis: Bei Geschäften des täglichen Lebens vollzieht sich der Vertragsschluss nicht bereits mit der Äußerung des Kunden, er wolle eine bestimmte Ware erwerben, sondern regelmäßig erst an der Kasse mit Bezahlung und Entgegennahme des erworbenen Gegenstandes. Mit der widerspruchslosen Entgegennahme und Bezahlung der Ware (Erfüllungsgeschäft) erklärt der Kunde sein Einverständnis mit der Geltung der AGB.

Cem Gültekin muss den erhöhten Kaufpreis nicht zahlen. Klauseln über Preiserhöhungen innerhalb von **vier Monaten** nach Vertragsschluss (kurzfristige Preiserhöhungen) sind unwirksam (§ 309 Zi. 1 BGB).

Aufgabe 6 Allgemeine Geschäftsbedingungen

1. Diese Gerichtsstandsklausel ist für einen Verbrauchsgüterkauf (= Vertrag zwischen Unternehmer und Verbraucher) unwirksam. Nach § 29 (2) ZPO kann der Gerichtsstand rechtswirksam lediglich unter Kaufleuten – nicht aber zwischen Kaufleuten und Privatleuten (Verbrauchern) – vereinbart werden.
2. Die Vereinbarung dieser Geschäftsbedingung ist zulässig (§ 357 (2) S. 3 BGB). Fehlt es an dieser Vereinbarung, so müsste der Verkäufer die Kosten der Rücksendung übernehmen (§ 357 (2) S. 2 BGB).
3. Die Verkürzung der Gewährleistungsfrist in AGBs auf einen kürzeren Zeitraum als gesetzlich vorgesehen (24 Monate bei Kaufverträgen über Neuwaren und 12 Monate bei Gebrauchtwaren zwischen gewerblichem Händler und Verbraucher) ist unzulässig und abmahnfähig (§ 475 (2) BGB).

   Hinweis: Die Frist für die Verjährung beginnt mit der Ablieferung der Sache beim Kunden und nicht mit dem Rechnungsdatum oder mit der Übergabe der Ware an die Transportperson.
4. Lösung identisch mit Lösung zu Ziffer 3
5. Diese Klausel verstößt gegen § 439 (2) BGB, wonach der Verkäufer zwingend die zum Zwecke der Nacherfüllung erforderlichen Aufwendungen, insbesondere Transport-, Wege-, Arbeits- und Materialkosten zu tragen hat. Nach § 309 8b) cc) BGB ist eine solche Klausel unwirksam.

   Hinweis: Mit der gleichen Begründung ist auch nachstehende Klausel unwirksam: „Der Käufer hat die im Falle einer Nachbesserung erforderlichen Transport- und Fahrtkosten zu tragen."
6. Eine solche Klausel ist geeignet, den Verbraucher davon abzuhalten, seine gesetzlichen Rechte geltend zu machen, falls Rechnung und Originalverpackung nicht mehr vorhanden sind (§ 307 BGB). Eine Berechtigung, die Erfüllung der Mängelhaftungsrechte von der Zusendung der Ware in Originalverpackung und unter Vorlage der Originalrechnung abhängig zu machen, besteht nicht. Eine solche Verfahrensweise kann höchstens als Bitte formuliert werden.
7. Diese Klausel stellt eine unzulässige Einschränkung des Widerrufsrechts dar, da die Forderung der Rücksendung der Ware in unversehrter Originalverpackung dem abschließenden Ausnahmekatalog des § 312d (4) BGB widerspricht und damit gegen § 307 (2) BGB verstößt (s. oben). Der Verkäufer hat aber die Möglichkeit, gegebenenfalls Wertersatz nach § 357 (3) BGB geltend zu machen.
8. Diese Vereinbarung ist zulässig. Auch ohne Aufnahme in die Allgemeinen Geschäftsbedingungen ist der Käufer verpflichtet, gegebenenfalls Wertersatz zu leisten, wenn durch die Benutzung der Sache eine Verschlechterung eingetreten ist (§ 357 (3) BGB).
9. Bei Verträgen über die Lieferung neu hergestellter Sachen sind Klauseln, durch die der Verwender die eigene Haftung ausschließt und den Kunden auf Ansprüche gegen Dritte verweist, nach § 309 Nr. 8b, aa) unwirksam.
10. Beim Verbrauchsgüterkauf geht die Gefahr für eine Beschädigung oder den Untergang der Sache gem. § 474 (2) BGB erst dann auf den Käufer über, wenn dieser tatsächlich den Besitz der gekauften Ware erlangt hat. Die Vorschrift des § 447 BGB (Gefahrenübergang beim Versendungskauf) gilt nicht im Falle des Verbrauchsgüterkaufs (Fernabsatzvertrag gilt als Verbrauchsgüterkauf, da es sich beim Käufer um einen Verbraucher handelt).

Aufgabe 7 AGB und Verbraucherinformation

Zu Nr. 7.2 und 7.3: Nach BGB gibt es keine Untersuchungs- oder Prüfpflicht. Vielmehr kann der Käufer innerhalb der zweijährigen Verjährungsfrist für Mängelansprüche (§ 438 (1) Nr. 3 BGB) jederzeit seine Rechte geltend machen. Bei Verbrauchsgüterkäufen gilt innerhalb der ersten 6 Monate die Beweislastumkehr gem. § 476 BGB. Aus Gründen der Beweissicherung sollte ein Käufer einen Mangel allerdings sobald wie möglich reklamieren.

Eine gesetzliche Untersuchungspflicht gilt gem. § 377 HGB nur für zweiseitige Handelskäufe.

zu Kapitel 2.2 Erfüllung des Kaufvertrages

ANWENDUNGS- UND ÜBUNGSAUFGABEN

Aufgabe 1 Verpflichtungs- und Erfüllungsgeschäfte

1. **Verpflichtungsgeschäft:**
   - Auslage des Kirchenführers = Angebot zum Abschluss eines Kaufvertrages an jedermann, der den vollen Kaufpreis entrichtet (= Anpreisung);
   - Entnahme und Bezahlung des Kirchenführers (konkludentes Handeln) = Annahme des Angebotes;

   Wirkung: zustande gekommener Kaufvertrag begründet die Verpflichtung des Verkäufers zur mangelfreien Übergabe und Übereignung des Kirchenführers (§ 433 (2) BGB). Kaufvertrag bewirkt nicht, dass Käufer Eigentümer der Sache und Verkäufer Eigentümer des Geldscheins wird.

   Erfüllungsgeschäft:
   - Übereignung (Einigung über den Eigentumsübergang und Übergabe) von Kirchenführer.

   Im vorliegenden Fall fallen Verpflichtungs- und Erfüllungsgeschäft zeitlich zusammen. Rechtlich sind sie jedoch zu trennen (Abstraktionsprinzip).

2. Im Fall eines Automatengeschäftes gilt folgende Regelung: In der Aufstellung eines Automaten liegt regelmäßig **ein bindendes Verkaufsangebot** des Aufstellers vor. Es ist auf den im Automaten vorhandenen Vorrat beschränkt und setzt seine Funktionsfähigkeit voraus. Die Annahme erfolgt durch den Einwurf eines gültigen Geldstücks.

Aufgabe 2 Verpflichtungen aus einem Kaufvertrag – Transport- und Verpackungskosten

1. Ja. Da eine Leistungszeit weder bestimmt noch aus den Umständen zu entnehmen ist, kann Monica Ambrosini die Leistung sofort verlangen (§ 271 (1) BGB).

2. Der Käufer (§ 448 (1) BGB). Kosten der Übergabe trägt der Verkäufer, die Kosten der Abnahme und des Versandes nach einem anderen Ort als dem Erfüllungsort trägt der Käufer.

3. Monica Ambrosini muss nicht zahlen. Bei einem Verbrauchsgüterkauf reist die Ware auf Gefahr des Verkäufers (§§ 474 (2), 447 (1) BGB).

4. Nein. Geldschulden sind **Bringschulden** (§ 270 (1) BGB). Frau Ambrosini muss dafür sorgen, dass der Gläubiger (Verkäufer) am Fälligkeitstag (11. April) über den Geldbetrag verfügen kann. Da sie aber erst an diesem Tag den Überweisungsauftrag erteilt hat, liegt eine verspätete Zahlung vor. Der Geldgläubiger könnte gegebenenfalls Verzugszinsen verlangen. Wegen der nur geringen Verzögerung wird er dies im vorliegenden Fall nicht tun.

   *Hinweis: Nach einer Entscheidung des Europäischen Gerichtshofes (EuGH – C-306/06 vom 03.04.2008) gilt die rechtzeitige Vornahme der Überweisung nicht **mehr in jedem Fall** als fristwahrend.*

   Der europäische Gerichtshof hat die EU-Zahlungsverzugsrichtlinie dahingehend ausgelegt, dass bei einer Zahlung durch Banküberweisung der geschuldete Betrag dem Konto des Gläubigers rechtzeitig gutgeschrieben sein muss, wenn das Entstehen von Verzugszinsen vermieden werden soll. Das EuGH-Urteil ist für deutsche Gerichte verbindlich, sein Anwendungsbereich ***gilt für Zahlungen zwischen Unternehmen bzw. zwischen Unternehmen und der öffentlichen Hand und zwischen Unternehmen und Verbrauchern.***

Geldschulden sind damit Bringschulden. Die früher aus § 270 (1) BGB abgeleitete Regelung, dass Geldschulden Schickschulden sind, gilt nicht mehr.

Aufgabe 3 Sachmangel bei Gefahrenübergang

Die Bäckerei Bosch kann die Zahlung nicht verlangen, da sie ihre Vertragspflichten gem. § 433 (1) BGB (Übergabe der Torte) noch nicht erfüllt hat. Gem. § 446 geht die Gefahr des zufälligen Untergangs oder der zufälligen Verschlechterung erst mit der Übergabe an den Käufer über. Da im vorliegenden Fall die Übergabe nicht erfolgt ist, kann Susanne Bieber auf Vertragserfüllung (Übergabe einer anderen Torte) bestehen. Andernfalls kann sie unter bestimmten Voraussetzungen die Zahlung verweigern.

Hinweis: Das Recht auf Verweigerung der Zahlung hat Susanne Bieber erst, nachdem sie die Bäckerei in Lieferungsverzug gesetzt hat und vom Vertrag zurückgetreten ist.

zu Kapitel 2.3 Schenkungsvertrag

ANWENDUNGS- UND ÜBUNGSAUFGABE

Aufgabe 1 Rechtliche Bindung an ein Schenkungsversprechen

1. Dirigent Fognini ist nicht an sein Schenkungsversprechen gebunden, da es nicht notariell beurkundet wurde (§ 518 (1) BGB).
2. Durch die Bewirkung der Schenkung wird der Mangel der Form geheilt (§ 518 (2) BGB). Da der Dirigent jedoch unmittelbar nach der Konzertreise entlassen wurde, kann er die Schenkung wegen groben Undanks widerrufen (§ 530 BGB).

zu Kapitel 2.4 Darlehensvertrag

ANWENDUNGS- UND ÜBUNGSAUFGABE

Aufgabe 1 Analyse eines Darlehensvertrages

PDF DIGITAL+

1. Ziffer 3.1: Darlehensnennbetrag 30.000 EUR
2. Ziffer 4.4: Vertragslaufzeit = 60 Monate (5 Jahre) oder über die Berechnung:
   Tilgung 1/4-jährlich 1.500 EUR
   30.000 : 1.500 EUR = 20 Raten à 1.500 EUR
   Laufzeit: 5 Jahre (20 Quartale)
3. Ziffer 3.2: Verzinsung
   4,5 % von 30.000 EUR = 1.350 EUR/Jahr
   1.350 EUR / 12 Monate · 3 Mo. (1 Quartal) = 337,50 EUR
   Ziffer 4.3: Zahlungsbedingungen, Rückzahlung
   20 % jährlich von 30.000 EUR (Darlehensbetrag) = 6.000 EUR
   6.000 EUR / 12 Monate · 3 Mo. (1 Quartal) = 1.500 EUR
   Das Konto von Herrn Vogt wird am 31.12. 2021 mit insgesamt 337,50 EUR (Zins) + 1.500 EUR (Tilgung) = 1.837,50 EUR belastet.

4. Für die Laufzeit und damit auch für die Höhe der Tilgung spielen die Einkommensverhältnisse des Darlehensnehmers eine Rolle. Vom verfügbaren Einkommen hängt die Höhe der Übernahme der Rückzahlungsverpflichtung (Tilgung) ab.
5. Ziffer 4.3: Zahlungsbedingungen, Rückzahlung
   „Darlehen mit Ratentilgung"
6. Ziffer 5: Sicherheiten
   Durch die Übernahme einer Bürgschaft des Vaters des Darlehensnehmers.

zu Kapitel 3 Besonderheiten beim Abschluss von Kaufverträgen mit Verbrauchern

Warensendung trotz Widerruf

Ein Online-Kunde hatte eine Bestellung bereits einen Tag später widerrufen und zehn Tage später sicherheitshalber einen erneuten Widerruf abgeschickt. Trotzdem schickte der Händler dem Kunden die Ware zu. Das OLG Koblenz erkannte darin einen Verstoß gegen das Gesetz gegen den unlauteren Wettbewerb (UWG) und eine unzumutbare Belästigung des Online-Kunden.

Oberlandesgericht Koblenz (AZ: 9 U 120/09)

zu Kapitel 3.2 Verbrauchsgüterkaufverträge: Ausgewählte Beispiele

ERARBEITUNGSAUFGABE

EA 1 Bestellung eines Lautsprechers bei einem Elektroversand

1. Der Elektroversand Romer GmbH ist laut § 14 BGB ein Unternehmer und Philipp Kranich nach § 13 BGB ein Verbraucher. Wird ein Vertrag zwischen einem Unternehmer und einem Verbraucher ausschließlich über Fernkommunikationsmittel (hier: E-Mail) abgeschlossen, handelt es sich gemäß § 312c BGB um einen Fernabsatzvertrag.
2. Philipp Kranich hat das Recht, seine auf Abschluss eines Fernabsatzvertrages abgegebene Willenserklärung innerhalb von 14 Tagen zu widerrufen. Er muss bei Inanspruchnahme dieses Rechts die abgegebene Willenserklärung per Brief, Fax, Telefon oder E-Mail widerrufen und den Lautsprecher zurückschicken (§§ 312g (1), 355 (1) u. (2) BGB).
   (Musterwiderrufsformular siehe nächste Seite)
3. Der Unternehmer muss die Kosten übernehmen, da er Philipp Kranich zuvor nicht über eine Kostenübernahme durch den Verbraucher informiert hat (§ 312e BGB).

zu Kapitel 3.2 Verbrauchsgüterkaufverträge: Ausgewählte Beispiele

ANWENDUNGS- UND ÜBUNGSAUFGABEN

Aufgabe 1 Widerruf einer Bestellung

1. Ja. Federica Ventola ist Verbraucher nach § 13 BGB. Demnach steht ihr für den Fernabsatzvertrag ein Widerrufsrecht von 14 Tagen (§§ 312g (1), 355 (1) BGB) zu. Innerhalb dieser Frist kann sie – ohne Angabe von Gründen – ihre Willenserklärung widerrufen. Der geschlossene Vertrag ist bis zum Ende der Frist **schwebend wirksam**.
2. Bei der Lieferung von Waren beginnt die Widerrufsfrist nicht vor dem Tag ihres Eingangs beim Empfänger (§ 356 (2) Nr. 1a) BGB). Die Widerrufsfrist ist eine Ereignisfrist i. S. von § 187 BGB. Die 14-tägige Widerrufsfrist erlischt, wenn die abgegebene Willenserklärung nicht spätestens am 28. April widerrufen wird (Annahme: kein Sonn- oder Feiertag).

zu EA 1 vorherige Seite

Wenn Sie den Vertrag widerrufen wollen, dann füllen Sie bitte dieses Formular aus und senden Sie es zurück.

Elektroversand **Romer**

An Elektroversand Romer
Am Bahndamm 14
79540 Lörrach

Tel.: (+49) (0) ..., Fax: (+49) (0) ...
info@elektroromer.net

Muster-Widerrufsformular

Hiermit widerrufe(n) ich/wir den von mir/uns abgeschlossenen Vertrag über und den Kauf der folgenden Waren/die Erbringung der folgenden Dienstleistung

1 Lautsprecher

Bestellt am *25.11. ...* /erhalten am *27.11. ...*

Name des/der Verbraucher(s) *Philipp Kranich*

Anschrift des/der Verbraucher(s)

...

...

...

01.12. ... *Philipp Kranich*

Datum Unterschrift des/der Verbraucher(s) (nur bei Mitteilung auf Papier)

Hintergrundinformationen zur Berechnung von Fristen (§§ 187 ff. BGB)

Arten von Fristen

Ereignisfrist

Für den Beginn der Frist ist ein Ereignis maßgebend.

Bsp.: Die Vertragspartner vereinbaren, dass die Zahlung vierzehn Tage nach der Lieferung erfolgen soll. Liefertermin ist der 19.03. d. J.

Der erste Tag der 14-Tage-Frist ist der 20.03., denn der Tag der Lieferung (Ereignistag) wird nicht mitgezählt § 187 (1) BGB). Der letzte Tag der Ereignisfrist ergibt sich durch Abzählen:

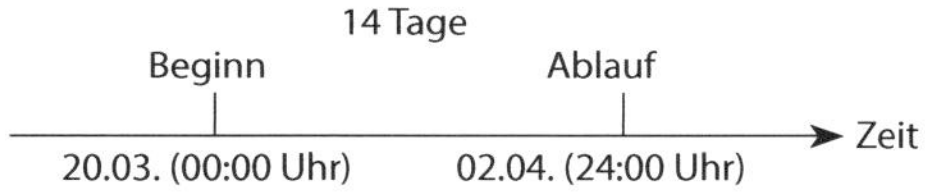

Beginnfrist

Der Beginn eines Tages stellt den für den Anfang einer Frist maßgebenden Zeitpunkt dar.

Bsp. 1: Kurt Klippert mietet am 02.04., 14:00 Uhr einen Pkw für 10 Tage. Er muss den Pkw spätestens am 11.04. zurückbringen, wenn sonst keine anderweitigen Vereinbarungen getroffen wurden.

Der erste Tag der 10-Tagesfrist (02.04.) ist der für den Anfang der Frist maßgebende Zeitpunkt. Dieser Tag wird demnach mitgezählt (§ 187 (2) BGB).

Bsp. 2: Hans ist am 23.09.1991 (11:30 Uhr) geboren. Er vollendet sein 18. Lebensjahr am 22.09.2009 (24:00 Uhr). Der Tag seiner Geburt wird mitgezählt (§ 187 (2) S. 2 BGB).

Besonderheiten bei der Berechnung von Fristen

Wird eine Frist nach Wochen, Monaten oder Jahren bestimmt, so ist ihr Ende im Falle einer Ereignisfrist an dem Tag, der durch seine ***Benennung oder seine Zahl dem Ereignistag*** *entspricht (§ 188 (2) BGB).*

Beispiele:

1. *Karl hat einen amtlichen Bescheid erhalten, gegen den er gemäß der beigefügten Rechtsmittelbelehrung innerhalb von 1 Monat nach dem Zugang Widerspruch erheben kann. Der Bescheid ist ihm am* ***Dienstag,*** *12. Mai, zugegangen. Die Widerspruchsfrist ist am* ***Freitag,*** *12. Juni (24:00 Uhr), abgelaufen.*
2. *Hans hat sich beim Kauf eines Grundstücks vertraglich verpflichtet, den Kaufpreis in Höhe von 200.000 EUR vier Monate nach Vertragsabschluss zu zahlen. Der Kaufvertrag wurde am* ***17.*** *Dezember abgeschlossen. Der Kaufpreis ist demnach fällig am 17. April des nächsten Jahres.*
3. *Katja hat am 07. Jan. d. J. einen Fernabsatzvertrag geschlossen. Am* ***08. Jan.*** *d. J.* ***(Donnerstag)*** *erhält sie zusammen mit der Lieferung eine ordnungsgemäße Belehrung über ihr Widerrufsrecht gem. § 355 (2) BGB. Das 14-tägige Widerrufsrecht erlischt, wenn sie nicht spätestens am* ***22. Jan.*** *d. J.* ***(Donnerstag)*** den Fernabsatzvertrag widerruft.

Aufgabe 2 Kosten der Ingebrauchnahme bei Fernabsatzvertrag

1. Es handelt sich um einen Fernabsatzvertrag gem. § 312c BGB. Deshalb hat Federica Ventola das Recht, ihre abgegebene Erklärung innerhalb von 14 Tagen ohne Begründung zu widerrufen (§ 312g (1) BGB i. v. m. § 355 (2) BGB). Die 14-tägige Widerrufsfrist beginnt gem. § 356 (2) Nr. 1a) am 03.09. d. J. (= erster Tag der Frist) und endet am 16.09. d. J. um 24:00 Uhr. Bis zu diesem Zeitpunkt müsste Federica Ventola ihre Erklärung widerrufen haben.
2. a) Gem. § 312e BGB muss der Verkäufer diese Kosten tragen, da es an einer vertraglichen Vereinbarung bzw. einer Vorabinformation fehlt, nach der die Kosten vom Käufer zu tragen sind.
   b) Gem. § 357 (7) BGB muss der Verkäufer den vollen Betrag erstatten, weil der Aufbau des Wasserbetts und die Befüllung der Matratze mit Wasser lediglich eine Prüfung der Sache darstellen. Der Käufer muss keinen Wertersatz für die eingetretene Wertminderung leisten.

BGH-Urteil zur Wertersatzpflicht bei Abschluss eines Fernabsatzvertrages über ein Wasserbett

BGH, Urteil vom 03.11.2010 – VIII ZR *337/09*; Vorinstanzen: AG Berlin-Wedding, Urteil vom 09.04.2009 – 17 C 683/08; LG Berlin, Urteil vom 18.11.2009 – 50 S. 56/09

MIR 2010, Dok. 154, Rz. 1

Bei dem fristgerechten Widerruf eines Fernabsatzvertrages hat der Verbraucher keinen Wertersatz zu leisten, wenn er die Ware (nur) zu Prüfzwecken in Gebrauch genommen hat. Dies gelte selbst dann, wenn eine solche Ingebrauchnahme zu einer Wertminderung der Ware führe, so der BGH mit Urteil vom 03.11.2010 (VIII ZR 337/09).

Zur Sache

Die Parteien schlossen im August 2008 per E-Mail einen Kaufvertrag über ein Wasserbett zum Preis von EUR 1.265,00. Das Angebot des Beklagten, der die Wasserbetten über das Internet zum Verkauf anbot, war dem Kläger per E-Mail als angehängte PDF-Datei übersandt worden. Der Text der E-Mail enthält eine Widerrufsbelehrung. Im weiteren Text der E-Mail heißt es:

„Im Hinblick auf die o. g. Widerrufsbelehrung weisen wir ergänzend darauf hin, dass durch das Befüllen der Matratze des Wasserbettes regelmäßig eine Verschlechterung eintritt, da das Bett nicht mehr als neuwertig zu veräußern ist."

Das Wasserbett wurde gegen Barzahlung beim Käufer angeliefert. Nachdem der Käufer das Wasserbett aufgebaut und mit Wasser befüllt hatte, übte er – fristgerecht – sein Widerrufsrecht aus. Nach Abholung des Wasserbetts forderte er den Verkäufer zur Rückzahlung des Kaufpreises auf. Der Verkäufer erstattete lediglich einen Betrag von EUR 258,00. Das Bett sei nicht mehr verkäuflich. Lediglich die Heizung im Wert von EUR 258,00 sei wieder verwertbar.

Nachdem das Amtsgericht der auf Rückzahlung des restlichen Kaufpreises von EUR 1.007,00 gerichteten Klage stattgegeben hatte, wies das Landgericht die Berufung des Verkäufers zurück.

Entscheidung des BGH: Keine Wertersatzpflicht im Fernabsatz bei Ingebrauchnahme zu Prüfzwecken

Die Revision des Verkäufers hatte keinen Erfolg. Der Käufer könne trotz des möglicherweise eingetretenen Wertverlusts den vollen Kaufpreis zurückverlangen, da er die Ware nur geprüft habe, so der BGH.

Ein fristgerecht erklärter Widerruf des Verbrauchers beim Fernabsatzvertrag habe zur Folge, dass die empfangenen Leistungen von den Vertragsparteien zurückzugewähren sind. Soweit der empfangene Gegenstand sich verschlechtert hat oder untergegangen ist, muss der Schuldner statt der Rückgabe Wertersatz leisten. Dabei müsse der Verbraucher nach § 357 Abs. 3 Satz 1 BGB[1] auch Wertersatz für eine durch die bestimmungsgemäße Ingebrauchnahme entstandene Verschlechterung leisten, wenn er spätestens bei Vertragsschluss in Textform auf diese Rechtsfolge und eine Möglichkeit hingewiesen worden ist, sie zu vermeiden. Die Wertersatzpflicht bestehe jedoch nach § 357 Abs. 3 Satz 3 BGB[1] dann nicht, wenn die Verschlechterung ausschließlich auf die Prüfung der Sache zurückzuführen sei. Letzteres sei nach Ansicht des BGH vorliegend der Fall. Der Aufbau des Wasserbetts und die Befüllung der Matratze mit Wasser stellen lediglich eine Prüfung der Sache dar.

Weil der Verbraucher im Fernabsatz die Ware vor Abschluss des Vertrags nicht sehen kann, solle er nach Art. 6 der Richtlinie 97/7/EG (Fernabsatzrichtlinie) und der sie umsetzenden deutschen Regelung grundsätzlich die Gelegenheit haben, die gekaufte Ware zu prüfen und auszuprobieren. Dies schließe auch die Ingebrauchnahme ein, soweit sie zu Prüfzwecken erforderlich ist, selbst wenn sie zu einer Wertminderung der Ware führt.

(tg) – PM Nr. 210/2010 des BGH vom 03.11.2010

Aufgabe 3 Rückgabe einer CD bei Internetkauf

Nein. Ein Widerrufs- und Rückgaberecht bei einem Fernabsatzvertrag besteht nicht, wenn es sich um die Lieferung einer Audio- oder Videoaufzeichnung handelt, sofern die gelieferten Datenträger vom Verbraucher entsiegelt worden sind (§ 312g (2) Nr. 6).

1 Aktuelle Rechtsquelle: § 357 (7) BGB – ab 13. Juni 2014

zu Kapitel 4 Störungen bei der Erfüllung von Verbrauchsgüterkaufverträgen

zu Kapitel 4.1 Arten von Erfüllungsstörungen im Überblick

ERARBEITUNGSAUFGABE

EA 1 Arten von Störungen bei der Erfüllung von Kaufverträgen

1. Verkäufer liefert falsche Ware, Laserpatrone anstatt einer Tintenpatrone (= Schlechtleistung)
2. Die Käuferin Marianne Kern nimmt statt der bestellten 1 600 l Heizöl nur 1 200 l ab (= Annahmeverzug)
3. Keine Störung des Kaufvertrages; gemäß Kaufvertrag muss der Lieferer erst am 1. August liefern
4. Käufer Horst Müller zahlt seine Rechnung nicht wie vereinbart innerhalb von zwei Wochen nach der Lieferung (= Nicht rechtzeitige Zahlung)

zu Kapitel 4.2 Schlechtleistung

ERARBEITUNGSAUFGABE

EA 1 Schlechtleistung – Arten von Sachmängeln

1. Da sich die Farbe nicht für den nach dem Vertrag vorausgesetzten Zweck (Streichen im Außenbereich) eignet, liegt ein Sachmangel vor (§ 434 (1) Nr. 2 S. 3).

Anspruchskonkurrenz zwischen Anfechtung und der Inanspruchnahme von Gewährleistungsrechten

Wie ist Teilaufgabe 1 a) zu lösen, wenn eine Anfechtungsmöglichkeit (z. B. bei Irrtum über eine wesentliche Eigenschaft) bei gleichzeitigem Vorliegen eines Sachmangels gegeben ist?

Ergebnis: Die Möglichkeit der Anfechtung durch den Käufer ist bei Vorliegen eines Sachmangels ausgeschlossen, damit die Gewährleistungsfrist nicht unterlaufen wird.

Begründung: Wäre bei einem Kaufvertrag nach Gefahrenübergang (Übergabe der verkauften Sache) die Anfechtung nach § 119 (2) BGB zugelassen, dann könnten dadurch die speziellen Vorschriften über die Sachmängelhaftung (§§ 434 ff. BGB) ausgehebelt werden, da der Vertrag mit der Anfechtung von Anfang ungültig wird. Daher wird § 119 (2) BGB nach allgemeiner Ansicht beim Vorliegen eines Sachmangels i. S. d. § 434 BGB durch die spezielleren §§ 434 ff. BGB verdrängt.

2. Die tatsächliche Beschaffenheit der Äpfel entspricht nicht der im Vertrag vereinbarten Beschaffenheit (§ 434 (1) S. 1 BGB). Daher liegt ein Sachmangel vor.
3. Aufgrund der Falschaussage in der Werbung ist das Nahrungsergänzungsmittel für den vorgesehenen Vertragszweck nicht geeignet. Daher liegt ein Sachmangel vor (§ 434 (1) S. 3 BGB).
4. Die Montageanleitung ist auch dann fehlerhaft, wenn sie unverständlich ist. Es kann nicht erwartet werden, dass Herr Duffner einen Übersetzungsdienst beauftragt.
   Daher liegt ein Sachmangel gem. § 434 (2) BGB vor.
5. Die Lieferung einer zu geringen Menge stellt einen Sachmangel dar (§ 434 (3) BGB).

zu Kapitel 4.2 Schlechtleistung

ANWENDUNGS- UND ÜBUNGSAUFGABEN

Aufgabe 1 Rechte bei Schlechtleistung – Beweislastumkehr

1. Ein Sachmangel liegt vor, wenn einer Sache bei **Gefahrenübergang** die vereinbarte Beschaffenheit fehlt (§ 434 BGB). Zum **Schutz des Verbrauchers** gilt jedoch die **Vermutung**, dass eine Sache bereits bei Gefahrenübergang mangelhaft war, wenn sich **innerhalb von sechs Monaten** seit Gefahrenübergang ein Sachmangel zeigt. Gäbe es diese Bestimmung nicht, so müsste der Käufer beweisen, dass der Mangel bereits zum Zeitpunkt des Gefahrenübergangs vorhanden war. Auch dann, wenn das Gerät zum Zeitpunkt des Gefahrenübergangs z. B. für kurze Zeit funktionsfähig war, wird zugunsten des Verbrauchers (Herr Ruckeisen handelt als Verbraucher, da er das Gerät nicht für sein Unternehmen kauft) ein Sachmangel bereits zu diesem Zeitpunkt vermutet. Nur wenn der Verkäufer ein einwandfreies Funktionieren zum Zeitpunkt des Gefahrenübergangs beweisen kann (das wird ihm im Normalfall nicht gelingen), liegt ausnahmsweise kein Sachmangel vor (**Beweislastumkehr gem.** § 476 BGB).

   Unter den gegebenen Voraussetzungen handelt es sich im vorliegenden Fall um einen Sachmangel.

2. Vorrangig steht Herrn Ruckeisen zunächst nur das Recht auf **Nacherfüllung** zu (§§ 437, 439 BGB). Im Rahmen dieses Rechts kann er wählen zwischen

   (1) Beseitigung des Mangels **(Nachbesserung)** und

   (2) Lieferung einer mangelfreien Sache **(Ersatzlieferung)**.

   Vom Vertrag kann er nur dann **zurücktreten**, wenn er dem Verkäufer **erfolglos** eine angemessene Nachfrist gesetzt hat (§ 437 Nr. 2, § 323 (1) BGB).

   Herr Ruckeisen kann unter den gegebenen Voraussetzungen zunächst nicht das Geld zurückverlangen. Er muss dem Verkäufer zunächst die Möglichkeit der Nachbesserung (hier: Ersatzlieferung) einräumen.

   Hinweis zum Rücktritt bei einem Kauf mangelhafter Ware

   Kunden dürfen einen Kauf rückgängig machen, falls die Ware Mängel aufweist und der Verkäufer sie nicht auf seine Kosten repariert oder Ersatz liefert – allerdings nur, falls der Fehler erheblich ist. Betragen die Reparaturkosten mindestens 5 Prozent des Kaufpreises, darf der Kunde sein Geld zurückverlangen. (Az. VIII ZR 94/13).

3. In diesem Fall liegt kein Verbrauchsgüterkauf (§ 474 BGB) vor. Damit gilt auch nicht die Beweislastumkehr gem. § 476 BGB. Um die Rechte aus einer Schlechtleistung geltend machen zu können, müsste Herr Ruckeisen beweisen, dass der Haartrockner bereits zum Zeitpunkt der Übergabe schadhaft war.

Aufgabe 2 Rechte bei Schlechtleistung

1. **Unverständliche Montageanleitung**

   Trotz mangelhafter Montageanleitung kann Kern den Kaufvertrag nicht rückgängig machen, weil es ihm gelungen ist, das Kinderturngerät fehlerfrei zu montieren (§ 434 (2) S. 2 BGB). Wäre ihm das nicht gelungen, so könnte er nach Ablauf einer angemessenen Nachfrist vom Vertrag zurücktreten (§ 323 (1) BGB).

2. **Rechte bei Falschaussage in der Werbung**

   Da der tatsächliche Benzinverbrauch von dem vereinbarten abweicht, liegt ein Sachmangel nach § 434 (1) S. 1 BGB vor. Dass der Wert des Wagens durch den minimalen Mehrverbrauch an Benzin nur unerheblich und die Gebrauchstauglichkeit gar nicht beeinträchtigt wird, steht der Annahme eines Mangels nicht entgegen.

   Demnach stehen Ronja Dreyer folgende Rechte zu:

   1) Nacherfüllung gem. §§ 437 Nr. 1, 439 (1) BGB. Nach § 439 (1) BGB hat sie dabei grundsätzlich die Wahl zwischen Nachbesserung und Ersatzlieferung. Dreyer kann also als Nacherfüllung die Lieferung eines neuen Exemplars des gleichen Modells mit dem vereinbarten Benzinverbrauch verlangen.
   2) Rücktritt vom Vertrag: Nicht möglich, da der Mehrverbrauch an Benzin minimal und die Verwendung des Autos in keiner Weise beeinträchtigt ist. Bei einer nur unerheblichen Pflichtverletzung ist Rücktritt ausgeschlossen (§ 323 (5) S. 2 BGB).
   3) Minderung: Ronja Dreyer kann nach § 437 Nr. 2 und § 441 (1) BGB den Kaufpreis durch einseitige Erklärung gegenüber Vollmer mindern. Den überzahlten Betrag kann sie nach § 441 (4) BGB herausverlangen.

   Hinweis: Grundsätzlich müssen nach § 441 BGB für ein Minderungsrecht die Voraussetzungen für ein Rücktrittsrecht erfüllt sein („Statt zurückzutreten"). Im vorliegenden Falle scheitert ein Rücktritt aber an § 323 (5) BGB wegen der Geringfügigkeit des Mangels. Allerdings ist dieser Ausschlussgrund nach § 441 (1) S. 2 auf das Minderungsrecht nicht anwendbar.

3. **Rechte bei Kauf eines Neuwagens bei aufgetretenem Motorschaden**

   Im vorliegenden Falle handelt es sich um einen Verbrauchsgüterkauf (§ 474 BGB). Daher gilt die Beweislastumkehr, wonach zugunsten des Verbrauchers vermutet wird, dass der Sachmangel bereits zum Zeitpunkt des Gefahrenübergangs bestand, wenn sich innerhalb von sechs Monaten nach Gefahrenübergang ein Sachmangel zeigt (§ 476 BGB). Unter den gegebenen Voraussetzungen kann Tezcan daher Nacherfüllung nach § 439 BGB verlangen. Vom Vertrag zurücktreten (§ 323 (1) BGB) oder den Kaufpreis mindern (§ 441 BGB) kann Tezcan erst, wenn er dem Vertragshändler erfolglos eine Nacherfüllungsfrist gesetzt hat.

4. **Rechte bei Kauf eines Gebrauchtfahrzeuges mit Getriebeschaden**

   Es handelt sich um einen Verbrauchsgüterkauf (§ 474 (1) BGB). Auch bei gebrauchten Sachen kann nicht von den kaufrechtlichen Gewährleistungsvorschriften abgewichen werden (§ 475 (1) BGB). Der Gebrauchtwagenhändler kann sich daher nicht auf den Gewährleistungsausschluss berufen.

   Da Käufer und Verkäufer im Kaufvertrag weder eine besondere Beschaffenheit vereinbart noch eine bestimmte Verwendung vorausgesetzt haben, kommt es darauf an, ob sich das Fahrzeug für die gewöhnliche Verwendung eignet, die bei Sachen gleicher Art üblich ist und der Käufer erwarten kann (§ 434 (1) Zi. 2 BGB). Vergleichsmaßstab ist dabei aber nicht eine entsprechende neuwertige, sondern eine gebrauchte Sache gleicher Art. Da bei einem zehn Jahre alten Fahrzeug Verschleißerscheinungen nicht ungewöhnlich sind, liegt kein Sachmangel i. S. d. § 434 (1) Nr. 2 BGB vor, so dass der Gebrauchtwagenhändler keine Gewähr zu leisten hat. Neumann hat daher keinen Anspruch auf Rückzahlung des Kaufpreises.

Aufgabe 3 Schlechtleistung: Ersatzlieferung – Umtausch – Nacherfüllung

Ja. Gem. § 433 BGB hat der Verkäufer dafür zu sorgen, dass die Sache zum Zeitpunkt des Gefahrenübergangs nicht mit Mängeln behaftet ist. Die Autoalarmanlage ist wegen eines Kontaktfehlers, der von Anfang an bestand, nicht funktionsfähig und demnach fehlerhaft. Bei Verbrauchsgüterkäufen (BGB § 474) gilt während der ersten 6 Monate eine Beweislastumkehr (BGB § 476).

Lorenzo Conti kann verlangen, dass ihm an Stelle der mangelhaften Sache eine mangelfreie geliefert wird (Nacherfüllung gem. § 439 BGB). Dieser Anspruch ist noch nicht verjährt (§ 438 BGB). Das vom Verkäufer eingeräumte Recht auf Umtausch bezieht sich nicht auf den Fall einer mangelhaften Lieferung.

Zu beachten ist der Unterschied zwischen „Ersatzlieferung" und „Umtausch":

Ersatzlieferung/Umtausch

Ersatzlieferung	Umtausch
= gesetzlicher Anspruch des Käufers auf Nacherfüllung beim Vorliegen von Sachmängeln (§ 439 (1) BGB)	liegt vor, wenn der Kunde eine andere Ware haben will, weil ihm die gekaufte Ware z. B. nicht gefällt, nicht passt, oder – im Fall einer Autoalarmanlage – nicht eingebaut werden kann; ein gesetzlicher Anspruch auf Umtausch besteht nicht, sondern ist allenfalls Gegenstand einer vertraglichen Vereinbarung oder einer späteren Kulanzregelung.

Aufgabe 4 Schlechtleistung: Einschränkung von Rechten durch Allgemeine Geschäftsbedingungen und Garantieerklärung

1. Das Gerät wies zum Zeitpunkt des Gefahrenübergangs einen Sachmangel gem. BGB § 434 auf. Die Verjährungsfrist von 2 Jahren (BGB § 438) ist noch nicht abgelaufen. Daher stehen Herrn Lang gem. § 437 grundsätzlich folgende Rechte zu: Nacherfüllung und unter bestimmten Voraussetzungen Rücktritt, Minderung, Schadenersatz, Ersatz vergeblicher Aufwendungen.

2. Lieferung einer mangelfreien Sache gem. § 439 BGB.

3. Häufig sehen die Allgemeinen Geschäftsbedingungen des Verkäufers, ohne deren Anerkennung durch den Käufer ein Vertrag nicht zustande kommt, nur ein Nachbesserungsrecht vor. Das ist grundsätzlich zulässig. Eine solche Vereinbarung ist aber unwirksam, wenn dem Käufer nicht ausdrücklich bei Fehlschlagen der Nachbesserung nach seiner Wahl das Minderungs- oder Rücktrittsrecht vorbehalten wird (BGB § 309 Nr. 8bb). Eine Nachbesserung gilt nach dem zweiten erfolglosen Versuch als fehlgeschlagen (BGB § 440). Die für die Nachbesserung erforderlichen Aufwendungen (z. B. Transport-, Arbeits- und Materialkosten) sind vom zur Nachbesserung verpflichteten Verkäufer zu tragen (BGB § 439 (2)).

   Bei der vorliegenden AGB-Klausel fehlt die ausdrückliche Zusicherung weiterer Rechte bei Fehlschlägen der Nachbesserung. Daher ist diese Klausel nichtig. Die Vereinbarung einer Nachbesserung anstelle der gesetzlichen Gewährleistungsansprüche ist damit hinfällig. Herr Lang kann somit die ihm gem. §§ 437 ff. BGB zustehenden Rechte geltend machen.

4. a) Bei Garantieerklärungen ist streng zu trennen zwischen einer Händler- und einer Herstellergarantie (vgl. BGB § 443). Beide Garantieformen sind freiwillig und unabhängig von der gesetzlichen Gewährleistung des Händlers nach BGB §§ 437 ff. In der Praxis wird die Garantieerklärung meistens vom Hersteller gegeben.

   In der Garantieerklärung muss u. a. ausdrücklich auf die weiterhin bestehenden gesetzlichen Rechte hingewiesen werden (BGB § 477).

Der Käufer hat bei Sachmängeln somit wahlweise seine gesetzlichen Rechte aus §§ 437 ff. BGB gegen den verkaufenden Händler oder seine Rechte aus dem Garantievertrag. Das heißt, dass der ausschließliche Verweis auf den Hersteller zur Mangelbehebung nicht zulässig ist.

b) Wenn die Ansprüche gegen den Verkäufer nicht mehr geltend gemacht werden können, sei es, dass die Ansprüche verjährt sind (Ablauf der 2-Jahresfrist gem. § 438 (1) BGB) oder der Verkäufer in ein Insolvenzverfahren geraten ist, bestehen die Ansprüche gegen den Hersteller trotzdem bis zum Ende der Garantiezeit weiter.

zu Kapitel 4.3 Nicht rechtzeitige Zahlung und Zahlungsverzug

ERARBEITUNGSAUFGABE

EA 1 Zahlungsverzug – Eintritt – Rechte

1. Es liegen zwei übereinstimmende Willenserklärungen (Bestellung des Stereo Receivers HC9 und Lieferung dessen) vor. Es handelt sich um ein Schuldverhältnis (gültiger Kaufvertrag gem. 433 BGB).

2. Kleinert erhält die Rechnung am 22.08. + 30 Tage (gezählt wird ab dem 23.08. lt. § 187 (1) BGB) = 21.09.

   Das Geld hätte spätestens am 21.09. auf dem Konto des Internethändlers verbucht sein müssen.

3. Torsten Kleinert befindet sich am 23.09. d. J. in Zahlungsverzug (erster Verzugstag: 22.09.).

   Nichtleistung trotz Fälligkeit (§§ 271, 286 (1), § 286 (3) BGB): Torsten Kleinert hat nicht rechtzeitig geleistet:

   Geldschulden sind Bringschulden. Das bedeutet, dass der Geldschuldner seine Verpflichtung erfüllt, wenn der Gläubiger den Geldbetrag innerhalb der Zahlungsfrist erhalten hat. Da das Geld am 21.09. noch nicht im Verfügungsbereich des Internethändlers ist, hat Torsten Kleinert seine Zahlungsverpflichtung aus dem Kaufvertrag nicht rechtzeitig erfüllt.

4. Bei Fehlen anders lautender vertraglicher Vereinbarungen ist der Rechnungsbetrag sofort nach Lieferung fällig (§ 271 (1) BGB). Der Schuldner (Torsten Kleinert) kommt aber bei Fehlen eines fest vereinbarten Zahlungstermins nicht schon mit Fälligkeit, sondern erst mit der Mahnung am 31.08. d. J. in Verzug (§ 286 (1) BGB).

5. Der Internethändler ist berechtigt, bei Zahlungsverzug zusätzlich zur Zahlung Schadenersatz für die verzögerte Zahlung zu verlangen (§ 280 (1) BGB). Der Verzugszins beträgt Stand Jan. 2021: – 0,88 % + 5 %-Punkte = 4,12 % (= Basiszinssatz + 5 %-Punkte) gem. § 288 (1) BGB.

   Verzugstage: erster Tag der Verzugsfrist ist der 22.09., letzter Tag der Verzugsfrist ist der 10.10.; daraus errechnen sich 19 Verzugstage.

   $$\text{Verzugszinsen}^{1} = \frac{595{,}50 \cdot 4{,}12 \cdot 19}{100 \cdot 365} = 1{,}28 \text{ EUR}$$

   Die Forderung in der angegebenen Höhe ist nicht berechtigt. Der Internethändler kann lediglich 2,78 EUR verlangen:

   Zinsen 1,28 EUR + Mahngebühren (für Porto und Papier) 1,50 EUR = 2,78 EUR

1 Die Verzugszinsen werden im Normalfall nach der act/act – Methode (Zinsmonat und Zinsjahr kalendergerecht) berechnet.

6. Der Internethändler kann vom Vertrag zurücktreten (§ 323 (1) BGB) und statt der Leistung Schadenersatz verlangen (§§ 280 (1) und (3), 281 BGB), da er eine angemessene Nachfrist (10.9. d. J.) für die Bezahlung gesetzt hat und diese erfolglos verstrichen ist. Somit müsste Kleinert den Stereo Receiver zurückgeben und den entstandenen Schaden ersetzen.

zu Kapitel 4.3 Nicht rechtzeitige Zahlung und Zahlungsverzug

ANWENDUNGS- UND ÜBUNGSAUFGABEN

PDF DIGITAL+

Aufgabe 1 Eintritt von Zahlungsverzug

	Vertragspartner	Klausel/Vereinbarung im Kaufvertrag	Datum des Zugangs der Rechnung bzw. Zahlungsaufforderung (z. B. Mahnung)	Eintritt des Zahlungsverzugs am ...	Begründung
1.	**Unternehmer – Verbraucher**	Hinweis auf Eintritt des Zahlungsverzugs	Rechnungsdatum: 15.05. d. J. Rechnungszugang 19.05. d. J.	*18.06. d. J. 24:00 Uhr (Beginn: 19.06. 0:00 Uhr)*	*30 Tage (Kalendertage) nach Rechnungszugang;*
2.	**Unternehmer – Verbraucher**	keine	Rechnungsdatum: 15.05. d. J. Rechnungszugang 19.05. d. J.	*Erst mit Mahnung*	*Schuldner ist Verbraucher; Hinweis gem. § 286 (3) BGB fehlt;*
3.	**Unternehmer – Unternehmer**	keine	Rechnungsdatum: 15.05. d. J. Rechnungszugang 19.05. d. J.	*18.06. d. J. 24:00 Uhr (Beginn: 19.06. 0:00 Uhr)*	*30 Tage (Kalendertage) nach Rechnungszugang; Hinweis auf Eintritt des Zahlungsverzugs nicht erforderlich, da Schuldner Unternehmer;*
4.	**Unternehmer – Verbraucher**	„Zahlbar sofort bei Erhalt der Ware netto Kasse"	keine Rechnung/keine Zahlungsaufforderung	*zunächst noch kein Zahlungsverzug*	*Rechnungszugang etc. fehlt; Verzug tritt erst 30 Tage nach Zugang einer Rechnung oder Zahlungsaufforderung (z. B. Mahnung) ein.*
5.	**Unternehmer – Verbraucher**	▪ „Zahlbar 20 Tage ab Rechnungsdatum" ▪ Hinweis auf Eintritt des Zahlungsverzugs	Rechnungsdatum: 15.05. d. J. Rechnungszugang 19.05. d. J.	*04.06. d. J. 24:00 Uhr (Beginn: 05.06. 0:00 Uhr)*	*20 Tage nach Rechnungsdatum (§ 286 (2) BGB); Rechnungszugang unerheblich, da Terminvereinbarung*
6.	**Unternehmer – Verbraucher**	▪ Hinweis auf Eintritt des Zahlungsverzugs	Rechnungsdatum: 15.05. d. J. Rechnungszugang 19.05. d. J. Mahnung: 05.06. d. J.	*05.06. d. J. 24:00 Uhr (Beginn: 06.06. 0:00 Uhr)*	*Verzug tritt ein durch Mahnung des Gläubigers (§ 286 (1) BGB);*

Schadenersatzberechnung bei Zahlungsverzug

Schadenersatzberechnung bei Zahlungsverzug

Befindet sich ein Verbraucher in Verzug, so hat er dem Gläubiger grundsätzlich den dadurch entstandenen Schaden zu ersetzen. Jedoch sind hinsichtlich der Berechnung der Schadenshöhe Grenzen gesetzt. So dürfen für ein **zweites Mahnschreiben** nur die **tatsächlich angefallenen Kosten** für Porto und Papier in Rechnung gestellt werden. Alternativ kann ein Pauschalbetrag von höchstens 2,50 Euro berechnet werden. **Arbeits- oder Bearbeitungsgebühren dürfen hingegen nicht angesetzt werden**. Auch die Kosten für ein Inkassobüro sind nach oben hin begrenzt. Die Rechtsprechung hat anerkannt, dass diese nicht höher sein dürfen als die Kosten für einen Rechtsanwalt, dessen Gebühren gesetzlich vorgegeben sind.

Vertragsstrafen in allgemeinen Geschäftsbedingungen, wonach ein Verbraucher im Zahlungsverzug eine Strafe zu zahlen habe, verstoßen gegen § 309 Nr. 6 BGB und sind daher unwirksam. Häufig sehen allgemeine Geschäftsbedingungen vor, dass im Fall einer nicht einlösbaren Lastschrift eine pauschale Bearbeitungsgebühr zu zahlen sei. Hierdurch versuchen Unternehmen oft, die bei der Bearbeitung der Rücklastschrift entstehenden Personalkosten auf den Verbraucher abzuwälzen. Dieser weit verbreiteten Praxis haben die Gerichte allerdings einen Riegel vorgeschoben. So urteilte das Oberlandesgericht Hamm, dass eine pauschale Rücklastschriftgebühr von 50 Euro in den **Geschäftsbedingungen einer Billigfluglinie** unzulässig ist (Az.: 17 U 112/07). Gleiches gilt bei **Mobilfunkverträgen**, in denen Bearbeitungsgebühren für nicht einlösbare Lastschriften pauschal höher angesetzt sind als die anfallenden Bankgebühren von 7,50 Euro.

Verbraucher haben also guten Grund, genau hinzusehen, wenn ihnen Mahnkosten berechnet werden.

(Quelle: FAZ vom 17.12.08)

Aufgabe 2 Eintritt des Zahlungsverzugs – Verzugszinsen

1. Schuster kommt ohne Mahnung in Zahlungsverzug. Der Verzug tritt spätestens ein, wenn der Schuldner 30 Tage nach Fälligkeit (04.11. d. J. 24:00 Uhr) und Zugang der Rechnung seine Verbindlichkeiten noch nicht beglichen hat – § 286 (3) BGB. Beginn des Zahlungsverzugs: 05.11. d. J. 0:00 Uhr. Das Autohaus könnte – ohne jede weitere Vorwarnung – 30 Tage nach Fälligkeit das gerichtliche Mahnverfahren in Gang setzen. Dabei gingen alle entstehenden Kosten zu Lasten von Schuster.

2. Das Autohaus Lauer kann während des Verzugs Verzugszinsen in Höhe von 5 Prozentpunkten über dem Basiszinssatz (01.07.2021: – 0,88 %) – derzeit also 4,12 % – verlangen – § 288 (1) BGB.

   Hinweis: Diese Regelung gilt auch für Handelsgeschäfte (Verzugszins, wenn ein Verbraucher nicht beteiligt ist: Basiszinssatz + 9 Prozentpunkte).

Aufgabe 3 Zinsberechnung im Zusammenhang mit Zahlungsverzug

1. Verzugstag: 21.03.; (März: 12 Tage, April: 30 Tage, Mai: 16 Tage) zu berücksichtigen: 58 Zinstage

   $$\text{Zinsen} = \frac{2.480 \cdot 4{,}12 \cdot 58}{100 \cdot 365} = 16{,}24 \text{ EUR}$$

   Überweisungsbetrag: 2.480 EUR + 16,24 EUR = 2.496,24 EUR

2. Verzugszinsen = 28,00 EUR – 1,50 EUR = 26,50 EUR

   $$K = \frac{26{,}50 \cdot 100 \cdot 365}{4{,}12 \cdot 62} = 3.786{,}60 \text{ EUR Rechnungsbetrag}$$

3. Eintritt des Zahlungsverzugs: 13.04. d. J. (erster Verzugstag: 14.04. d. J.)
   Verzugstage: 17 (April) + 31 (Mai) + 25 (Juni) = 73 Tage
   Berechnete Verzugszinsen = 14.430,61 EUR – 14.200 EUR = 230,61 EUR

   $$p = \frac{230{,}61 \cdot 100 \cdot 365}{14.200 \cdot 73} = 8{,}12\,\%$$

   Heinz Zipf ist kein Verbraucher, denn der Zinssatz von 8,12 % bedeutet 9 Prozentpunkte über dem Basiszinssatz und dieser gilt laut § 288 (2) BGB für Rechtsgeschäfte, an denen ein Verbraucher nicht beteiligt ist.

4. $$t = \frac{2{,}18 \cdot 100 \cdot 365}{840 \cdot 4{,}12} = 22{,}9 \text{ Tage} \approx 23 \text{ Tage}$$

   Die Rechnung war am 26.03. d. J. fällig. Erster Verzugstag war der 27.03. d. J.

5. 365 Tage = 4,12 %
   110 Tage = x

   $$x = \frac{4{,}12 \cdot 110}{365} = 1{,}24\,\%$$

   101,24 % = 30.372,49 EUR
   100 % = x

   $$x = \frac{30.372{,}49 \cdot 100}{101{,}24} = 30.000{,}48 \text{ EUR}$$

   Rechnungsbetrag: 30.000,48 EUR

Aufgabe 4 Zahlungsverzug – Eintritt – Rechtsfolgen

1. **Eintritt des Zahlungsverzugs – Verzugszinsen**

   Die Zahlung ist sofort nach Lieferung (30.04. d. J.) fällig – §§ 271 (1), 273 (1) BGB.
   Die Medicom GmbH kann Verzugszinsen verlangen. Obwohl Kerstin Scharf ihrer Bank innerhalb der 30 Tagesfrist (§ 286 (3) BGB) den Überweisungsauftrag erteilt hat, trägt sie die Verzögerungsgefahr (Geldschulden = Bringschulden) gem. § 270 (1) BGB.

2. **Zahlungsverzug – Rücktritt vom Vertrag**

   a) Peter Kaiser kommt mit der Mahnung (26.06. d. J.) in Zahlungsverzug. Die Forderung ist zwar sofort fällig. Da aber für die Zahlung keine Zeit nach dem Kalender bestimmt oder bestimmbar ist (§ 286 (2) BGB), ist eine Mahnung erforderlich, um den Schuldner in Verzug zu setzen. Aus der Vereinbarung „sofortige Zahlung" lässt sich eine eindeutige Bestimmung des Zahlungstermins nicht ableiten.

   b) Krasniqi kann erst dann vom Vertrag zurücktreten, wenn er Kaiser eine angemessene Frist zur Zahlung gesetzt hat (§ 323 (1) BGB). Eine Mahnung ohne Nachfristsetzung berechtigt noch nicht zum Rücktritt.

   Hinweis: Für den Gläubiger empfiehlt es sich, bereits mit der Mahnung eine angemessene Nachfrist zu setzen. Damit ist er berechtigt, nach Ablauf der Nachfrist sofort vom Vertrag zurücktreten, falls die sonstigen Rücktrittsvoraussetzungen erfüllt sind.

zu Kapitel 5 Mahnverfahren und Zwangsvollstreckung

zu Kapitel 5.1 Mahnverfahren

ANWENDUNGS- UND ÜBUNGSAUFGABE

Aufgabe 1 Zahlungsverzug – Mahnverfahren – Vollstreckungsbescheid

1. Hubert Göllner kommt mit der Mahnung am 04. Mai d. J. in Zahlungsverzug (§ 286 (2) BGB).

2. a) Die Widerspruchsfrist beträgt zwei Wochen seit der Zustellung des Mahnbescheids (§ 692 (1) Zi 3 ZPO).

   b) Der Widerspruch wird erfolgreich sein, wenn der Fehler tatsächlich nicht auf falsche Bedienung zurückzuführen ist. Zugunsten des Verbrauchers wird vermutet, dass ein Mangel, der innerhalb von sechs Monaten nach Übergabe der Sache auftritt (Gefahrenübergang), bereits bei Übergabe vorhanden war. Dem Verkäufer gegenüber können nur dann keine Gewährleistungsansprüche durchgesetzt werden, wenn dieser beweisen kann, dass die Sache zum Zeitpunkt des Gefahrenübergangs einwandfrei war (Beweislastumkehr – § 476 BGB).

zu Kapitel 5.2 Zwangsvollstreckung und Pfändung

ANWENDUNGS- UND ÜBUNGSAUFGABE

Aufgabe 1 Vollstreckungsbescheid und Pfändung

1. Ja. Der Antrag auf Vollstreckungsbescheid wurde rechtzeitig gestellt. Der Mahnbescheid ist noch in Kraft, weil die 6-Monatsfrist des § 701 ZPO noch nicht verstrichen ist. Der Vollstreckungsbescheid wurde von der Stadtsparkasse Heilbronn auch nicht zu früh beantragt, weil die dem Schuldner (Renz) gem. § 699 (1) ZPO zustehende Widerspruchsfrist von 2 Wochen abgelaufen ist.

2. a) Keinen Einspruch einlegen, denn dieser wäre zwecklos. Die Zahlungsverpflichtung ergibt sich aus dem Sachverhalt eindeutig. Renz würde einen Prozess verlieren und müsste dann noch die Gerichtskosten tragen. Sinnvoll wäre zu zahlen oder mit der Bank über eine Stundung oder Ratenzahlung zu verhandeln.

   b) Da § 700 ZPO den Vollstreckungsbescheid einem für vorläufig vollstreckbaren Versäumnisurteil gleichstellt, beträgt die Einspruchsfrist 2 Wochen (§§ 338, 339 ZPO)

3. a) Briefmarkensammlung, orientalischer Teppich
   Gem. § 811 ZPO sind die dem persönlichen Gebrauch, der Berufstätigkeit oder dem Haushalt dienenden Sachen sowie die auf 4 Wochen erforderlichen Nahrungs- und Beleuchtungsmittel nicht pfändbar.

   b) Briefmarkensammlung, § 808 (1) ZPO.

4. Pfandsiegel, § 808 (2) ZPO.

5. a) Hat der Gerichtsvollzieher Gegenstände aus dem Besitz des Schuldners gepfändet, an denen der Schuldner kein Eigentumsrecht besitzt, dann kann der Eigentümer Widerspruchsklage gegen die Pfändung einreichen, um sein Eigentum zurückerhalten. Die Frist gibt dem Schuldner auch Gelegenheit, die Schuld zu begleichen und danach die gepfändeten Gegenstände zurückzuerhalten.

   b) Ort und Zeit der Versteigerung müssen bekannt gemacht werden, damit möglichst viele Bieter zur Versteigerung erscheinen. Nur so kann ein günstiger Versteigerungserlös erzielt werden. Schuldner und Gläubiger können mitbieten.

6. Kernfrage: Ist Rücksichtnahme auf bisherigen Lebensstandard des Schuldners sozial?
   Gefahr: Aufgrund der gesetzlichen Regelung könnte der Fall eintreten, dass dem Schuldner ein höherer Lebensstandard gesichert wird als dem Gläubiger.

zu Kapitel 6 Überschuldung privater Haushalte und Verbraucherinsolvenz

zu Kapitel 6.1 Gründe für die Überschuldung privater Haushalte

ANWENDUNGS- UND ÜBUNGSAUFGABEN

DIGITAL+

Aufgabe 1 Persönlicher Haushaltsplan

Schülerabhängige Lösung

Aufgabe 2 Auswertung eines Haushaltsplanes

Kreditbetrag	8.000,00 EUR
48 · 0,6 % = 28,8 % Zinsen	2.304,00 EUR
Darlehensverpflichtung	10.304,00 EUR
Monatsraten	48
Monatsrate	214,66 EUR

Ergebnis: Aus dem monatlichen Überschuss von 269,17 EUR lässt sich die Monatsrate aus dem Ratenkredit in Höhe von 214,66 EUR decken.

Aufgabe 3 Internetrecherche

Schülerabhängige Lösungen

Aufgabe 4 Schuldnerberatung

Schülerabhängige Lösung

zu Kapitel 6.2 Verbraucherinsolvenz

ERARBEITUNGSAUFGABE

EA 1 Ablauf eines Verbraucherinsolvenzverfahrens

1. Auf der Grundlage des Schuldenbereinigungsplanes unter gleichzeitiger Vorlage der Einkommens- und Vermögensverhältnisse des Schuldners versucht der Schuldnerberater, eine außergerichtliche Einigung zu erzielen. Gegenstand einer solchen Einigung sind i. d. R. Teilerlass der Forderungen und/oder Stundung.
2. Mit der außergerichtlichen Schuldenbereinigung soll versucht werden, eine Verbraucherinsolvenz und das damit verbundene gerichtliche Verfahren zu verhindern.
3. Die außergerichtliche Schuldenbereinigung gilt als angenommen, wenn keiner der Gläubiger widerspricht.
4. - Bescheinigung einer geeigneten Person oder Stelle, aus der sich ergibt, dass eine außergerichtliche Einigung erfolglos war.
   - Antrag auf Erteilung der Restschuldbefreiung.
   - Vermögens- und Einkommensverzeichnis.
   - Schuldenbereinigungsplan (vgl. § 305 InsO).
5. Grundsätzlich müssen alle Gläubiger zustimmen. Das Gericht kann aber Gläubigereinwendungen auf Antrag eines Gläubigers oder des Schuldners ersetzen, wenn
   - mehr als die Hälfte der Gläubiger dem Schuldenbereinigungsplan zustimmen und
   - die Ansprüche der zustimmenden Gläubiger mehr als 50 % der Gesamtsumme der benannten Gläubiger betragen.
6. Zusammen mit dem Antrag zur Eröffnung des Insolvenzverfahrens stellt der Schuldner einen Antrag auf Restschuldbefreiung. Im Verbraucherinsolvenzverfahren wird das pfändbare Vermögen des Schuldners veräußert bzw. an die Gläubiger verteilt. Der Schuldner erhält die Auflage, sich zu bemühen, innerhalb der nächsten sechs Jahre (Wohlverhaltensperiode) seine noch ausstehenden Verbindlichkeiten so weit wie möglich zu erfüllen. Erfüllt er diese Auflagen, so ist er am Ende der Wohlverhaltensperiode auch vom Rest seiner Schulden befreit.

   Die Frist von sechs Jahren verringert sich auf **drei Jahre**, wenn der Schuldner in diesem Zeitraum mindestens 35 % der angemeldeten Schulden sowie die gesamten Verfahrenskosten begleicht (§ 300 (1) Nr. 2 InsO). Gelingt es dem Schuldner innerhalb von **fünf Jahren**, die gesamten Verfahrenskosten zu begleichen, so kann er auch nach dieser Zeit bereits Restschuldbefreiung erlangen (InsO § 300 (1) Nr. 3).

zu Kapitel 6.2 Verbraucherinsolvenz

ANWENDUNGS- UND ÜBUNGSAUFGABE

Aufgabe 1 Internetrecherche – Verbraucherinsolvenzen

Schülerabhängige Antworten

Learning area D
Business divisions and activities of an MNC

for chapter 1 Business objectives and motives for internationalisation

INTRODUCTORY EXERCISE

IE 1 Business objectives of a multinational automotive supplier

1./2.

- Proximity to the North American market → sales market
- Availability of skilled labour → production
- Low labour costs → production
- Production for the Mexican market and for export to numerous countries → sales market
- Major automakers manufacture in Mexico → sales market
- Suppliers invest in Mexico → procurement market
- Profit from innovations, e.g. 23 patents → production

3.
- Investment → operational objective since all criteria are defined, though not short-term
- R&D centre → strategic objective since it is not directly measurable and the results of research tend to be rather long-term
- Number of engineers → operational objective since all criteria are defined and rather short-term

4. Ecological objectives are not mentioned here. However, there are two social objectives in the text: Continental is an **important employer** with a workforce numbering more than 24,000 and offers its staff a high degree of flexibility and **development opportunities**.

for chapter 1 Business objectives and motives for internationalisation

TASKS FOR APPLICATION AND PRACTICE

Task 1 Business objectives

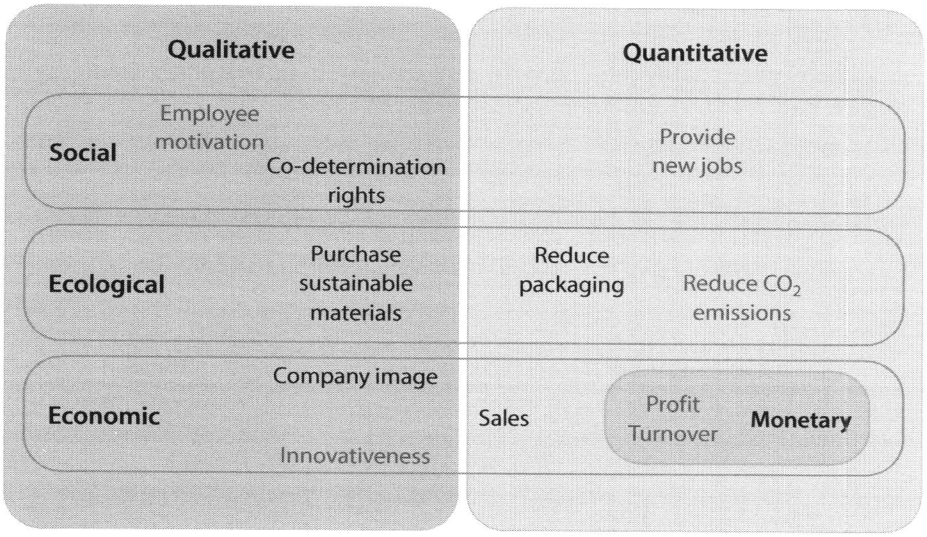

Task 2 Ecological objectives

1. Companies are linked to the surrounding ecosystem in many different ways. For one thing, this is true of the use of natural resources such as raw materials, energy, land and air, which affects the environment. Furthermore, the production process causes environmental problems such as waste, noise, and harmful emissions contaminating the air, soil and water. Many consequences of pollution are borne by society as social costs because they are not covered by companies' cost accounting (externalisation of social costs). If a company fails to meet its environmental responsibility, this could harm both its reputation and its sales figures. By contrast, adopting an environmentally beneficial policy may be a marketing advantage. In addition, it is also in the company's best interests as an environmental disaster could well destroy the basis of its existence.

2.
   - R&D: developing eco-friendly products
   - Purchasing: short transport routes
   - Sales: reducing packaging
   - Investments: investing in technology to save energy
   - Production: reducing and recycling waste

3.
   - Higher production costs for eco-friendly products
   - Lack of technology or expertise for manufacturing eco-friendly products
   - Lack of acceptance among employees (e.g. business trips by train instead of a company car, video conferences instead of face-to-face meetings)

Task 3 Operationalisation of objectives

1 The objective of the central management. (Increase of sales to 7 million euros, increase of profits by at least 25%).

2. Marketing: Increasing sales of kitchen appliances (fridges, washing machines, dishwashers) by 15% in the following business year.

   Production: Reducing production costs by at least 6% in the following business year by streamlining production.

3. Operationalised objectives enable the degree of achievement to be identified. Operational objectives provide direction concerning the achievement of a task.

4.

	Profit	Environmental pollution	Customer relationships
Operational objectives	Increasing profits by 5% per year on average within the next 5 years.	Increasing recyclable parts of our household appliances to 90% within two years.	Decreasing the number of late deliveries to retailers by 30% by next year.
	Realising a return on equity of at least 20% in each year.	Decreasing emissions by 5% within the next 5 years.	Increasing customer contacts (retailer) by 10% for consulting reasons within six months.

Task 4 Relationships between objectives

1. These objectives are complementary because an increase in sales volume usually leads to both a higher market share and a higher turnover. (However, if the increase in market share was brought about by lowering prices, turnover might also decrease. In that case they would be competing objectives.)
2. These objectives are complementary because increasing turnover contributes to higher profit (if we assume that costs remain the same).
3. These objectives are complementary because lowering costs contributes to higher profit (if we assume that turnover remains the same).
4. These objectives are complementary. The higher the quality, the better the image.
5. These objectives are competitive (in the short run) since a reduction of pollution entails additional investments and costs, which lower profit. However, measures such as saving energy or reducing toxic waste also save money. In this respect, the objectives may be as well complementary. Moreover, a better image may eventually increase turnover and hence profit.
6. These objectives are complementary. The higher the market power, the safer the jobs since the company does not face much competition.
7. These objectives are competitive since more company cars will hinder the reduction of the carbon footprint (unless the company offers only electric cars).

Task 5 Production cost as a motive for internationalisation

1. Labour productivity = Production volume/working hours

   Labour productivity$_{GER}$ = 100,000 shirts/12,500 hours = 8 shirts per hour

   Labour productivity$_{GER}$ = 100% → 8 shirts

Labour $productivity_{BUL} = 44.9\% \rightarrow X \rightarrow X = 8/100 \cdot 44.9 = 3.59$ shirts

Labour $productivity_{BUL} = 3.59 = 100{,}000/w \rightarrow$ in Bulgaria 27,855 working hours are needed.

Total labour $cost_{GER} = 12{,}500 \cdot 41.01 =$ €512,657.73

Total labour $cost_{BUL} = 27{,}855 \cdot 4.64 =$ €129,111.97

Total labour costs in Germany are almost four times as high as in Bulgaria, even if labour productivity is much higher in Germany. The main difference is in the hourly wage. As labour costs are the main part of production costs, ShowRiginals will probably decide to establish the new factory in Bulgaria.

2. On the procurement market, there may be cost advantages, too. Suppliers may be closer to Bulgaria than to Germany and services like maintenance may also be cheaper there.

   The Bulgarian sales market may offer new opportunities and reduce the risk of relying exclusively on the German market. Customised shirts may be a market niche in Bulgaria with less competition than in Germany. However, if ShowRiginals plans to sell the shirts in Germany, additional transportation cost would have to be considered.

Task 6 International companies in your region

(Open answer)

for chapter 2 The value chain and types of production

TASKS FOR APPLICATION AND PRACTICE

Task 1 Functional organisation of an enterprise

a) Calculate the minimum price of a product. → Accounting

b) Compare offers of suppliers. → Procurement

c) Hire new employees. → Human Resources

d) Store finished goods until they are sold. → Logistics

e) Negotiate a bank loan. → Finance

f) Visit customers and inform them about new products. → Sales & Distribution

g) Ensure product quality. → Production

h) Invent a new product. → Research & Development

Task 2 Exploring a local enterprise

(Open answer)

PDF

DIGITAL+

Task 3 Cooperation of functional business areas

Situation	Procurement	Production	Sales & Distribution	Logistics	Research & Development	Human Resources	Accounting	Finance
1	X	X		X			X	X
2	X	X		X			X	X
3	X	X				X	X	X
4	X		X				X	
5			X	X		X	X	X
6	X	X	X	X	X	X	X	X
7	X	X	X	X			X	
8	X	X	X	X		X	X	
9		X					X	X

Task 4 The value chain of a manufacturer

1. The **research and development** department is responsible for developing a robot window cleaner. Maybe they can profit from previous research on robots.

2. After the development of a robot window cleaner, the **production** department sets up and optimises a production process to manufacture the new product.

   The **finance** department negotiates a credit agreement with a bank to finance new machines and other equipment needed for manufacturing.

   There may be some new material requirements defined by the R&D department. Therefore, the **procurement** department needs to look for suitable suppliers and compare their offers.

   The **human resources** department recruits suitable personnel for the new production line.

   The **logistics** department plans the amounts of raw materials and finished products that have to be stored as well as their transportation.

   The department of **accounting** documents all necessary expenses as well as the revenues that will be generated.

3. The cheaper the raw materials purchased, the higher the value added. Moreover, **procurement** contributes to value creation by choosing a reliable supplier that ensures that production never stands still due to shortages.

   Sales and distribution contributes by creating good advertising campaigns. If customers know about the quality and special features of a product, they are prepared to pay higher prices. That means the product is more valuable.

Task 5 Application of different types of production

Note for the teacher: Students may use the support material provided in their book (QR-Code).

1. Mass production would only be possible by reducing the number of different models. Series production makes it possible to offer products that match most of consumer wants and needs. Individual production would be even better in this respect. However, VisioWire could not profit from economies of scale in that case. That would make their TV sets very expensive and hence not very attractive to consumers. Summing up, series production is a good compromise for a product like TV sets.

2. a) Flow production leads to a higher output and productivity. That means that more TV sets can be produced by the same number of workers. Workers can perform specific tasks better and faster due to specialisation. There is no need to transport or store the products during production as all tasks are done at one assembly line. If a correct cycle time is set, there are no delays and the lead time (from starting to produce till finishing a certain product) is very short.

   b) Aspects discussed may include the following:

Management	Shareholders	Labour union	Mayor of the city
▪ Fully automatic production is our goal. Flow production helps us to achieve that goal. ▪ First of all, our customers will profit, because we will be able to offer very good quality at competitive prices. ▪ But also our employees will profit, because innovation secures their jobs and offers challenging new tasks.	▪ We like the idea of higher productivity and reducing labour cost. ▪ But on the other hand, we fear that costs will increase with all these machines and robots. In case of an economic downturn it is not easy to reduce costs.	▪ We value that automation reduces highly repetitive work on an assembly line. ▪ However, we fear that jobs are lost. Especially our low-skilled colleagues will have problems finding a job.	▪ I agree with the labour union. We must avoid job losses under all circumstances, because high unemployment in our city will make it less attractive and affect other businesses like restaurants and retailing as well. ▪ Still, we should also keep in mind that our citizens want to buy TV sets at a reasonable price.

Task 6 Types of production in paper plane production

PDF DIGITAL+

Instructions can be found in the teacher's digital resources.

Result may vary. Here is a list of possible observations:

- Flow production looks like a street.
- Workshop production looks like three islands.
- All jobs are done manually.
- As all planes are of the same type, this is mass production.
- Productivity is probably higher using flow production.
- This may be due to delays when workshop production is used.
- There is much more need for transportation (from one workshop to the other) using workshop production.

- The lead time using flow production is probably lower.
- The flow production team will probably request more capital as scissors are needed in the beginning and in the end of the process.
- In flow production there is a high degree of specialisation in one particular task. However, specialisation is also possible in workshop production.
- To reduce delays, stocks between the different workshops are needed.
- Workshop production is more flexible, e.g. when something goes wrong.
- Quality depends more on other factors than the type of production.

for chapter 3 Digitalisation in manufacturing companies

TASKS FOR APPLICATION AND PRACTICE

Task 1 Industrial revolutions

Industrial revolutions			
Mechanisation	**Electrification**	**Computerisation**	**Digitalisation**
Industry 1.0	Industry 2.0	Industry 3.0	Industry 4.0
major inventions			
Steam engine	Assembly line	Personal computer	Cyber-physical production systems

Task 2 New business models based on Industry 4.0

1. A physical component (the saw), a smart component (sensors and a small computer) and a connectivity component (e.g. a network adapter for WiFi)
2.

	Current business model	New business model
Main activity of the company	Make and sell physical goods (saws)	Provide a service (sawing)
Sources of revenue	Sale of the products, maintenance charges, sale of spare parts	Usage fees (hours of machine usage)
Risk of failures (downtime etc.)	... borne by the customer	... mainly borne by our company, since we have no revenue if the saw is not working
Use of the data obtained	Not obtained yet	Optimising products according to their main usage; offer additional services

3. The evaluation may include the following points:

   Advantages for our company:
   - Regular and secure income (instead of fluctuating sales)
   - Lower costs for our customers in times of crisis and additional services, e.g. maintenance and spare parts included in the fee → competitive advantage for our company
   - We profit from improvements even more, since we receive the usage fee whether maintenance is necessary or not.

Potential drawbacks:

- Investment in smart technology needed
- Uncertainty as to whether carpentry workshops will value the Saw-as-a-Service model.
- Depending on the contract, customers can easily switch from one provider to the other.

Key for users of the support material (QR-Code):

1)

Smart products		
Physical component	**Smart component**	**Connectivity component**
Saw	Sensors and a small computer	Network adapter for WiFi

2)

	Current business model	New business model
Main activity of the company	Make and sell physical goods (saws)	Provide a service (sawing)
Sources of revenue	Sale of the products, maintenance charges, sale of spare parts	Usage fees (hours of machine usage)
Risk of failures (downtime etc.)	... borne by the customer	... mainly borne by our company, since we have no revenue if the saw is not working
Use of the data obtained	Not obtained yet	Optimising products according to their main usage; offer additional services

3)

	Advantages for our company	Potential drawbacks
Financial impacts	Regular and secure income (instead of fluctuating sales)	Investment in smart technology needed
Customer reaction	Lower costs for our customers in times of crisis and they receive additional services, e.g. maintenance included → competitive advantage for our company	Uncertainty as to whether carpentry workshops will value the Saw-as-a-Service model.
Other impacts	We profit from improvements even more, since we receive the usage fee whether maintenance is necessary or not.	Depending on the contract, customers can easily switch from one provider to the other.

Task 3 Communication infrastructure as a precondition for digitalisation

(Open answer)

Task 4 ERP systems as a precondition for Industry 4.0

1. Enterprise resource planning (ERP) systems like SAP or Oracle collect and combine all the data of a company in one single database which comprises for example the orders the procurement department has placed, the orders the sales and distribution department has received as well as data from the production planning, human resources, and finance departments.

2. As the table below shows, production has to be stopped on 6 June, since Powerslide LLP is running out of wheels. As a result, the company can only deliver 180 skateboards on 10 June. If no new orders are placed, similar problems can be expected in the second half of June.

3. First of all, ERP systems save a lot of time, since they automate many calculations like the ones you did in subtask 2. Moreover, they reduce the number of errors made in calculations. A further basic feature of ERP systems is that you can print documents like orders or invoices without much extra work as all data is already part of the database.

4. Previously, ERP systems were used separately from operations technology and automation technology. Industry 4.0 integrates these systems. The flow of information within the company has become much faster. For example, if orders are changed, the production process will be adjusted immediately.

	Wheel June orders	**Stock of Wheels***	**/4****	**Daily production**	**Stock of skateboards***	**Skateboard orders**
		1.000	250		80	
1		800	200	50	130	
2		600	150	50	180	
3		400	100	50	30	200
4		200	50	50	80	
5		0	0	50	130	
6		0	0	**0**	30	100
8	1.000	800	200	50	80	
9		600	150	50	130	
10		400	100	50	**– 20**	200
11		200	50	50	30	
12		0	0	50	80	
14		600	150	50	30	100
15	800	400	100	50	80	

* stock at the end of the day
** divided by 4 because four wheels are needed for each skateboard

Task 5 Bullwhip effect

1.

Battery manufacturer → Torch manufacturer → Wholesaler → Supermarket chain

2. $500 \cdot 1.3 \cdot 1.2 \cdot 2 = 1.560$ batteries

3. Probably zero. The discounter has ordered enough to stock a number of branches. Even if more batteries are required the wholesaler will have enough on stock. And in any case, the torch manufacturer will order nothing because he already has included next month's demand in his order because of the good price.

4. The further we move along the supply chain, the bigger the variations in demand are. Timelags, bulk orders to benefit from volume discounts, speculation about the fluctuation of prices and the fear concerning the risk of supply shortages lead to seemingly random order volume even though consumer demand is relatively stable.

5. ▪ Higher stock levels → higher cost
   ▪ Delivery bottlenecks despite higher stock levels
   ▪ Poor capacity utilisation
6. Supply chain management helps to improve the flow of information along the supply chain. In effect, a manufacturer upstream will know at which time which quantities will be needed by his customers' buyers. The aim of SCM is to optimise production and logistics processes, e.g. minimising stock levels and delivery times while at the same time safeguarding production.
7. They are competing objectives: If you try to achieve on the one you jeopardise the other.
8. (Individual experiences in the *beer game*)

Task 6 Disruptive technologies

(Open answer)

Task 7 Data security and acceptance of increasing digitalisation

1. Attackers and possible motives:
   - Hackers → fame or political reasons, e.g. "Anonymous" hacktivists
   - Cybercriminals → blackmail someone using ransomware or sell stolen data, e.g. for marketing purposes
   - Insiders → take revenge for being fired
   - Competitors or other countries → weaken a certain company or country, e.g. Stuxnet
2. Negative effects of cyberattacks:
   - Loss of productivity, e.g. because of a production stop
   - Financial loss, e.g. cost of data recovery, IT consulting, public relations and legal costs
   - Reputation damage, e.g. if customer data was published
3. Simple cybersecurity techniques:
   System updates, secure passwords, backups
6. (Open answer), Hint: https://www.bbc.com/news/topics/cp3mvpdp1r2t/cyber-attacks
7. Cybersecurity issues as a risk for the acceptance of increasing digitalisation:
   With every news message of customer data including credit card numbers having been stolen from large online shops, consumers lose confidence in the cybersecurity measures promised. Some consumers will stop certain online activities. But even if consumer data is obtained legally (although many times without the user's knowledge) many people are uncomfortable about the possible use of their data. If a company knows exactly which goods you buy, which films you watch and which kind of information you look up, it most likely knows more about you than any secret service.
8. Further problems that need to be solved for the acceptance of increasing digitalisation:
   - Ethical issues, for example when decisions are left to machines
   - Health and security issues, when robots and humans work closely together
   - Problems on the job market, when workers are replaced by robots
   - Environmental problems, since smart products usually consume more energy and specific resources which are hard to obtain

Task 8 Just-in-Time

1. With the introduction of JiT the cost levels are higher (194,400 euros). However, the implementation cost will be incurred only once. Starting from the second year of implementation, JiT will save costs, since its annual costs only amount to 90,400 euros in comparison to 168,000 euros without the introduction of JiT (see table below).
2. JiS requires the material to be delivered in the order of assembly. That means for example that housings prepared for cappuccino creamers and housings without that feature would be delivered in a certain order.
3. JiT requires more orders and hence more deliveries. As a result, more trucks are needed that will produce more CO_2. On the other hand, the amount of storage space decreases which means that more land can be left to nature.

Stock without JiT		**Cost in €**	
2 000	pallets	120 000	cost of warehousing
1 600 000	value of materials	48 000	cost of capital lockup
		168 000	**sum total**

Stock with JiT		**Cost in €**	
600	pallets	36 000	cost of warehousing
4 800 000	value of materials	14 400	cost of capital lockup
		40 000	additional delivery cost/lower volume discount
		90 400	**subtotal excluding implementation cost**
		100 000	cost of implementing JiT
		190 400	**sum total**

Task 9 Cyber-physical production systems

1. Components needed to make a machine "smart": computers, actuators, sensors
2. A self-organising machine processes the information it gets and responds to changing requirements.
3. Using a digital twin, production can be simulated before it begins. The cyber-physical production system first checks whether the product is feasible. Basically, the machine tests whether it can fulfil the requirements or not. Then, it determines the best possible order of the necessary steps.
4. The following technologies can be used:
   - RFID for the recognition of the product,
   - intelligent sensors to avoid accidents involving workers and
   - speech recognition or user interfaces for the communication between worker and machine.
5. Machines collect data to learn from them. They evaluate which settings work best, cause the lowest number of errors and require the least amount of material for instance. The machine then uses this data to improve production.

6. A customised product is "tailor-made", i.e. made specifically for an individual or a small number of customers, e.g. a wardrobe that exactly fits into a corner of your room. The latter is also called "batch size 1".

Task 10 Digitalisation in furniture retailing

1)

Prior to sale	Information/Advice	Purchase and payment	After the sale
Offer an **online shop** so customers can obtain information before visiting the furniture store, or order goods straight away. Moreover, customers could customise a product by themselves.	Use a **chatbot** to provide basic information and save costs at the same time.	Use **self-checkout terminals** to save staff cost and reduce queues.	Use **RFID** to provide "track & trace" in order to inform customers about progress at the delivery stage.
Use **social commerce** to inspire future customers, e.g. using Instagram, facebook or pinterest.	Use **beacons and in-store-navigation** to provide further information on the smartphone of the customers about the product they are looking at.	Use **NFC** for mobile and contactless payment to provide more service to customers	Use a **service app** to stay in contact with customers.
	Use **electronic shelf labels** to change prices quickly.		Use a **loyalty programme app** with discounts, coupons etc. to retain customers
	Use **QR-codes** for each piece of furniture to provide further information on alternative colours etc.		
	Use **augmented reality** to give a customers an impression of how a sofa would fit into their living room.		

2) Providing an **online shop** is a good opportunity to gain new customers that live further away from your furniture store. But there are also some risks. Regular customers might use our online shop but also compare prices with those of other online shops. Instead of looking for a sofa in our shop and ending up buying pillows, dishes, and a pan on the way, they might just order the sofa.

Beacons and in-store navigation initially cause high costs. Whether customers value this service equally high is not clear. Maybe they would rather look around or want to protect their data. However, it may be very helpful to have all the possible colours and forms of a sofa available on your smartphone when you stand in front of it. That might differentiate your furniture store from others.

3) You receive more data from online customers than from regular customers, e.g. their address and bank details or items they have been looking at but in the end did not buy. Beacons tell you about the path a customer takes in your store, e.g. whether someone has first been looking for special offers or the restaurant. You can use that data to create and retain a long-term customer base which after all, is the aim of CRM. Thus, you can arrange your product display in such a manner that the average customer passes by products that he is not looking for but then ends up buying them anyway.

   Moreover, you can make sure an online customer will see the product he looked at but did not buy yet on your website as soon as he opens your site. Furthermore, he will see online ads for this specific product when he visits other websites, e.g. news pages.

Task 11 Pros and cons of Industry 4.0

(Open answer)

for chapter 4 Cultural diversity

INTRODUCTORY EXERCISE

IE 1 Cultural diversity management at Shell

1. Becoming a world-class investment opportunity.
2. The customers of a multinational company like Shell are very diverse. Hiring people with diverse backgrounds may help to understand these customers' wants and needs as well as their behaviour.

   A second reason why diversity management may lead to higher profits is that people who work in a place where everyone feels welcome are more committed and perform better in their roles.
3. Women, ethnic minorities, people with disabilities, LGBT people
4. The company set targets especially for the number of women and locals in senior roles. They introduced global and local talent plans and outlined ways to measure their performance. Moreover, Shell introduced flexible working hours and benefits for their employees' partners. A so-called diversity and inclusion index measures how employees actually feel about diversity. Employee networks are meant to provide a framework for underrepresented groups to support each other. Shell's Women's Career Development Programme is a company programme to help female employees to balance career and family.
5. Shell states they have a culture of respect, understanding and inclusion. Diversity is in line with these. These values, especially non-discrimination, are included in the Shell Code of Conduct that is accessible to every employee and the public.
6. (Open answer)

for chapter 4 Cultural diversity

TASKS FOR APPLICATION AND PRACTICE

Task 1 Our own intercultural experiences

(Open answer)

Task 2 Cultural misunderstandings

Both tried to be polite and acted adequately in their own cultural context. However, the cultural norms and values are different in this case. To a Chinese person, a second offer would be necessary and not pushy at all. To a German, "No, thank you." means nothing else than "No, thank you."

cf. Wang, L., Wenn Konfuzius Schulz von Thun trifft… in: Kumbier, Schulz von Thun (Hg.), Interkulturelle Kommunikation (2006), S. 190f

Task 3 Culture as a system of orientation – short role play

DIGITAL+

Instructions on how to play and further materials for the role play can be found in the teacher's digital resources.

Task 4 German cultural standards

1. Match the following examples to the corresponding German cultural standards.

A software engineer: "That code will never work".	Directness/truth
A technician: "I won't leave until your heating is fixed."	Internalised control
A manager: "He's obnoxious. But a good lawyer. Let's hire him."	Task orientation
An angry department manager: "Where would we be if everyone did as they liked?"	Rules and regulations
A clerk: "Please don't disturb. I'll call you when I've finished."	Time management
A German proverb: "Dienst ist Dienst und Schnaps ist Schnaps."	Separation of the personal and public domains
A mother to her son: "Don't talk to strangers."	Interpersonal distance

2. Because of their simplicity, cultural standards may lead to prejudices. Moreover, they may be biased by the authors' perspective. However, cultural standards are not meant to tell "how Germans are", for example. In fact, they are merely there to master critical intercultural interactions.

Task 5 American cultural standards

1./2. There is no information given that points to answer (a). They indeed lack the expertise in mechanical engineering like in (b) but they would surely ask if that was the main problem. Mistranslations (c) as in the case of "prototype" as a "false friend" can always happen, although there is no indication of other language problems here. The American cultural standard "**easy going**" is key to understand why Americans prefer to produce a quick solution first and troubleshoot later (d). They feel that this strategy is much better because it leads to faster results. Although there are stereotypes, Americans do not have special reservations about Germans. There is no information about gender discrimination (e) either. The fact that women have rather better career chances in the US than in Germany seems to point in the opposite direction. Answer (f) is based on the American cultural standard of "**action orientation**". In a brainstorming session, it is against the rules to dismiss an idea outright. This is considered rude. Americans are rather optimistic and will at least try out some of the ideas.

3. Strategy: Sophia needs to understand the concept of brainstorming. It's about visions for the future rather than concrete plans. She could come up with proposals to overcome problems she expects to arise or alternative plans. Moreover, she could suggest holding a German-style discussion after a brainstorming session to evaluate the ideas.

   Concerning the quality of the software for testing, she either accepts that typical American approach or raises the issue with her colleagues. In a joint venture, both sides have to be clear about their goals and methods.

KEY for users of the support material (QR-Code):

1)

Possible explanation for the behaviour of the American partners	Information in the text	My assessment of the statement
a) They are not qualified enough for the job.	Software developers	☐ likely ☒ unlikely because there is no information given that points to a lack of qualifications.
b) They did not react to her statement because they lack expertise in mechanical engineering.	Software developers	☐ likely ☒ unlikely because they indeed lack the expertise in mechanical engineering, but they would surely ask if that was the main problem.
c) They are having some other misunderstandings because Sophia is not a native English speaker.	"Prototype" is a "false friend".	☐ likely ☒ unlikely because no other examples of language difficulties are mentioned in the text.
d) They would rather like to find a quick solution first and troubleshoot later.	Many proposals were not suitable; they were not thoroughly discussed prior to implementation.	☒ likely ☐ unlikely because it fits to the American cultural standard "**easy going**". They feel that this strategy is much better because it leads to faster results.
e) They don't like to work together with her as a German and a woman.	No information on the atmosphere in the team	☐ likely ☒ unlikely because although there are stereotypes, Americans do not have special reservations about Germans. There is no information about gender discrimination either.
f) They don't take her seriously because she always appears to be pessimistic concerning new ideas.	Sophia points at some problems concerning the ideas and drafts put forward by her American counterparts.	☒ likely ☐ unlikely because according to the cultural standard of "**action orientation**", Americans are rather optimistic and try out at least some of the ideas. In a brainstorming session, it is against the rules to dismiss an idea outright. This is considered rude.

2) ☒ Action orientation ☒ Easy going

3)
- Adapting to the American approach, e.g. understanding the concept of brainstorming. It's about visions for the future rather than concrete plans.
- Combining American optimism with Sophia's German step-by-step approach, e.g. coming up with possible ways to overcome problems she expects or proposing alternative plans.
- Introducing German methods, e.g. holding a German-style discussion after a brainstorming session to evaluate the ideas.
- Raising intercultural issues within the team, e.g. the stage of development a software has to have before testing. In a joint venture, both sides have to be clear about their goals and methods.

Task 6 Chinese cultural standards

1. Hierarchy fits best. A business unit (BU) leader is not in a position to request anything directly from another BU leader. To a smaller extent, saving face might be important.

2. From Mr Wang's perspective, he did everything to preserve social harmony. Changing topics prevented a conflict. He didn't like the embarrassment of having to admit a mistake. But he showed Mrs Neu that he had understood. Mrs Neu disturbed harmony with her repeated questions. Apparently, she was just looking for someone to blame. In his view, she also didn't do her job as a manager properly because she should have checked everything her staff members did. Mr Wang would never criticise her for that because that's also against the cultural standard of hierarchy.
3. As a boss, Mrs Neu is responsible for solving the problems of her subordinates according to the cultural standard of hierarchy. She doesn't blame Mr Wang to save her and his face. Instead, she praises him for something else. The personal introduction to the supplier's management helps Mr Wang to build Guanxi (personal networks).

Task 7 Prejudices in a VUCA world

1. (Open answer)
2. Prejudices reduce complexity and give orientation and security even when you lack adequate information about another culture. Hence, in a VUCA world, prejudices are likely to spread. We must be aware of the fact that prejudices very often lead to conflicts.
3. Just like prejudices, cultural standards can reduce complexity and give orientation in cultural interaction which is very helpful in a world so complex and ambiguous. But unlike prejudices, cultural standards do not oversimplify and are based on both scientific research and the experiences of many people. As a result, they can be used to avoid conflicts and lead to a better understanding of other cultures.

Task 8 Core skills for intercultural competence – role-play

Answers may vary. Key skills are the ability to take a polycentrist rather than an ethnocentrist view, the ability to communicate and the ability to fix limits to acceptance. But also the following may be relevant: ambiguity tolerance, cultural knowledge, empathy and the ability of meta-communication.

Task 9 Core skills for intercultural competence

The first core skill to mention is **cultural knowledge.** In the elevator scene, Fabian apparently did not know that controversial topics like politics must not be mentioned in small talk. At the same time, his **ethnocentrism** offended his American counterpart. Taking a negative view of everything in comparison to your home culture is not a good starting point for intercultural communication.

Ambiguity tolerance would have helped him when talking to his colleague. When he asked him to visit, he should have given a friendly reply without pressing for a date. An invitation may just be a way of being nice without any actual intent. If his colleague had invited him and mentioned a certain date and time, he would have been sure that he actually wanted him to visit. His friendly indirect reply "busy" in fact meant "no".

In the meeting, Fabian criticised his boss publicly. That is clearly beyond any **level of acceptance**. His proposal would have been a lot better like this: "What about giving customers some options from which they can choose?"

However, Fabian seems to have good skills in **meta-communication**. Probably, his boss understood in that conversation that Fabian did not want to be offensive. He probably told him that being nice and positive is very important and know-it-alls are not very popular in the United States.

KEY for users of the support material (QR-Code):

Scene	(Lack of) core skills for intercultural competence	Explanation
Discussion in elevator	Cultural knowledge, ethnocentrism	Fabian apparently did not know that controversial topics like politics must not be mentioned in small talk. Taking a negative view of everything in comparison to your home culture is not a good starting point for intercultural communication.
Invitation to visit a colleague's family	Ambiguity tolerance	Fabian should have given a friendly reply without pressing for a date. An invitation might just be a way of being nice without any actual intent. If his colleague had invited him and mentioned a certain date, he would have been sure that he actually wanted him to visit. His friendly indirect reply "busy" in fact meant "no".
Meeting	Fixing levels of acceptance	Fabian criticised his boss publicly. That is not acceptable to his American boss. His proposal would have been a lot better like this: "What about giving customers some options from which they can choose?"
Apology	Meta-communication	Fabian seems to have good skills in meta-communication. Probably, his boss understood in that conversation that Fabian did not want to be offensive. He probably told him that being nice and positive is very important and know-it-alls are not very popular in the United States.

Task 10 Outcomes of intercultural competence

Outcomes of intercultural competence (according to A. Thomas)			
Action security	**Action flexibility**	**Action creativity**	**Transfer of action**
If methods are not clear from the beginning, problems will occur. For instance, Germans will take a method of clear time management for granted, Americans will press for quick results and the Chinese will work on different topics at the same time.	German team members may have experienced that direct communication leads to quick results. However, if they cannot adapt to totally different approaches in China and the USA, the team spirit will suffer.	The team misses an opportunity if they do not use Guanxi. These networks may help the team to get in touch with interested production companies.	Even though members of the team may have the ability to use the other three outcomes of intercultural competence, cultural misunderstandings will certainly arise. If the team members fail to sort these out in team meetings or even with a coach, they will not succeed.

Task 11 Managing diversity

1. a) At the moment, 2 of 10 employees have a migration background. The resulting quota of 20% matches the overall percentage of people with a migration background (19.5%) very well.

   However, a single employee represents 10% of the department, which implies that the Turkish and the Italian employees are already overrepresented with respect to the national percentages of Italian (1%) and Turkish (3.6%) backgrounds.

   Thus, in this particular situation, taking on the applicant with a German background would decrease the percentage of people with a migration background to $2 : 11 \cdot 100 = 18.2\%$, while the Russian applicant would cause an increase to $3 : 11 \cdot 100 = 27.3\%$. Employees with Russian backgrounds would then equal 9.1% of the marketing staff – again an overrepresentation.

   b) It is very difficult – especially in small organisational units – to set up staffs that reflect the composition of the total population in terms of ethnic backgrounds. Also, if this is the only criterion used, applicants cannot be selected according to their performance.

2. a) Since the company wants to enter the Russian market, it would take on the Russian applicant, assuming that she could help understand the Russian business partners and also have some valuable knowledge about her home country.

   b) If an applicant feels that she is just welcomed due to her ethnic background, she might feel devalued and discriminated against, even if it is in a positive way. Moreover, a person with a Russian background might not know more about Russian business matters than a German employee with expert skills in tapping new markets.

3. The management could analyse the different characteristics of their employees. This does not only include ethnic backgrounds, but also education and personal experience. In a next step, the management would have to think about how such differences could be made valuable for the company. For example, the management could set up a multi-cultural and multi-functional team that prepares the entry into Russian markets. However, there might be communication problems and emotional conflicts due to the heterogeneity of the team.

Lernbereich E
Einführung in das externe Rechnungswesen

zu Kapitel 1 Aufgaben des Rechnungswesens – Kontoführung am Beispiel der Veränderung des Bargeldbestandes

ANWENDUNGS- UND ÜBUNGSAUFGABEN

Aufgabe 1 Kassenbuch und Kassenkonto führen

1.

Kassenbuch				
Datum	**Buchungstext**	**Beleg-Nr.**	**Einnahme**	**Ausgabe**
03.01...	Anfangsbestand	AB	2.860,00 EUR	
03.01...	Büromaterial	KB6		80,00 EUR
03.01...	Vorschuss	KB7		200,00 EUR
03.01...	Rechnung	KB8	5.000,00 EUR	
03.01...	Bareinzahlung	KB9		4.000,00 EUR
		Summe	7.860,00 EUR	4.280,00 EUR

2. Istbestand laut Zählliste = **3.580 EUR**
Buchbestand laut Aufzeichnungen =
2.860 EUR + 5.000 EUR – (80 EUR + 200 EUR + 4.000 EUR) = **3.580 EUR**

Soll	Kasse		Haben
Anfangsbestand	**2.860,00**	KB 6: Büromaterialien	80,00
KB 8: Rechnung	5.000,00	KB 7: Vorschuss	200,00
		KB 9: Einzahlung	4.000,00
		Schlussbestand	**3.580,00**
	7.860,00		7.860,00

3. Mögliche Ursachen für Kassendifferenzen
   - Diebstahl
   - Bestand falsch gezählt
   - Wechselgeld fehlerhaft (z. B. Zahlendreher)
   - Beleg liegt nicht vor
   - Beleg wurde nicht gebucht
   - doppelte Buchung eines Belegs
   - falsche Buchungsseite
   - falscher Betrag
   - falsche Summenbildung
   - Trinkgeld

4. Vermeidung von Kassendifferenzen durch ...
   - Kasse bzw. Büro bei Abwesenheit abschließen
   - Zählen mit Zählliste
   - zweimal zählen
   - Wechselgeld besonders kontrollieren
   - Belege nummerieren
   - Buchungsregeln beachten und konzentriert arbeiten

Aufgabe 2 Buch-Ist-Vergleich beim Kassenabschluss

1. Buchbestand = 820,00 EUR + 1.600,00 EUR – 2.280,00 EUR = 140,00 EUR
2. Buchbestand könnte nicht mit dem tatsächlichen Bestand (Istbestand) übereinstimmen.
3. Fehlbetrag = 140,00 EUR – 100,00 EUR = 40,00 EUR
   Ggf. Korrekturbuchung im Kassenkonto im Haben.

zu Kapitel 2 Von der Inventur zur Eröffnungsbilanz Wertveränderung in der Bilanz

ANWENDUNGS- UND ÜBUNGSAUFGABEN

Aufgabe 1 Bestandsaufnahme

Grundsätzlich hat der Istbestand bei Abweichungen Vorrang. Da es sich beim Kontoauszug der Sparkasse um den Istbestand handelt, ist dieser Wert in das Inventar aufzunehmen.
Ausweis im Inventar: 150.700 EUR

Hinweis: Im Falle eines fehlerhaften Kontoauszugs müsste das Unternehmen bei der kontoführenden Bank eine Korrektur verlangen.

Aufgabe 2 Ermittlung des Eigenkapitals

	GJ 01	GJ 02
Vermögen	780.000 EUR	940.000 EUR
– Schulden	540.000 EUR	550.000 EUR
= Eigenkapital (Reinvermögen)	240.000 EUR	390.000 EUR

Aufgabe 3 Erstellung eines Inventars und einer Bilanz

1. **Inventar der Konservenfabrik Wußler und Sohn OHG, 79098 Freiburg, zum 31.12... (in EUR)**

A. Vermögen		
I. Anlagevermögen		
1. Grundstücke und Bauten		600.000,00
2. Maschinen lt. bes. Verzeichnis		420.000,00
3. Fahrzeuge laut bes. Verzeichnis		190.000,00
4. Geschäftsausstattung lt. bes. Verzeichnis		92.000,00
II. Umlaufvermögen		
1. Vorräte		
Frischgemüse lt. bes. Verzeichnis	2.900,00	
Konserven lt. bes. Verzeichnis	9.600,00	12.500,00
2. Forderungen aus Lieferungen und Leistungen		
lt. OP-Liste der Schuldner (Debitoren)		49.000,00
3. Flüssige Mittel		
Kasse	4.580,00	
Bankguthaben: Deutsche Bank Kto. Nr. 888575	14.890,00	
Bankguthaben: Freiburger Gewerbebank Kto. Nr. 7236	24.100,00	43.570,00
Summe Vermögen		**1.407 070,00**
B. Schulden		
1. Verbindlichkeiten gegenüber Kreditinstituten		
Freiburger Gewerbebank	320.000,00	
Sparkasse Freiburg	6.500,00	326.500,00
2. Verbindlichkeiten aus Lieferungen und Leistungen		
lt. OP-Liste der Gläubiger (Kreditoren)		88.160,00
Summe Schulden		**414.660,00**

2.

Ermittlung des Reinvermögens (Eigenkapital)

	Vermögen	zum 31.12...	1.407.070,00
–	Schulden	zum 31.12...	414.660,00
=	Eigenkapital (Reinvermögen)	zum 31.12...	992.410,00

Das Reinvermögen (Eigenkapital) gibt den Betrag an, der dem Eigentümer eines Unternehmens bei angenommener Auflösung des Unternehmens nach Begleichung aller Schulden zufließen würde.

3. Aus Gründen der Übersichtlichkeit werden gleichartige Positionen wie z. B. Vorräte zusammengefasst. In den besonderen Verzeichnissen ist eine detaillierte Auflistung der Einzelpositionen (genaue Bezeichnung, Stückzahl, Stückpreis) zu finden.

4.

Bilanz der Konservenfabrik Wußler und Sohn OHG zum 31. Dezember ...

Aktiva		Passiva	
I. Anlagevermögen		**I. Eigenkapital**	992.410,00
1. Grundstücke und Bauten	600.000,00	**II. Fremdkapital**	
2. Maschinen	420.000,00	1. Verbindlichkeiten gegenüber Kreditinstituten	326.500,00
3. Fuhrpark	190.000,00	2. Verbindlichkeiten aus L.u.L.	88.160,00
4. BGA	92.000,00		
II. Umlaufvermögen			
1. Vorräte	12.500,00		
2. Forderungen aus L.u.L.	49.000,00		
3. Flüssige Mittel	43.570,00		
Bilanzsumme	**1.407.070,00**	**Bilanzsumme**	**1.407.070,00**

Aufgabe 4 Erstellung einer Bilanz

1.

Eröffnungsbilanz

Aktiva		Passiva	
I. Anlagevermögen		**I. Eigenkapital**	14.000,00 €
1. Geschäftsausstattung	12.500,00 €	**II. Fremdkapital**	
2. Fuhrpark	15.000,00 €	1. Verbindlichkeiten gegenüber Kreditinstituten	20.000,00 €
II. Umlaufvermögen			
1. Vorräte (Handelsware)	5.000,00 €		
2. Flüssige Mittel	1.500,00 €		
Bilanzsumme	**34.000,00 €**	**Bilanzsumme**	**34.000,00 €**

2. Von Shirin und Valerij müsse je 7.000,00 aufgebracht werden. Das Eigenkapital ist eine Restgröße, die sich aus der Differenz zwischen Vermögen und Schulden ergibt. Das Eigenkapital bringt die Bilanz zum Ausgleich, so dass beide Bilanzseiten gleich groß sind (Bilanzgleichung). Da die Passivseite die Mittelherkunft angibt, steht das von den Eigentümern zur Verfügung gestellte Eigenkapital auf der Passivseite.

3. Ja, das ist möglich. Bankguthaben und Eigenkapital stehen nicht in einem unmittelbaren Zusammenhang.

Beispiel:

Aktiva	Bilanz		Passiva
I. Anlagevermögen	**320.000,00 €**	**I. Eigenkapital**	**50.000,00 €**
II. Umlaufvermögen		**II. Fremdkapital**	**350.000,00 €**
Bankguthaben	80.000,00 €		
Bilanzsumme	**400.000,00 €**	**Bilanzsumme**	**400.000,00 €**

Aufgabe 5 Werteveränderung in der Bilanz

Nr.	Auswirkungen auf die Bilanz		
1	Geschäftsausstattung nimmt um Verbindlichkeiten nehmen um	3.000 EUR zu 3.000 EUR zu	→ **Aktiv-Passiv-Mehrung**
2	Verbindlichkeiten nehmen um Bankguthaben nimmt um	3.000 EUR ab 3.000 EUR ab	→ **Aktiv-Passiv-Minderung**
3	Bankguthaben nimmt um Forderungen nehmen um	7.000 EUR zu 7.000 EUR ab	→ **Aktivtausch**
4	Darlehen nimmt um Bank nimmt um	20.000 EUR ab 20.000 EUR ab	→ **Aktiv-Passiv-Minderung**
5	Forderungen nehmen um Fuhrpark nimmt um	8.000 EUR zu 8.000 EUR ab	→ **Aktivtausch**

Aufgabe 6 Bilanzveränderungen

Nr.	
a	Möglich, da **Aktiv-Passiv-Mehrung**
b	Nicht möglich, da kein Grundfall der Bilanzveränderung vorliegt
c	
d	Möglich, da **Passivtausch**

zu Kapitel 3 Buchen auf Bestandskonten unter Einhaltung der Grundsätze ordnungsmäßiger Buchführung

ANWENDUNGS- UND ÜBUNGSAUFGABEN

Aufgabe 1 Grundsätze ordnungsmäßiger Buchführung

1. Verstoß gegen die Grundsätze ordnungsmäßiger Buchführung: Aufbewahrungspflicht für Buchungsbelege gemäß § 147 (1) AO: 10 Jahre.
2. Verstoß gegen die Grundsätze ordnungsmäßiger Buchführung: Das Kassenbuch sollte gemäß § 146 (1) AO täglich aufgezeichnet werden.
3. Kein Verstoß gegen die Grundsätze ordnungsmäßiger Buchführung: Laufende Nummerierung ist Voraussetzung für ordnungsmäßige Ablage/Archivierung
4. Verstoß gegen den Grundsatz der Vollständigkeit, da kein wahrheitsgemäßer Ausweis der Schulden.
5. Verstoß gegen den Grundsatz der Wahrheit, da kein wahrheitsgemäßer Ausweis des Vermögens.

Aufgabe 2 Kontoauszug buchen

1. und 2.

Soll	Bank		Haben
Anfangsbestand	**25.919,08**	❷ Kfz-Steuer	460,00
❶ Re 14986	783,02	**Schlussbestand**	**26.248,50**
❸ Zinsen Festgeld	6,40		
	26.708,50		26.708,50

Kontostand (neu) laut eigener Kontenführung = **26.248,50 EUR**
Kontostand (neu) laut Kontoauszug der Bank = **26.248,50 EUR**

Aufgabe 3 Allgemeine Buchungsregeln am Beispiel von Geschäftsvorfällen

PDF

DIGITAL+

❶ Barabhebung vom Bankkonto für die Geschäftskasse: 1.000 EUR		
Welche Konten sind zu berücksichtigen?	Kasse	Bank
Auf welcher Seite des Kontos wird gebucht?	Soll	Haben
Welche Beträge sind zu buchen?	1.000 EUR	1.000 EUR

❷ Kauf eines Computers gegen Überweisung: 1.300 EUR		
Welche Konten sind zu berücksichtigen?	Geschäfts-ausstattung	Bank
Auf welcher Seite des Kontos wird gebucht?	Soll	Haben
Welche Beträge sind zu buchen?	1.300 EUR	1.300 EUR

❸ Ein Kunde bezahlt eine fällige Rechnung per Überweisung: 7.500 EUR		
Welche Konten sind zu berücksichtigen?	Bank	Forderungen
Auf welcher Seite des Kontos wird gebucht?	Soll	Haben
Welche Beträge sind zu buchen?	7.500 EUR	7.500 EUR

❹ Bareinzahlung auf das Bankkonto aus der Geschäftskasse: 2.500 EUR		
Welche Konten sind zu berücksichtigen?	Bank	Kasse
Auf welcher Seite des Kontos wird gebucht?	Soll	Haben
Welche Beträge sind zu buchen?	2.500 EUR	2.500 EUR

❺ Kassenbeleg:1.000 EUR für Unbehandelte T-Shirts (Vorprodukte) 920 EUR und Härter (Hilfsstoffe) 80 EUR		
Welche Konten sind zu berücksichtigen?	Vorprodukte/ Hilfsstoffe	Kasse
Auf welcher Seite des Kontos wird gebucht?	Soll Soll	Haben
Welche Beträge sind zu buchen?	920 EUR 80 EUR	1.000 EUR

Aufgabe 4 Allgemeine Buchungsregeln

	Soll	Haben	
Gegeben	3.000,00	4.200,00	
Gesucht	**1.200,00**		→ Fehlende Buchung im Soll in Höhe von 1.200,00 EUR
Summe	4.200,00	4.200,00	→ Begründung: Summe Soll = Summe Haben

Aufgabe 5 Konto Rohstoffe führen und abschließen

Soll	Rohstoffe		Haben
❶ **Anfangsbestand**	**1.600,00**	❸ Verbrauch	3.000,00
❷ Einkauf	2.000,00	❹ Rücksendung	400,00
❺ Einkauf	2.000,00	❻ **Schlussbestand**	**2.200,00**
	5.600,00		5.600,00

Aufgabe 6 Konto Darlehen führen und abschließen

Soll	Rohstoffe		Haben
❷ Tilgung	4.000,00	❶ **Anfangsbestand**	**50.000,00**
❺ Tilgung	4.000,00	❸ Darlehen	30.000,00
❻ **Schlussbestand**	**72.000,00**		
	80.000,00		80.000,00

Aufgabe 7 Einfache Buchungssätze – Bestandskonten

1.

	Konto	Soll/EUR	Haben/EUR
❶	Kasse an Bank	500,00	500,00
❷	Darlehen an Bank	8.200,00	8.200,00
❸	Handelswaren an Verbindlichkeiten aus L.u.L.	900,00	900,00
❹	Bank an Forderungen aus L.u.L.	18.560,00	18.560,00
❺	Rohstoffe an Verbindlichkeiten aus L.u.L.	9.628,00	9.628,00
❻	Verbindlichkeiten aus L.u.L. an Bank	9.628,00	9.628,00

2.

Soll	Bank		Haben
Anfangsbestand	**34.700,00**	❶	500,00
❹	18.560,00	❷	8.200,00
		❻	9.628,00
		Schlussbestand	**34.700,00**
	53.260,00		53.260,00

Soll	Verbindlichkeiten aus L.u.L.		Haben
❻	9.628,00	**Anfangsbestand**	**8.468,00**
Schlussbestand	**9.368,00**	❸	900,00
		❺	9.628,00
	18.996,00		18.996,00

Aufgabe 8 Zusammengesetzte Buchungssätze – Bestandskonten

	Konto	Soll/EUR	Haben/EUR
❶	Rohstoffe Hilfsstoffe an Verbindlichkeiten aus L.u.L.	1.600,00 400,00	 2.000,00
❷	Verbindlichkeiten aus L.u.L. an Kasse Bank	2.000,00	 500,00 1.500,00

Aufgabe 9 Bestandskonten: Eröffnung – Buchungen – Abschluss

1. Eröffnungsbilanz

Aktiva	Eröffnungsbilanz zum ...		Passiva
I. Anlagevermögen		**I. Eigenkapital**	70.000,00
1. Fuhrpark	19.000,00	**II. Fremdkapital**	
2. BGA	28.300,00	1. Darlehen	60.000,00
II. Umlaufvermögen		2. Verbindlichkeiten aus L.u.L.	20.000,00
1. Handelswaren	47.200,00		
2. Forderungen aus L.u.L.	13.000,00		
3. Flüssige Mittel	42.500,00		
	150.000,00		**150.000,00**

2. Buchungssätze

	Konto	Soll/EUR	Haben/EUR
❶	Bank an Kasse	5.000,00	5.000,00
❷	Handelswaren an Verbindlichkeiten L.u.L.	5.800,00	5.800,00
❸	Bank an Forderungen L.u.L.	9.000,00	9.000,00
❹	Darlehen an Bank	5.000,00	5.000,00
❺	BGA an Kasse	700,00	700,00
❻	Verbindlichkeiten L.u.L. an Bank	11.000,00	11.000,00
❼	Verbindlichkeiten L.u.L. an Handelswaren	2.000,00	2.000,00
❽	Verbindlichkeiten L.u.L. an Darlehen	12.000,00	12.000,00
❾	Fuhrpark an Verbindlichkeiten L.u.L.	38.000,00	38.000,00

3.

Aktivkonten

Fuhrpark

Soll			Haben
AB	19.000	SBK	**57.200**
❾	38.000		
	57.000		57.000

BGA

Soll			Haben
AB	28.300	SBK	**29.000**
❺	700		
	29.000		29.000

Handelswaren

Soll			Haben
AB	47.200	❼	**2.000**
❷	5.800	SBK	51.000
	53.000		53.000

Forderungen L.u.L.

Soll			Haben
AB	13.000	❸	9.000
		SBK	**4.000**
	13.000		13..000

Kasse

Soll			Haben
AB	18.500	❶	5.000
		❺	700
		SBK	**12.800**
	18.500		18.500

Bank

Soll			Haben
AB	24.000	❹	5.000
❶	5.000	❻	11.000
❸	9.000	SBK	**22.000**
	38.000		38.000

Passivkonten

Darlehen

Soll			Haben
❹	5.000	AB	60.000
SBK	**67.000**	❽	12.000
	72.000		72.000

Verbindlichkeiten L.u.L.

Soll			Haben
❻	11.000	AB	20.000
❼	2.000	❷	5.800
❽	12.000	❾	38.000
SBK	**38.800**		
	63.800		63.800

Eigenkapital

Soll			Haben
SBK	**70.000**	AB	70.000
	70.000		70.000

Schlussbilanzkonto

Soll			Haben
Fuhrpark	57.000	Darlehen	67.000
BGA	29.000	Verbindlichkeiten L.u.L.	38.800
Handelswaren	51.000	Eigenkapital	70.000
Forderungen L.u.L.	4.000		
Kasse	12.800		
Bank	22.000		
	175.800		175.800

zu Kapitel 4 Buchen von Eigenkapitalveränderungen unter Berücksichtigung des gesamten Kontensystems

ERARBEITUNGSAUFGABE

EA 1 Buchen nach Belegen – Bestands- und Ergebniskonten

1. Geschäftsvorfälle

❶ Die fällige Abschlagszahlung unseres Stromanbieters in Höhe von 1.200 EUR wird per Lastschrift abgebucht.
❷ Wir überweisen die Miete für unser Büro in Heidelberg in Höhe von 800 EUR.
❸ Die Gebäudeversicherung zieht den Dezember-Beitrag in Höhe von 100 EUR von unserem Konto ein.
❹ Wir erhalten Zinsen in Höhe von 40 EUR für unser Guthaben.
❺ Die Kfz-Steuer in Höhe von 390 EUR wird abgebucht.

2. Von den Bilanzkonten werden folgende benötigt:

- Bank
- Eigenkapital

3.

S	Bank		H
AB	20.000 EUR	❶	1.200 EUR
❹	40 EUR	❷	800 EUR
		❸	100 EUR
		❺	390 EUR
		SBK	17.500 EUR
	20.040 EUR		20.040 EUR

S	Eigenkapital		H
❶	1.200 EUR	AB	75.000 EUR
❷	800 EUR	❹	40 EUR
❸	100 EUR		
❺	390 EUR		
SBK	72.550 EUR		
	75.040 EUR		75.040 EUR

Ermittlung des AB beim Eigenkapital: 190.000 – 90.000 – 25.000 = 75.000 EUR.

4. Buchungssätze

❶	Eigenkapital an Bank	1.200 EUR
❷	Eigenkapital an Bank	800 EUR
❸	Eigenkapital an Bank	100 EUR
❹	Bank an Eigenkapital	40 EUR
❺	Eigenkapital an Bank	390 EUR

5. Eigenkapitalvergleich

	Eigenkapital (neu)	72.550 EUR	
–	Eigenkapital (alt)	75.000 EUR	
=	Kapitalminderung	– 2.450 EUR	= Verlust

6. Selbst bei kleinen Unternehmen gibt es hunderte Geschäftsvorfälle in einem Jahr, die zu einer Veränderung des Eigenkapitals führen. Würden sie alle direkt über das Konto Eigenkapital gebucht, wäre dies sehr unübersichtlich. Man könnte beispielsweise nicht auf einen Blick erkennen, wie hoch die Stromkosten insgesamt waren. Es wäre damit sehr schwierig zu analysieren, warum es zu einem Gewinn oder Verlust in einer bestimmten Höhe gekommen ist.

Daher werden Unterkonten des Eigenkapitals gebildet, auf die Aufwendungen und Erträge der gleichen Art zusammengefasst werden, z. B. Mietaufwendungen, Zinsaufwendungen, Umsatzerlöse.

zu Kapitel 4 Buchen von Eigenkapitalveränderungen unter Berücksichtigung des gesamten Kontensystems

ANWENDUNGS- UND ÜBUNGSAUFGABEN

Aufgabe 1 Buchen auf Bestands- und Ergebniskonten

1.

	Konto	Soll/EUR	Haben/EUR	4. Ergebniswirksam?	
❷	Geschäftsausstattung an Verbindlichkeiten aus L.u.L.	1.500,00	 1.500,00	Nein	Kein Aufwands- und kein Ertragskonto
❸	Hilfsstoffe an Verbindlichkeiten aus L.u.L.	1.200,00	 1.200,00	Nein	Kein Aufwands- oder Ertragskonto
❶	Personalaufwendungen an Bank	800,00	 800,00	Ja	Aufwandskonto

2. Bei den Geschäftsvorfällen 1. und 2. ändert sich das Eigenkapital nicht. Die Geschäftsvorfälle sind nicht ergebniswirksam, da kein Ertrags- oder Aufwandskonto betroffen ist.

   Die Ausbildungsvergütung stellt dagegen einen Personalaufwand dar. Sie wird auf dem Aufwandskonto Personalaufwendungen gebucht. Sie mindert das Eigenkapital.

3.

	Konto	Soll/EUR	Haben/EUR	4. Ergebniswirksam?	
❹	Kontoführungsgebühren an Bank	30,00	 30,00	Ja	Aufwandskonto
❺	Reparaturaufwendungen an Verbindlichkeiten aus L.u.L.	140,00	 140,00	Ja	Aufwandskonto
❻	Geschäftsausstattung an Kasse	1.390,00	 1.390,00	Nein	Kein Aufwands- und kein Ertragskonto
❼	Verbindlichkeiten aus L.u.L. Verbindlichkeiten aus L.u.L. an Bank	1.500,00 1.200,00	 2.700,00	Nein	Kein Aufwands- und kein Ertragskonto
❽	Eigenkapital (Privat) an Kasse	500,00	 500,00	Nein	Kein Aufwands- und kein Ertragskonto

Aufgabe 2 Erstellung eines Gewinn- und Verlustkontos

1. u. 2.

Soll	Gewinn- und Verlustkonto		Haben
Benzinaufwendungen	600,00	Mieterträge	800,00
Löhne und Gehälter	10.000,00	Zinserträge	200,00
Rohstoffaufwendungen	8.000,00	Umsatzerlöse Erzeugnisse	20.000,00
Telefonaufwendungen	500,00		
Eigenkapital (Gewinn)	1.900,00		
	21.000,00		21.000,00

	Konto	Soll/EUR	Haben/EUR
	GuV an Eigenkapital	1.900,00	 1.900,00

Aufgabe 3 Buchungssätze im Zusammenhang mit Telekommunikation

	Konto	Soll/EUR	Haben/EUR
❶	Geschäftsausstattung an Verbindlichkeiten aus L.u.L.	2.000,00	 2.000,00
❷	Telefonaufwendungen an Verbindlichkeiten aus L.u.L.	580,00	 580,00
❸ a)	Verbindlichkeiten aus L.u.L. an Bank	2.000,00	 2.000,00
❸ b)	Verbindlichkeiten aus L.u.L. an Bank	580,00	 580,00
❹	Telefonaufwand an Bank	750,00	 750,00

Aufgabe 4 Buchen nach Belegen – Bestands- und Ergebniskonten

	Konto	Soll/EUR	Haben/EUR
❶	Stromaufwendungen Mietaufwendungen Versicherungsaufwendungen an Bank	1.200,00 800,00 100,00	 2.100,00
❷	Bank an Zinserträge	40,00	 40,00
❸	Eigenkapital (Privat) an Bank	4.000,00	 390,00
❹	Kfz-Steueraufwendungen an Bank	390,00	 390,00

oder: Drei Einzelbuchungen

Aufgabe 5 Buchen nach Belegen

	Konto	Soll/EUR	Haben/EUR
❶	Benzinaufwendungen an Kasse	61,00	 61,00
❷	Portoaufwendungen an Kasse	10,00	 10,00
❸	Geschäftsausstattung Büromaterialaufwendungen an Kasse	220,00 196,00	 416,00

Aufgabe 6 Konto Privat führen und Buchungssätze bilden

	Konto	Soll/EUR	Haben/EUR
❶	Privat	500,00	
	an Kasse		500,00
❷	Bank	40.000,00	
	an Privat		40.000,00
❸	Privat	7.000,00	
	an Bank		7.000,00
❹	Geschäftsausstattung	999,00	
	Privat	999,00	
	an Bank		1.998,00

Aufgabe 7 Doppelte Ergebnisermittlung

Eigenkapital zum 31.12.01	=	Eigenkapital zum 01.01.01	=	Ergebnis im Geschäftsjahr 01
216.100 EUR	=	170.000 EUR	=	46.100 EUR → **Gewinn**

Eigenkapital = Vermögen − Schulden
zum 31.12.01 355.500 EUR − 139.400 EUR = 216.100 EUR

Soll	GuV-Rechnung von Textildruck Shirt-Shop Ehret e. Kfm.		Haben
Aufwendungen für Rohstoffe	92.000	Umsatzerlöse Erzeugnisse	690.500
Aufwendungen für Hilfsstoffe	2.100	Zinserträge	100
Aufwendungen für Betriebsstoffe	1.200		
Löhne	280.000		
Gehälter	160.500		
Mietaufwendungen	66.000		
Büromaterialaufwendungen	3.700		
Werbeaufwendungen	12.500		
Telefonaufwendungen	10.800		
Kfz-Steuer	2.100		
Zinsaufwendungen	13.600		
Saldo (Gewinn)	46.100		
	690.600		**690.600**

Aufgabe 8 Buchen auf Bestands- und Ergebniskonten

1. Eröffnungsbilanz

Aktiva	Eröffnungsbilanz zum ...		Passiva
I. Anlagevermögen		**I. Eigenkapital**	157.600,00
1. Fuhrpark	39.000,00	**II. Fremdkapital**	
2. BGA	60.000,00	1. Darlehen	40.000,00
II. Umlaufvermögen			
1. Rohstoffe	50.000,00		
2. Forderungen aus L.u.L.	22.000,00		
3. Flüssige Mittel	26.600,00		
	197.600,00		**197.600,00**

2. Einrichtung der Konten siehe nächste Seite

3. Buchungssätze

	Konto	Soll/EUR	Haben/EUR
1	Bank an Zinserträge	200,00	200,00
2	Zinsaufwendungen an Bank	1.000,00	1.000,00
3	Darlehen an Bank	3.000,00	3.000,00
4	BGA an Verbindlichkeiten aus L.u.L.	27.000,00	27.000,00
5	Rohstoffaufwendungen an Rohstoffe	7.000,00	7.000,00
6	Kfz-Reparaturen an Verbindlichkeiten aus L.u.L.	680,00	680,00
7	Benzin an Kasse	80,00	80,00
8	Forderungen aus L.u.L. an Umsatzerlöse	22.800,00	22.800,00
9	Bank an Forderungen aus L.u.L.	12.800,00	12.800,00
10	Mietaufwendungen an Bank	900,00	900,00
11	Telefon an Bank	720,00	720,00
12	Bank an Mietaufwendungen	100,00	100,00
13	Personalaufwendungen an Bank	6.300,00	6.300,00

2., 4., 7.

Aktivkonten

Fuhrpark

Soll			Haben
AB	39.000	**SBK**	**39.000**
	39.000		39.000

BGA

Soll			Haben
AB	60.000	**SBK**	**87.000**
❹	27.000		
	87.000		87.000

Rohstoffe

Soll			Haben
AB	50.000	❺	7.000
		SBK	**43.000**
	50.000		50.000

Forderungen L.u.L.

Soll			Haben
AB	22.000	❾	12.800
❽	22.800	**SBK**	**32.000**
	44.800		44.800

Kasse

Soll			Haben
AB	14.900	❼	80
		SBK	**14.820**
	14.900		14.900

Bank

Soll			Haben
AB	11.700	❷	1.000
❶	200	❸	3.000
❾	12.800	❿	900
⓬	100	⓫	720
		⓭	6.300
		SBK	**12.880**
	24.800		24.800

Passivkonten

Darlehen

Soll			Haben
❸	3.000	AB	40.000
SBK	**37.000**		
	40.000		40.000

Verbindlichkeiten L.u.L.

Soll			Haben
SBK	**27.680**	❹	27.000
		❻	680
	27.680		27.680

Eigenkapital

Soll			Haben
SBK	**164.020**	AB	157.600
		GuV-Konto	6.420
	164.020		164.020

Schlussbilanzkonto

Soll			Haben
Fuhrpark	39.000	Darlehen	37.000
BGA	87.000	Verbindlichkeiten L.u.L.	27.680
Rohstoffe	43.000	Eigenkapital	164.020
Forderungen L.u.L.	32.000		
Kasse	14.820		
Bank	12.889		
	228.700		228.700

4., 5.

Aktivkonten

Soll	Benzin		Haben
❼	80	GuV-Konto	**80**
	80		80

Soll	Personalaufwendungen		Haben
⓭	6.300	GuV-Konto	**6.300**
	6.300		6.300

Soll	Mietaufwendungen		Haben
❿	900	⓬	100
		GuV-Konto	**800**
	900		900

Soll	Rohstoffaufwendungen		Haben
❺	7.000	GuV-Konto	7.000
			7.000
	7.000		7.000

Soll	Kfz-Reparaturen		Haben
❺	680	GuV-Konto	**680**
	680		680

Soll	Telefon		Haben
⓫	720	GuV-Konto	**720**
	720		720

Soll	Zinsaufwendungen		Haben
❷	1.000	GuV-Konto	**1.000**
	1.000		1.000

Passivkonten

Soll	Umsatzerlöse		Haben
GuV-Konto	**22.800**	❽	22.800
	22.800		22.800

Soll	Zinserträge		Haben
GuV-Konto	**200**	❶	200
	200		200

Soll	GuV-Konto		Haben
Benzin	80	Umsatzerlöse	22.800
Personalaufwendungen	6.300	Zinserträge	200
Mietaufwendungen	800		
Rohstoffaufwendungen	7.000		
Kfz-Reparaturen	680		
Telefon	720		
Zinsaufwendungen	1.000		
Eigenkapital (Gewinn)	**6.420**		
	23.000		23.000

6.

Konto	Soll/EUR	Haben/EUR
GuV	6.420,00	
an Eigenkapital		6.420,00

Aufgabe 9 Zusammenfassende Aufgabe zu Buchungen im Kontensystem

1.

Aktiva	Eröffnungsbilanz zum 01.01...		Passiva
I. Anlagevermögen		**I. Eigenkapital**	35.000,00
1. Fuhrpark	20.000,00	**II. Fremdkapital**	
II. Umlaufvermögen		1. Darlehen	10.000,00
1. Bank	25.000,00		
	45.000,00		**45.000,00**

Soll	Fuhrpark		Haben
AB	20.000		

Soll	Eigenkapital		Haben
		AB	35.000

Soll	Bank		Haben
AB	25.000		

Soll	Darlehen		Haben
		AB	10.000

2. **Laufende Buchung der Geschäftsvorfälle**

	Konto	Soll/EUR	Haben/EUR
❶	BGA an Verbindlichkeiten aus L.u.L.	8.000	 8.000
❷	Kasse an Bank	900	 900
❸	Mietaufwendungen an Bank	400	 400
❹	Kfz-Steueraufwendungen an Bank	450	 450
❺	Versicherungsaufwendungen an Bank	320	 320
❻	Büromaterialien an Kasse	600	 600
❼	Leasingaufwendungen an Bank	1.500	 1.500
❽	Bank an Umsatzerlöse aus Fahrten	3.520	 3.520
❾	Privat an Kasse	200	 200
❿	Verbindlichkeiten aus L.u.L. an Bank	8.000	 8.000
⓫	Werbeaufwendungen an Verbindlichkeiten aus L.u.L.	1.400	 1.400
⓬	Benzinaufwendungen an Verbindlichkeiten aus L.u.L.	1.760	 1.760
⓭	Bank an Umsatzerlöse aus Fahrten	5.280	 5.280

	Konto	Soll/EUR	Haben/EUR
⓮ 1	Darlehen an Bank	1.000	1.000
⓮ 2	Zinsaufwendungen an Bank	50	50
⓮ 3	Privat an Bank	2.000	2.000
⓮ 4	Bank an Zinserträge	20	20

2., 3 c) **Bestandskonten: Eröffnung – Buchung – Abschluss**

Aktivkonten

Soll	Bank		Haben
AB	25.000	❷	900
❽	3.250	❸	400
⓭	5.280	❹	450
⓮ 4	20	❺	320
		❼	1.500
		❿	8.000
		⓮ 1	1.000
		⓮ 2	50
		⓮ 3	2.000
		SBK	**19.200**
	33.800		33.800

Soll	BGA		Haben
❶	8.000	**SBK**	**8.000**

Soll	Kasse		Haben
❷	900	❻	600
		❾	200
		SBK	**100**
	900		900

Soll	Fuhrpark		Haben
❶	20.000	**SBK**	**20.000**

Passivkonten

Soll	Darlehen		Haben
Privat	2.200	AE	35.000
SBK	**35.140**	GuV-Konto	2.340
	37.340		37.340

Soll	Darlehen		Haben
⓮ 1	1.000	AB	10.000
SBK	**9.000**		
	10.000		10.000

Soll	Verbindlichkeiten		Haben
❿	8.000	❶	8.000
SBK	**3.160**	⓫	1.400
		⓬	1.760
	11.160		11.160

Soll	Privat		Haben
❾	200	**Eigen-kapital**	**2.200**
⓮ 3	2.000		
	2.200		2.200

3 e)
- Inventurbestand „Zählliste“ stimmt mit Buchbestand Konto Kasse überein.
- Inventurbestand „Kontoauszug“ stimmt mit Buchbestand Konto Bank überein.

→ Somit können die Buchwerte übernommen werden.

3 d)

Soll	Schlussbilanzkonto zum 31.01...		Haben
Fuhrpark	20.000	Eigenkapital	35.100
BGA	8.000	Darlehen	9.000
Kasse	19.200	Verbindlichkeiten	3.160
Bank	100		
	47.300		**47.300**

↓ Übertrag

3 f)

Soll	Schlussbilanz zum 31.01...		Haben
I. Anlagevermögen		I. Eigenkapital	35.100
1. Fuhrpark	20.000	II. Fremdkapital	
2. BGA	8.000	1. Darlehen	9.000
II. Umlaufvermögen		2. Verbindlichkeiten	3.160
1. Flüssige Mittel	19.300		
	47.300		**47.300**

2., 3 a) Ergebniskonten: Buchungen – Abschluss

Aufwandskonten

Soll	Mietaufwendungen		Haben
❸	400	GuV-Konto	80

Soll	Kfz-Steueraufw.		Haben
❹	450	GuV-Konto	**450**

Soll	Versicherungsaufw.		Haben
❺	320	GuV-Konto	**320**

Soll	Büromaterialien		Haben
❻	600	GuV-Konto	**600**

Soll	Leasingaufwendungen		Haben
❼	1.500	GuV-Konto	**1.500**

Soll	Benzinaufwendungen		Haben
⓬	1.760	GuV-Konto	**1.760**

Soll	Zinsaufwendungen		Haben
⓮ 2	50	GuV-Konto	**50**

Soll	Werbeaufwendungen		Haben
⓫	1.400	GuV-Konto	**1.400**

Ertragskonten

Soll	Umsatzerlöse aus Fahrten		Haben
GuV-Konto	**8.800**	❽	3.520
		⓭	5.280
	8.800		8.800

Soll	5710 Zinserträge		Haben
GuV-Konto	**20**	⓮ 4	20

3 b)

Aktiva	GuV-Konto 31.01...		Passiva
Mietaufwendungen	400	Umsatzerlöse aus Fahren	8.800
Kfz-Steueraufw.	450	Zinserträge	20
Versicherungsaufw.	320		
Büromaterialien	600		
Leasingaufwendungen	1.500		
Benzinaufwendungen	1.760		
Zinsaufwendungen	50		
Werbeaufwendungen	1.400		
Eigenkapital (Gewinn)	**2.340**		
	8.820		**8.820**

- Summe der Erträge > Summe der Aufwendungen
  → Saldo = Gewinn in Höhe von 2.340 EUR

zu 3 a) und 3 b) **Abschluss des Privatkontos auf das Eigenkapitalkonto**

	Konto	Soll/EUR	Haben/EUR
B 1	Eigenkapital an Privat	2.200,00	 2.200,00

Abschluss der Ergebniskonten auf das GuV-Konto

	Konto	Soll/EUR	Haben/EUR
B 2	GuV-Konto an Mietaufwendungen	400	 400
B 3	GuV-Konto an Kfz-Steueraufw.	450	 450
B 4	GuV-Konto an Versicherungsaufw.	320	 320
B 5	GuV-Konto an Büromaterialien	600	 600
B 6	GuV-Konto an Leasingaufwendungen	1.500	 1.500
B 7	GuV-Konto an Benzinaufwendungen	1.760	 1.760
B 8	GuV-Konto an Zinsaufwendungen	50	 50
B 9	GuV-Konto an Werbeaufwendungen	1.400	 1.400
B10	Umsatzerlöse aus Fahrten an GuV-Konto	8.800	 8.800
B11	Zinserträge an GuV-Konto	20	 20

Abschluss des GuV-Kontos auf das Eigenkapitalkonto

	Konto	Soll/EUR	Haben/EUR
B 12	GuV-Konto an Eigenkapital	2.340	 2.340

Abschluss der Bestandskonten auf das Schlussbilanzkonto

	Konto	Soll/EUR	Haben/EUR
B 13	Schlussbilanzkonto an BGA	8.000	 8.000
B 14	Schlussbilanzkonto an Kasse	100	 100
B 15	Schlussbilanzkonto an Bank	19.200	 19.200
B 16	Darlehen an Schlussbilanzkonto	9.000	 9.000
B 17	Verbindlichkeiten an Schlussbilanzkonto	3.160	 3.160
B 18	Eigenkapital an Schlussbilanzkonto	35.140	 35.140

4. *schülerindividuelle Antworten*
   z. B. Gewinn steht in einem „guten" Verhältnis zum Eigenkapital

zu Kapitel 5 Einfacher Jahresabschluss

ANWENDUNGS- UND ÜBUNGSAUFGABEN

Aufgabe 1 Buch-Ist-Vergleich

1. Saldo im Konto Kasse = 4.920,50 EUR
   → keine Korrekturbuchung, da Buchwert = Istwert

   Saldo im Konto Hilfsstoffe = 340,00 EUR
   → Korrekturbuchung im Haben, da Buchwert > Istwert

   Saldo im Konto Handelswaren = 2.649,50 EUR
   → Korrekturbuchung im Soll, da Buchwert < Istwert

Konto	Soll/EUR	Haben/EUR
Aufwendungen für Hilfsstoffe an Hilfsstoffe	49,50	 49,50
Handelswaren an Aufwendungen für Handelswaren	50,00	 50,00

2. Kasse: keine Veränderung
   Hilfsstoffe: Ergebnis verschlechtert sich, da Aufwandsbuchung im Soll
   Handelswaren: Ergebnis verbessert sich, da Aufwandsbuchung im Haben

Aufgabe 2 Aufstellung von Bilanz und GuV

1.

Buchung der laufenden Geschäftsvorfälle:					
❶	Kasse	200,00	an	Eigenkapital	200,00
❷	Materialbestand	120,00	an	Kasse	120,00
❸	Werbeaufwendungen	10,00	an	Kasse	10,00
❹	Materialaufwendungen	110,00	an	Materialbestand	110,00
❺	Kasse	180,00	an	Umsatzerlöse	180,00
Buchungssätze für den Abschluss der Ergebniskonten:					
❻	GuV-Konto	10,00	an	Werbeaufwendungen	10,00
❼	GuV-Konto	100,00	an	Materialaufwendungen	110,00
❽	Umsatzerlöse	180,00	an	GuV-Konto	180,00
Buchungssatz für den Abschluss des GuV-Kontos:					
❾	GuV-Konto	60,00	an	Eigenkapital	60,00
Buchungssätze für den Abschluss der Bestandskonten:					
❿	Schlussbilanzkonto	250,00	an	Kasse	250,00
⓫	Schlussbilanzkonto	10,00	an	Materialbestand	10,00
⓬	Eigenkapital	260,00	an	Schlussbilanzkonto	260,00

PDF
DIGITAL+

2. und 3.

Bestandskonten

Aktivkonten

Soll	Kasse		Haben
❶	200,00	❷	120,00
❺	180,00	❸	10,00
		❿ SBK	**250,00**
	380,00		380,00

Soll	Materialbestand		Haben
❷	120,00	❹	110,00
		❿ SBK	**10,00**
	120,00		120,00

Passivkonten

Soll	Eigenkapital		Haben
⓬ SBK	**260,00**	❶	200,00
		❾ GuV-Konto	**60,00**
	260,00		736.500,00

Ergebniskonten

Aufwandskonten

Soll	Werbeaufwendungen		Haben
❸	10,00	❻ GuV-Konto	**10,00**

Soll	Materialaufwendungen		Haben
❹	110,00	❼ GuV-Konto	**110,00**

Ertragskonten

Soll	Umsatzerlöse		Haben
❽ GuV-Konto	**180,00**	❺	180,00

Soll	Gewinn- und Verlustkonto		Haben
❻ Werbeaufwendungen	10,00	❽ Umsatzerlöse	180,00
❼ Materialaufwendungen	110,00		
❾ Eigenkapital (Gewinn)	60,00		
	180,00		**180,00**

Soll	Schlussbilanzkonto		Haben
❿ Kasse	250,00	⓬ Eigenkapital	260,00
⓫ Materialbestand	10,00		
	260,00		**260,00**

Inventur →

Aktiva	Schlussbilanz		Passiva
Materialbestand	10,00	Eigenkapital	260,00
Kasse	250,00		
	260,00		**260,00**

4. Die Teilnahme hat sich gelohnt, da laut GuV-Konto ein Gewinn in Höhe von 60 EUR erzielt wurde. Das Eigenkapital hat sich um diesen Beitrag erhöht.

Aufgabe 3 Bilanz-Erstellung und Ergebnisermittlung

Bilanz von Textildruck Shirt-Shop Ehret e. Kfm. zum 31.12.00

Aktiva		Passiva	
I. Anlagevermögen		**I. Eigenkapital**	170.000
1. Maschinen	145.824	**II. Fremdkapital**	
2. Fuhrpark	96.096	1. Verbindlichkeiten gegenüber Kreditinstituten	160.000
3. BGA	40.309	2. Verbindlichkeiten aus L.u.L.	20.480
II. Umlaufvermögen		3. Sonstige Verbindlichkeiten	2.900
1. Vorräte	22.647		
2. Forderungen aus L.u.L.	18.873		
3. Liquide Mittel	29.631		
Bilanzsumme	**353.380**		**353.380**

Eigenkapital zum 31.12.00	=	Eigenkapital zum 31.12. Vorjahr	=	Ergebnis im Geschäftsjahr 00
170.000 EUR	=	130.000 EUR	=	40.000 EUR

→ **Gewinn**

Aufgabe 4 GuV-Erstellung und Ergebnisermittlung

GuV-Konto von Textildruck Shirt-Shop Ehret e. Kfm.

Soll		Haben	
Aufwendungen für Rohstoffe	110.160,00	Umsatzerlöse Erzeugnisse	662.793,00
Aufwendungen für Hilfsstoffe	2.043,00	Umsatzerlöse Handelswaren	6.000,00
Aufwendungen für Betriebsstoffe	1.511,00	Zinserträge	60,00
Aufwendungen für Handelswaren	3.705,00		
Löhne	256.000,00		
Gehälter	153.900,00		
Mietaufwendungen	60.000,00		
Büromaterialaufwendungen	4.095,00		
Werbeaufwendungen	8.000,00		
Telefonaufwendungen	10.864,00		
Kfz-Steuer	2.565,00		
Zinsaufwendungen	16.000,00		
Saldo	40.000,00		
	668.843,00		**668.843,00**

Gewinn- und Verlustrechnung Textildruck Shirt-Shop Ehret e. Kfm.

Soll		Haben	
Materialaufwendungen	117.419 EUR	Umsatzerlöse	668.783 EUR
Personalaufwendungen	409.900 EUR	Zinsen und ähnliche Erträge	60 EUR
Sonst. betriebl. Aufwendungen	82.959 EUR		
Zinsen und ähnl. Aufwendungen	16.000 EUR		
sonstige Steuern	2.565 EUR		
Gewinn	**40.000 EUR**		
	668.843 EUR		**668.843 EUR**

zu Kapitel 6 Kontenrahmen und Kontenplan

ANWENDUNGS- UND ÜBUNGSAUFGABEN

Aufgabe 1 Zuordnung der Kontennummern

Konten	Bestandskonten		Ergebniskonten	
	Aktivkonto	Passivkonto	Aufwands-konto	Ertragskonto
Bank	2800			
Fuhrpark	0840	–	–	–
Telefon	–	–	6890	-
Eigenkapital	–	3000	–	–
Verbindlichkeiten aus L.u.L.	–	4400	–	–
Werbeaufwendungen	–	–	6870	–
Zinsaufwendungen	–	–	7510	–
Mieterträge	–	–	–	5080
Kontoführungsgebühren der Bank	–	–	6750	
Umsatzerlöse Fertigerzeugnisse	–	–	–	5000
Welche Kontenklassen?	0; 2	3; 4	6; 7	5

Aufgabe 2 Abgrenzung Kontenrahmen und Kontenplan

1. schülerindividuell; z. B.
   0270 EDV-Software; Aufteilung Fuhrpark 0840 Pkw und 0841 Lkw; Aufteilung 4200 Darlehen

2. 1) 0710 Maschinen
   2) 2020 Hilfsstoffe
   3) 0830 Sonstige Transportmittel
   4) 2040 Verpackungsmaterial
   5) 6130 Reparatur und Instandhaltung von techn. Anlagen
   6) 6051 Strom
   7) 0870 Büromöbel und sonstige Geschäftsausstattung
   8) 2010 Vorprodukte
   9) 0880 Ladeneinrichtung

Aufgabe 3 Bildung von Buchungssätzen mit Angabe der Kontennummern

	Nr.	Konto	Soll/EUR	Haben/EUR
1	0870	Geschäftsausstattung	840,00	
	an	2820 Kasse		840,00
2	2000	Rohstoffe	7.245,00	
	an	4400 Verbindlichkeiten L.u.L.		7.245,00
3	0840	Fuhrpark	58.000,00	
	an	4400 Verbindlichkeiten L.u.L.		58.000,00
4	4200	Darlehen	6.000,00	
	an	2800 Bank		6.000,00
5	7510	Zinsaufwendungen	800,00	
	an	2800 Bank		800,00
6	4400	4400 Verbindlichkeiten L.u.L.	2.960,00	
	an	2800 Bank		2.960,00
7	6800	Büromaterialien	145,00	
	an	2820 Kasse		145,00
8	6000	Rohstoffaufwendungen	580,00	
	an	2000 Rohstoffe		580,00

Aufgabe 4 Bildung von Buchungssätzen mit Angabe der Kontennummern

	Nr.	Konto	Soll/EUR	Haben/EUR
1	0870	Geschäftsausstattung	1.500,00	
	an	4400 Verbindlichkeiten aus L.u.L.		1.500,00
2	2020	Hilfsstoffe	1.200,00	
	an	4400 Verbindlichkeiten aus L.u.L.		1.200,00
3	6300	Personalaufwendungen	800,00	
	an	2800 Bank		800,00
4	6750	Kontoführungsgebühren	30,00	
	an	2800 Bank		30,00
5	6130	Reparaturaufwendungen	140,00	
	an	4400 Verbindlichkeiten aus L.u.L.		140,00
6	0870	Geschäftsausstattung	1.390,00	
	an	2820 Kasse		1.390,00
7	4400	Verbindlichkeiten aus L.u.L.	1.500,00	
	4400	Verbindlichkeiten aus L.u.L.	1.200,00	1.500,00
	an	2800 Bank		1.200,00
8	3000	Eigenkapital (oder 3001 Privat)	500,00	
	an	2820 Kasse		500,00

zu Kapitel 7 Umsatzsteuer

ANWENDUNGS- UND ÜBUNGSAUFGBABEN

Aufgabe 1 Ausstellung einer Rechnung

1. Rechnungsbetrag = ([40 · (35,00 EUR · 0,92)] + 25,00 EUR) · 1,19 = 1.562,47 EUR
2. Zahlungseingang = 1.562,47 EUR · 0,98 = 1.531,22 EUR
   Abzug von 2 % Skonto zulässig, da innerhalb von 10 Tagen

Aufgabe 2 Zum Mitnehmen oder hier essen?

1. 19 % USt: 5,95 / 1,19 = 5,00 EUR Nettobetrag USt 0,95 EUR
2. 7 % USt: 5,95 / 1,07 = 5,56 EUR Nettobetrag USt 0,39 EUR
3. ▪ Wenn der Preis zwischen beiden Verkäufen gleich ist, hat das Restaurant beim Straßenverkauf einen zusätzlichen Gewinn je Menü in Höhe von 0,56 EUR, da nur 0,39 EUR satt 0,95 EUR Umsatzsteuer an das Finanzamt abgeführt werden müssen..
   ▪ Beim Straßenverkauf entfallen die Tätigkeiten wie Reinigung der Tische, Reinigung der Toiletten, Reinigung von Tabletts, Entsorgung des Einmalgeschirrs

PDF DIGITAL+

Aufgabe 3 Buchen der Umsatz- und Vorsteuer/Abschluss der Konten

1.

	Nr.	Konto	Soll/EUR	Haben/EUR
❶	2000	Rohstoffe	2.200,00	
	2600	Vorsteuer	418,00	
	an	4400 Verbindlichkeiten aus L.u.L.		2.618,00
❷	2400	Forderungen aus L.u.L.	19.040,00	
	an	5000 Umsatzerlöse FE		16.000,00
		4800 Umsatzsteuer		3.040,00
❸	4400	Verbindlichkeiten aus L.u.L.	2.618,00	
	an	2800 Bank		2.618,00
	2800	Bank	19.040,00	
	an	2400 Forderungen aus L.u.L.		19.040,00
❹	2400	Forderungen aus L.u.L.	1.190,00	
	an	5010 Umsatzerlöse Handelswaren		1.000,00
		4800 Umsatzsteuer		190,00
❺	0870	Geschäftsausstattung	1.800,00	
	2600	Vorsteuer	342,00	
	an	4400 Verbindlichkeiten aus L.u.L.		2.142,00
❻	2820	Kasse	47,60	
	an	5010 Umsatzerlöse Handelswaren		40,00
		4800 Umsatzsteuer		7,60
❼	6700	Miete	1.200,00	
	an	2800 Bank		1.200,00
	2800	Bank	12,00	
	an	5710 Zinserträge		12,00
	6710	Leasing	560,00	
	2600	Vorsteuer	106,40	
	an	2800 Bank		666,40

2. u. 3.

2600 Vorsteuer

Soll		Haben	
❶	418,00	❽	866,40
❺	342,00		
❼	106,40		
	866,40		866,40

4800 Umsatzsteuer

Soll		Haben	
❽	866,40	❷	3.040,00
❾	2.371,20	❹	190,00
		❻	7,60
	3.237,60		3.237,60

2800 Bank

Soll		Haben	
		❾	2.371,20

	Nr. Konto	Soll/EUR	Haben/EUR
❺	4800 Umsatzsteuer an 2600 Vorsteuer	866,40	866,40
❻	4800 Umsatzsteuer an 2800 Bank	2.371,20	2.371,20

Aufgabe 4 Auswirkungen von Geschäftsvorfällen auf Zahllast und Unternehmensergebnis

	Auswirkung auf die Zahllast des Unternehmens		Auswirkung auf das Ergebnis des Unternehmens	
	Betrag	Begründung	Betrag	Begründung
❶	– 418 EUR	Vorsteuer ↑	0 EUR	kein Aufwands-/Ertragskonto
❷	+ 3.040 EUR	Umsatzsteuer ↑	+ 16000 EUR	Ertragskonto 5000
❸	0 EUR	keine VST/UST	0 EUR	kein Aufwands-/Ertragskonto
	0 EUR	keine VST/UST	0 EUR	kein Aufwands-/Ertragskonto
❹	+ 190 EUR	Umsatzsteuer ↑	+ 1000 EUR	Ertragskonto 5010
❺	– 342 EUR	Vorsteuer ↑	0 EUR	kein Aufwands-/Ertragskonto
❻	+ 7,60 EUR	Umsatzsteuer ↑	+ 40 EUR	Ertragskonto 5010
❼	0 EUR	keine VST/UST	– 1.200 EUR	Ertragskonto 6700
	0 EUR	keine VST/UST	+ 12 EUR	Ertragskonto 5010
	– 106,40 EUR	Vorsteuer ↑	– 560 EUR	Ertragskonto 6710

Aufgabe 5 Buchen von Geschäftsvorfällen mit Berücksichtigung der Umsatzsteuer

1.

Eröffnungsbilanz

Aktiva		Passiva	
I. Anlagevermögen		I. Eigenkapital	131.000
Maschinen	80.000	II. Fremdkapital	
Geschäftsausstattung	60.000	Darlehen	70.000
II. Umlaufvermögen		Verbindlichkeiten aus L.u.L.	23.000
Rohstoffe	30.000	Sonstige Verbindlichkeiten	6.000
Forderungen aus L.u.L.	40.000		
Bank	20.000		
	230.000		230.000

3.

	Nr.	Kontobezeichnung	Soll/EUR	Haben/EUR
❶	2000	Rohstoffe	5.800,00	
	2600	Vorsteuer	1.102,00	
	an	4400 Verbindlichkeiten aus L.u.L.		6.902,00
❷	4800	Umsatzsteuer	6.000,00	
	an	2800 Bank		6.000,00
❸	6000	Aufwendungen für Rohstoffe	8.000,00	
	an	2000 Rohstoffe		8.000,00
❹	0710	Maschinen	20.000,00	
	2600	Vorsteuer	3.800,00	
	an	4400 Verbindlichkeiten aus L.u.L.		23.800,00
❺	4400	Verbindlichkeiten aus L.u.L.	6.902,00	
	an	2800 Bank		6.902,00
❻	4200	Darlehen	1.000,00	
	7510	Zinsaufwendungen	350,00	
	an	2800 Bank		1.350,00
❼	0870	Geschäftsausstattung	2.000,00	
	2600	Vorsteuer	380,00	
	an	4400 Verbindlichkeiten aus L.u.L.		2.380,00
❽	6710	Leasing	1.800,00	
	2600	Vorsteuer	342,00	
	an	2800 Bank		2.142,00
❾	2400	Forderungen aus L.u.L.	49.980,00	
	an	5000 Umsatzerlöse Fertigerzeugnisse		42.000,00
		4800 Umsatzsteuer		7.980,00
❿	6050	Benzin	900,00	
	2600	Vorsteuer	171,00	
	an	4400 Verbindlichkeiten aus L.u.L.		1.071,00
⓫	6700	Miete	650,00	
	an	2800 Bank		650,00
⓬	6890	Telefon	500,00	
	2600	Vorsteuer	95,00	
	an	2800 Bank		595,00
⓭	2800	Bank	49.980,00	
	an	2400 Forderungen aus L.u.L.		49.980,00
⓮	6300	Gehälter	8.400,00	
	an	2800 Bank		8.400,00

4. und 5. Ergebniskonten führen und abschließen

Aufwandskonten

Soll	6000 Rohstoffaufw.		Haben
❸	8.000	GuV-Konto	8.000
	8.000		8.000

Soll	6050 Benzin		Haben
❿	900	GuV-Konto	900
	900		900

Soll	6300 Gehälter		Haben
⓮	8.400	GuV-Konto	8.400
	8.400		8.400

Soll	6700 Miete		Haben
⓫	650	GuV-Konto	650
	650		650

Soll	6710 Leasing		Haben
❽	1.800	GuV-Konto	1.800
	1.800		1.800

Soll	6890 Telefon		Haben
⓬	500	GuV-Konto	500
	500		500

Soll	7510 Zinsaufwendungen		Haben
❻	350	GuV-Konto	350
	350		350

Ertragskonten

Soll	5000 Umsatzerlöse FE		Haben
GuV-Konto	42.000	❾	42.000
	42.000		42.000

6. GuV-Konto führen und abschließen

Soll	8020 Gewinn- und Verlustkonto		Haben
6000 Rohstoffaufw.	8.000	5000 Umsatzerlöse FE	42.000
6050 Benzin	900		
6300 Gehälter	8.400		
6700 Miete	650		
6710 Leasing	1.800		
6890 Telefon	500		
7510 Zinsaufwendungen	350		
Eigenkapital (= Gewinn)	21.400		
	42.000		42.000

	Nr.	Konto	Soll/EUR	Haben/EUR
❶	8200	GuV-Konto	21.400,00	
	an	3000 Eigenkapital		21.400,00

2., 4., 7. Bestandskonten einrichten, führen und abschließen

Aktivkonten

Soll		0710 Maschinen	Haben
AB	80.000	**8010**	**100.000**
❹	20.000		
	100.000		100.000

Soll		0870 Geschäftsausstattung	Haben
AB	60.000	**8010**	**62.000**
❼	2.000		
	62.000		62.000

Soll		2000 Rohstoffe	Haben
AB	30.000	❸	8.000
❶	5.800	**8010**	**27.800**
	35.800		35.800

Soll		2400 Forderungen aus L.u.L.	Haben
AB	40.000	⓭	49.980
❾	49.980	**8010**	**40.000**
	89.980		89.980

Soll		2800 Bank	Haben
AB	20.000	❷	6.000
⓭	49.980	❺	6.902
		❻	1.350
		❽	2.142
		⓫	650
		⓬	595
		⓮	8.400
		8010	**43.941**
	69.980		69.980

Soll		2600 Vorsteuer (19 %)	Haben
❶	1.102	⓯	5.890
❹	3.800		
❼	380		
❽	342		
❿	171		
⓬	95		
	5.890		5.890

Passivkonten

Soll		3000 Eigenkapital	Haben
8010	**152.400**	AB	131.000
		GuV-Konto (8020)	21.400
	153.400		152.400

Soll		4200 Darlehen	Haben
❻	1.000	AB	70.000
8010	**69.000**		
	70.000		70.000

Soll		4400 Verbindlichkeiten aus L.u.L.	Haben
❺	6.902	AB	23.000
8010	**50.251**	❶	6.902
		❹	23.800
		❼	2.380
		❿	1.071
	57.153		57.153

Soll		4800 Umsatzsteuer (19 %)	Haben
❷	6.000	AB	6.000
⓯	5.890	❾	7.980
8010	**2.090**		
	7.980		7.980

Soll		8010 Schlussbilanzkonto	Haben
0710 Maschinen	100.000	3000 Eigenkapital	152.400
0870 Geschäftsausstattung	62.000	4200 Darlehen	69.000
2000 Rohstoffe	27.800	4400 Verbindlichkeiten aus L.u.L.	50.251
2400 Forderungen aus L.u.L.	40.000	4800 Umsatzsteuer (19 %)	2.090
2800 Bank	43.941		
	273.741		273.741

8. Zahllast für den abgelaufenen Monat

Zahllast = Umsatzsteuer – Vorsteuer
= 7.980 – 5.890
= 2.090

	Nr.	Konto	Soll/EUR	Haben/EUR
⓯	4800 an	Umsatzsteuer 2600 Vorsteuer	5.890,00	 5.890,00

Aufgabe 6 Buchen nach Belegen

	Nr.	Konto	Soll/EUR	Haben/EUR
1. Beleg 1	2010 2600 an	Vorprodukte Vorsteuer 4400 Verbindlichkeiten aus L.u.L.	364,00 69,16	433,16

	Nr.	Konto	Soll/EUR	Haben/EUR
2. Beleg 2	4400 an	Verbindlichkeiten aus L.u.L. 2800 Bank	433,16	433,16
	2800 an	Bank 2400 Forderungen aus L.u.L.	1.487,50	1.487,50
	4800 an	Umsatzsteuer 2800 Bank	3.640,00	3.640,00

3. Umsatzsteuer = 1.487,50 EUR / 119 · 19 = 237,50 EUR

Aufgabe 7 Kontrolle der Umsatzsteuer/Ermittlung der Zahllast

1.

		Netto	USt-Satz	Umsatzsteuer
5000	Umsatzerlöse für Fertigerzeugnisse	80.000,00	19	15.200,00
5010	Umsatzerlöse für Handelswaren	2.800,00	19	532,00
5410	Provisionserträge	1.600,00	19	304,00
				16.036,00
				⇕
4800	Umsatzsteuer			16.036,00

Errechnete Umsatzsteuer stimmt mit der ausgewiesenen Umsatzsteuer überein.

2. Zahllast = Umsatzsteuer – Vorsteuer = 16.036,00 EUR – 24.800,00 EUR = – 8.764,00 EUR
Es handelt sich um einen Vorsteuerüberhang.

Aufgabe 8 Zusammenfassende Aufgabe zur Umsatzsteuer

1.

	Nr.	Konto	Soll/EUR	Haben/EUR
Beleg 1	2010	Vorprodukte	11.900,00	
	2600	Vorsteuer	2.261,00	
	an	4400 Verbindlichkeiten aus L.u.L.		14.161,00
Beleg 2	2400	Forderungen aus L.u.L.	26.418,00	
	an	5000 Umsatzerlöse Fertigerzeugnisse		22.200,00
		4800 Umsatzsteuer		4.218,00

2. Beleg 1: Zahllast (= Umsatzsteuer – Vorsteuer) verringert sich um 2.261,00 EUR, da sich die Vorsteuer erhöht.
   Beleg 2: Zahllast erhöht sich um 4.218,00 EUR, da sich die Umsatzsteuer erhöht.

3. Beleg 1: Ergebnisneutral, da keine Ergebniskonten angesprochen werden
   Beleg 2: Gewinn erhöht sich um 22.200,00 EUR, da ein Ertragskonto angesprochen wird.

4. schülerindividuell;
   z.B. Umsatzsteuersatz, Anschrift des Rechnungsausstellers, Artikelbezeichnung

5. Rechnungsbetrag = 22.200,00 · 0,95 · 1,19 = 25.097,10 EUR
   Hinweis: Der mögliche Skontoabzug führt zu keiner Veränderung des Rechnungsbetrags.

6. Die Umsatzsteuer hat keine Auswirkungen auf den Gewinn.
   Es handelt sich um einen durchlaufenden Posten.

zu Kapitel 8 Buchungen von Beschaffungs-, Leistungserstellungs- und Verkaufsvorgängen in einem Industrieunternehmen

ANWENDUNGS- UND ÜBUNGSAUFGABEN

Aufgabe 1 Einkauf von Materialien (Roh-, Hilfs- und Betriebsstoffe)

PDF

DIGITAL+

	Nr.	Konto	Soll/EUR	Haben/EUR
❶	2000	Rohstoffe	2.200,00	2.618,00
	2600	Vorsteuer	418,00	
	an	4400 Verbindlichkeiten aus L.u.L.		
❷	2030	Betriebsstoffe	80,00	
	2600	Vorsteuer	15,20	
	an	4400 Verbindlichkeiten aus L.u.L.		95,20
❸	2020	Hilfsstoffe	320,00	
	2600	Vorsteuer	60,80	
	an	4400 Verbindlichkeiten aus L.u.L.		380,80

Aufgabe 2 Preisnachlässe buchen

	Konto		Soll/EUR	Haben/EUR
1.	4400	Verbindlichkeiten aus L.u.L.	135,66	
	an	6002 Preisnachlässe für Rohstoffe		114,00
		2600 Vorsteuer		21,66

	Text	Soll/EUR	Haben/EUR
2.	Preisnachlass von einem Lieferer	+ 21.66	Vorsteuer ↓

Aufgabe 3 Rücksendung in einer Ölmühle buchen

1.

	Sonnenblumenkerne	1.400,00 EUR
+	19 % Umsatzsteuer	266,00 EUR
=	Gutschrift zur Verrechnung	1.666,00 EUR

2. Die Gutschrift bezieht sich auf die zuvor gebuchten Nettoerlöse.
Die Nettoerlöse bilden die Bemessungsgrundlage für die zu berechnende Umsatzsteuer (= Entgelt). Somit ist bei jeder Gutschrift die Umsatzsteuer zum Zwecke einer Umsatzsteuerkorrektur zu berücksichtigen.

	Konto		Soll/EUR	Haben/EUR
3.	4400	Verbindlichkeiten aus L.u.L.	1.666,00	
	an	6002 Preisnachlässe für Rohstoffe		1.400,00
		2600 Vorsteuer		266,00

	Text	Zahllast-veränderung	Begründung
4.	Rücksendung an einen Lieferer	+ 266,00	Vorsteuer ↓

Aufgabe 4 Buchungssätze zum Materialverbrauch in einer Jeansfabrik

6000 Aufwendungen für Rohstoffe an 2000 Rohstoffe	32.000,00	 32.000,00
6020 Aufwendungen für Hilfsstoffe an 2020 Hilfsstoffe	1.200,00	 1.200,00
6010 Aufwendungen für Vorprodukte an 2010 Vorprodukte	800,00	 800,00
6020 Aufwendungen für Hilfsstoffe an 2020 Hilfsstoffe	1.600,00	 1.600,00

Aufgabe 5 Fortschreibungsmethode

1. Lagerbestand zum 28.02. = 190 Stück – 40 Stück + 120 Stück – 50 Stück – 20 Stück – 30 Stück = 170 Stück **(Buchbestand)**

   Materialverbrauch Februar = 40 Stück + 50 Stück + 20 Stück + 30 Stück = 140 Stück

2.

	Konto	Soll/EUR	Haben/EUR
MES 85	6000 Aufwendungen für Rohstoffe an 2000 Rohstoffe	1.200,00	 1.200,00
ER 20	2000 Rohstoffe 2600 Vorsteuer an 4400 Verbindlichkeiten aus L.u.L.	3.600,00 684,00	 4.284,00

3. u. 4. → Fehlmenge = 10 Stück
→ Inventurdifferenz wird ausgebucht: 10 Stück · 30 EUR / Stück = 300,00 EUR

	Konto	Soll/EUR	Haben/EUR
Korrektur-buchung	6000 Aufwendungen für Rohstoffe an 2000 Rohstoffe	300,00	 300,00

Soll — 2000 Rohstoffe — Haben

Soll		Haben	
AB	5.700,00	MES 85	1.200,00
ER 20	3.600,00	MES 92	1.500,00
		MES 98	600,00
		MES 102	900,00
		Korrektur	300,00
		SB	4.800,00
	9.300,00		9.300,00

Soll — 6000 Rohstoffaufwendungen — Haben

Soll		Haben	
MES 85	1.200,00	Saldo	4.500,00
MES 92	1.500,00		
MES 98	600,00		
MES 102	900,00		
Korrektur	300,00		
	4.500,00		4.500,00

Konto	Soll/EUR	Haben/EUR
8010 Schlussbilanzkonto an 2000 Rohstoffe	4.800,00	 4.800,00
8020 Gewinn- und Verlustkonto an 6000 Aufwendungen für Rohstoffe	4.500,00	 4.500,00

Aufgabe 6 Geschäftsvorfälle in einer Textildruckerei

1.

	Konto	Soll/EUR	Haben/EUR
❶	2400 Forderungen aus L.u.L.	1.785,00	
	an 5000 Umsatzerlöse Erzeugnisse		1.500,00
	4800 Umsatzsteuer		285,00
❷	2820 Kasse	199,00	
	an 5010 Umsatzerlöse Handelswaren		167,23
	4800 Umsatzsteuer		31,77
❸	2800 Bank	1.785,00	
	an 2400 Forderungen aus L.u.L.		1.785,00
❹	2210 Handelswaren	4.000,00	
	2600 Vorsteuer	760,00	
	an 4400 Verbindlichkeiten aus L.u.L.		4.760,00
❺	2400 Forderungen aus L.u.L.	9.996,00	
	an 5000 Umsatzerlöse Erzeugnisse		2.400,00
	5010 Umsatzerlöse Handelswaren		6.000,00
	4800 Umsatzsteuer		1.596,00
❻	2820 Kasse	10,00	
	an 5010 Umsatzerlöse Handelswaren		8,40
	4800 Umsatzsteuer		1,60

2. Zahllast erhöht sich um 285,00 EUR, da die Umsatzsteuer zunimmt.

3. Das Ergebnis verbessert sich um 8.400,00 EUR, da in dieser Höhe Umsatzerlöse (= Erträge) anfallen und gebucht werden.

   Allerdings darf dieser Betrag nicht mit dem erzielten Gewinn gleichgesetzt werden, da die entsprechenden Aufwendungen (Material, Personal) berücksichtigt werden müssen.

Aufgabe 7 Buchen von Geschäftsvorfällen in einem Industrieunternehmen

1.

Eröffnungsbilanz

Aktiva		Passiva	
I. Anlagevermögen		I. Eigenkapital	734.700
Bebaute Grundstücke	480.000	II. Fremdkapital	
Maschinen	230.000	Darlehen	290.000
Fuhrpark	90.000	Verbindlichkeiten aus L.u.L.	83.300
Geschäftsausstattung	60.000	Sonst. Verbindlichkeiten	17.000
II. Umlaufvermögen			
Rohstoffe	80.000		
Hilfsstoffe	16.000		
Forderungen aus L.u.L.	119.000		
Bank	50.000		
	1.125.000		1.125.000

2.

	Konto	Soll/EUR	Haben/EUR
❶	2000 Rohstoffe	8.800,00	
	2020 Hilfsstoffe	1.200,00	
	2600 Vorsteuer (19 %)	1.900,00	
	an 4400 Verbindlichkeiten aus L.u.L.		11.900,00
❷	2400 Forderungen aus L.u.L.	28.560,00	
	an 5000 Umsatzerlöse Fertigerzeugnisse		24.000,00
	4800 Umsatzsteuer (19 %)		4.560,00
❸	4800 Umsatzsteuer (19 %)	17.000,00	
	an 2800 Bank		17.000,00
❹	6000 Rohstoffaufwendungen	8.000,00	
	6020 Hilfsstoffaufwendungen	400,00	
	an 2000 Rohstoffe		8.000,00
	2020 Hilfsstoffe		400,00
❺	2000 Rohstoffe	2.000,00	
	2600 Vorsteuer (19 %)	380,00	
	an 4400 Verbindlichkeiten aus L.u.L.		2.380,00
❻	4400 Verbindlichkeiten aus L.u.L.	11.900,00	
	an 2800 Bank		11.900,00
❼	4200 Darlehen	10.000,00	
	7510 Zinsaufwendungen	1.200,00	
	an 2800 Bank		11.200,00
❽	2400 Forderungen aus L.u.L.	45.220,00	
	an 5000 Umsatzerlöse Fertigerzeugnisse		38.000,00
	4800 Umsatzsteuer (19 %)		7.220,00
❾	6890 Telefon	900,00	
	2600 Vorsteuer (19 %)	171,00	
	an 2800 Bank		1.071,00
❿	2800 Bank	28.560,00	
	an 2400 Forderungen aus L.u.L.		28.560,00
⓫	6200 Löhne	14.000,00	
	6300 Gehälter	8.200,00	
	an 2800 Bank		22.200,00
⓬	6000 Rohstoffaufwendungen	15.000,00	
	6020 Hilfsstoffaufwendungen	1.100,00	
	an 2000 Rohstoffe		15.000,00
	2020 Hilfsstoffe		1.100,00
⓭	6050 Strom	7.000,00	
	2600 Vorsteuer (19 %)	1.330,00	
	7020 Grundsteuer	1.400,00	
	7030 Kfz-Steuer	2.400,00	
	an 2800 Bank		12.130,00
⓮	6800 Büromaterialien	600,00	
	2600 Vorsteuer (19 %)	114,00	
	an 4400 Verbindlichkeiten aus L.u.L.		714,00

3. u. 4.

Aktivkonten

Soll	0500 Bebaute Grundstücke		Haben
AB	480.000,00	**8010**	**480.000,00**
	480.000,00		480.000,00

Soll	0710 Maschinen		Haben
AB	230.000,00	**8010**	**230.000,00**
	230.000,00		230.000,00

Soll	0840 Fuhrpark		Haben
AB	90.000,00	**8010**	**90.000,00**
	90.000,00		90.000,00

Soll	0870 Geschäftsausstattung		Haben
AB	60.000,00	**8010**	**60.000,00**
	60.000,00		60.000,00

Soll	2000 Rohstoffe		Haben
AB	80.000,00	❹	8.000,00
❶	8.800,00	⓬	15.000,00
❺	2.000,00	**8010**	**67.800,00**
	90.800,00		90.800,00

Soll	2020 Hilfsstoffe		Haben
AB	16.000,00	❹	400,00
❶	1.200,00	⓬	1.100,00
		8010	**15.700,00**
	17.200,00		17.200,00

Soll	2400 Forderungen		Haben
AB	119.000,00	❿	28.560,00
❷	28.560,00	**8010**	**164.220,00**
❽	45.220,00		
	192.780,00		192.780,00

Soll	2800 Bank		Haben
AB	50.000,00	❸	17.000,00
❿	28.560,00	❻	11.900,00
		❼	11.200,00
		❾	1.071,00
		⓫	22.200,00
		⓭	12.130,00
		8010	**3.059,00**
	78.560,00		78.560,00

Soll	2600 Vorsteuer (19 %)		Haben
❶	1.900,00	**4800**	**3.895,00**
❺	380,00		
❾	171,00		
⓭	1.330,00		
⓮	114,00		
	3.895,00		3.895,00

Passivkonten

Soll	3000 Eigenkapital		Haben
8010	**736.500,00**	AB	734.700,00
		GuV-Konto (8020)	1.800,00
	736.500,00		736.500,00

Soll	4200 Darlehen		Haben
❼	10.000,00	AB	290.000,00
8010	**280.000,00**		
	290.000,00		290.000,00

Soll	4400 Verbindlichkeiten		Haben
❻	11.900,00	**8010**	83.300,00
8010	**86.394,00**	❶	11.900,00
		❺	2.380,00
		⓮	714,00
	98.294,00		98.294,00

Soll	4800 Umsatzsteuer (19 %)		Haben
❸	17.000,00	AB	17.000,00
VSt.	3.895,00	❷	4.560,00
2600	**7.885,00**	❽	7.220,00
	28.780,00		28.780,00

Aufwandskonten

Soll	6000 Rohstoffaufwendungen		Haben
❹	8.000,00	**8020**	**23.000,00**
⓬	15.000,00		
	23.000,00		23.000,00

Soll	6020 Hilfsstoffaufwendungen		Haben
❹	400,00	**8020**	**1.500,00**
⓬	1.100,00		
	1.500,00		1.500,00

Soll	7510 Zinsaufwendungen		Haben
❼	1.200,00	**8020**	**1.200,00**
	1.200,00		1.200,00

Soll	6890 Telefon		Haben
❾	900,00	**8020**	**900,00**
	900,00		900,00

Soll	6200 Löhne		Haben
⓫	14.000,00	**8020**	**14.000,00**
	14.000,00		14.000,00

Soll	6300 Gehälter		Haben
⓫	8.200,00	**8020**	**8.200,00**
	8.200,00		8.200,00

Soll	6050 Strom		Haben
⓭	7.000,00	**8020**	**7.000,00**
	7.000,00		7.000,00

Soll	7020 Grundsteuer		Haben
⓭	1.400,00	**8020**	**1.400,00**
	1.400,00		1.400,00

Soll	7030 Kfz-Steuer		Haben
⓭	2.400,00	**8020**	**2.400,00**
	2.400,00		2.400,00

Soll	6800 Büromaterial		Haben
⓮	600,00	**8020**	**600,00**
	600,00		600,00

Ertragskonten

Soll	5000 Umsatzerlöse FE		Haben
8020	**62.000,00**	❷	24.000,00
		❽	38.000,00
	62.000,00		62.000,00

5. GuV-Konto bzw. SBK gemäß Kontenführung:

Soll	8020 Gewinn- und Verlustkonto		Haben
6000 Rohstoffaufwendungen	23.000	5000 Umsatzerlöse FE	62.000
6020 Hilfsstoffaufwendungen	1.500		
7510 Zinsaufwendungen	1.200		
6890 Telefon	900		
6200 Löhne	14.000		
6300 Gehälter	8.200		
6060 Strom	7.000		
7020 Grundsteuer	1.400		
7030 Kfz-Steuer	2.400		
6800 Büromaterial	600		
3000 Eigenkapital (= **Gewinn**)	**1.800**		
	62.000		62.000

Soll	8010 Schlussbilanzkonto		Haben
0500 Bebaute Grundstücke	480.000	3000 Eigenkapital	736.500
0710 Maschinen	230.000	4200 Darlehen	280.000
0840 Fuhrpark	90.000	4400 Verbindlichkeiten aus L.u.L.	86.394
0870 Geschäftsausstattung	60.000	4800 Umsatzsteuer (19 %)	7.885
2000 Rohstoffe	67.800		
2020 Hilfsstoffe	15.700		
2400 Forderungen aus L.u.L.	164.220		
2800 Bank	3.059		
	1.110.779		1.110.779

Aufgabe 8 Kundenskonto buchen

	Konto		Soll/EUR	Haben/EUR
1.	2400	Forderungen aus L.u.L.	2.975,00	
	an	5000 Umsatzerlöse Fertigerzeugnisse		2.500,00
		4800 Umsatzsteuer		475,00
2.	2800	Bank	2.975,00	
	5002	Kundenskonto	50,00	
	4800	Umsatzsteuer	9,50	
	an	2400 Forderungen aus L.u.L.		2.975,00

Aufgabe 9 Ausgangsrechnung und Kundenskonto buchen

1.

	Bruttobetrag	Nettobetrag	Umsatzsteuer	
Rechnungsbetrag	3.094,00	2.600,00	494,00	100 %
Skontobetrag	61,88	52,00	9,88	2 %
Überweisungsbetrag	3.032,12	2.548,00	484,12	98 %
	119 %	100 %	19 %	

PDF

DIGITAL+

2. **Darstellung in Kontenform** (ohne Kontenabschluss):

Soll	5000 UE Fertigerzeugnisse		Haben
		(a)	2.600,00

Soll	2400 Forderungen aus L.u.L.		Haben
(a)	3.094,00	(b)	3.094,00

Soll	5002 Kundenskonto		Haben
(b)	52,00		

Soll	4800 Umsatzsteuer		Haben
(b)	9,88	(a)	494,00

Soll	2800 Bank		Haben
AB	...		
(b)	3.032,12		

3.

	Konto	Soll/EUR	Haben/EUR
(a)	2400 Forderungen aus L.u.L.	3.094,00	
	an 5000 Umsatzerlöse Fertigerzeugnisse		2.600,00
	4800 Umsatzsteuer		494,00
(b)	2800 Bank	3.032,12	
	5002 Kundenskonto	52,00	
	4800 Umsatzsteuer	9,88	
	an 2400 Forderungen aus L.u.L.		3.094,00

4.

	Text	Zahllastveränderung	Begründung
(a)	Rechnungsausgang	+ 494,00	Umsatzsteuer ↑
(b)	Banküberweisung mit Skontierung	– 9,88	Umsatzsteuer ↓

zu Kapitel 9 Bestandsveränderungen an fertigen und unfertigen Erzeugnissen

ANWENDUNGS- UND ÜBUNGSAUFGABEN

Aufgabe 1 Bestandsveränderungen an fertigen Erzeugnissen

1.

Soll	GuV-Konto		Haben
Rohstoffaufwendungen	12.000,00	Umsatzerlöse Zucker	110.000,00
Fertigungslöhne	18.000,00		
Gehälter	15.000,00		
Sonst. Aufwendungen	33.000,00		
Eigenkapital (Gewinn)	**32.000,00**		
	110.000,00		110.000,00

2. Bestandszunahme an Zucker in Höhe von 4.000 EUR ist eine erbrachte Leistung (Mehrbestand); diese Leistung muss im laufenden Geschäftsjahr berücksichtigt werden.

3.

Konto	Soll/EUR	Haben/EUR
2200 Fertige Erzeugnisse	4.000,00	
an 5220 Bestandsveränderungen FE		4.000,00

4. 1) Summe Aktiva: .... + 4.000 EUR
   2) Jahresergebnis: .... + 4.000 EUR
   3) Summe Anlagevermögen: .... unverändert
   4) Eigenkapital: .... + 4.000 EUR

5. ▪ rückläufige Auftragslage; Auslastung wurde nicht verringert; somit Aufbau von Lagerbeständen
   ▪ Aufträge wurden bereits ausgeführt; die hergestellten Mengen befinden sich auf Lager; aber erst nach dem Jahreswechsel wird ausgeliefert

Aufgabe 2 Bestandsveränderung an unfertigen und fertigen Erzeugnissen

1. Jeansrohlinge Stufe 1: Buchung einer Bestandsmehrung (20 Stück zu je 10 EUR = 200 EUR)
2. Jeansrohlinge Stufe 2: keine Bestandsveränderung; somit keine Buchung
3. Jeans versandfertig: Buchung einer Bestandsminderung (30 Stück zu je 24 EUR = 720 EUR)

	Konto	Soll/EUR	Haben/EUR
❶	2100 Unfertige Erzeugnisse	200,00	
	an 5210 Bestandsveränderungen UE		200,00
❸	5220 Bestandsveränderungen FE	720,00	
	an 2200 Fertige Erzeugnisse		720,00

zu Kapitel 10 Anschaffung von Sachanlagen – Abschreibung

ERARBEITUNGSAUFGABE

EA 1

1.

	Listenpreis	35.000 EUR
+	Überführung und Zulassung	1.000 EUR
+	Werbeaufschrift	200 EUR
–	Rabatt 10 % auf den Listenpreis	3.500 EUR
=	Anschaffungskosten	32.700 EUR

Der Transporter muss regelmäßig betankt werden. Daher gehört die erste Tankfüllung nicht zu den Anschaffungskosten des Transporters.

2.

Konto		Soll/EUR	Haben/EUR
0840	Fuhrpark	32.700,00	
2600	Vorsteuer	6.213,00	
an	Verb. a. L.u.L.		38.913,00

3.

Bilanz zum 31.12.

Aktiva		Passiva	
Maschinen	70.000,00 €	Eigenkapital	75.000,00 €
Geschäftsausstattung*	**77.700,00 €**	Darlehensverbindlichkeiten	90.000,00 €
Rohstoffe	25.000,00 €	Verbindlichkeiten aus L.u.L.	63.913,00 €
Forderungen aus L.u.L.	30.000,00 €		
Vorsteuer	**6.213,00 €**		
Bank	20.000,00 €		
	228.913,00 €		**228.913,00 €**

* Fuhrpark ist ein Unterkonto der Betriebs- und Geschäftsausstattung

4. Der Transporter würde am Jahresende mit einem Wert von 32.700 EUR in der Bilanz stehen, wenn keine Korrekturbuchung erfolgt.

5. Der Transporter verliert vor allem durch Verschleiß an Wert. Nach einem Jahr im Gebrauch ließe er sich sicherlich nicht mehr zum Anschaffungspreis verkaufen. Der Wertverlust muss daher erfasst werden und ein entsprechend niedriger Wert in der Bilanz aufgeführt werden. Dies geschieht in der Buchhaltung durch Abschreibung. Die Anschaffungskosten werden auf die Jahre, in denen der Gegenstand genutzt werden kann, verteilt. Der Restwert des obigen Transporters würde bei 9 Jahren Nutzungsdauer bei 32.700 – (32.700/9) = 29.067 EUR liegen.

zu Kapitel 10 Anschaffung von Sachanlagen – Abschreibung

ANWENDUNGS- UND ÜBUNGSAUFGABEN

Aufgabe 1 Ermittlung und Buchung der Anschaffungskosten

1.

Anschaffungskosten	
Listenpreis	34.000,00 EUR
+ Autoradio	450,00 EUR
+ Überführung	200,00 EUR
+ Kfz-Kennzeichen	30,00 EUR
+ Anmeldegebühr	25,00 EUR
= Anschaffungskosten	34.705,00 EUR

	Konto	Soll/EUR	Haben/EUR
2.	0840 Fuhrpark	34.705,00	
	6050 Benzin	35,00	
	2600 Vorsteuer	6.589,20*	
	an 4400 Verbindlichkeiten aus L.u.L.		41.329,20
3.	4400 Verbindlichkeiten aus L.u.L.	41.329,20	
	an 2800 Bank		41.329,20

* Die Anmeldegebühr ist nicht umsatzsteuerpflichtig.

Aufgabe 2 Anschaffungskosten zuordnen

1.

Stanzmaschine	Anschaffungskosten?
Listenpreis	Ja
Transportversicherung	Ja
Kranentladung	Ja
Zoll	Ja
Kleinere Ersatzteile	Nein
Rabatt	nein, mindert die Anschaffungskosten
Errichtung eines Fundaments	ja, da zur Herstellung der Betriebsbereitschaft erforderlich

2.

Gebäude	Anschaffungskosten?
Kaufpreis	Ja
Notariatskosten	Ja
Grunderwerbsteuer	Ja
Grundsteuer	Nein, da wiederkehrende Zahlung
Grundbuchgebühren für Eigentumsübergang	Ja
Darlehenszinsen	nein, da Finanzierungskosten
Grundbuchgebühren für Grundschuld zur Darlehenssicherung	nein, da Finanzierungskosten

3.

Computer	Anschaffungskosten?
Listenpreis	Ja
bezahlte Vorsteuer*	Nein
Anlieferung	Ja
Vernetzung herstellen	
50 Rohlinge	Nein
Skonto	nein, mindert die Anschaffungskosten

* Annahme: Das Unternehmen ist vorsteuerabzugsberechtigt.

PDF

DIGITAL+

Aufgabe 3 Lineare Abschreibung mit Kontenführung

1.

Soll	0870 Geschäftsausstattung		Haben
❷	12.000,00	❹	539,00

Soll	4400 Verbindlichkeiten aus L.u.L.		Haben
❸	14.280,00	❷	14.800,00

Soll	6500 Abschreibung auf SA		Haben
❹	539,00		

Soll	2600 Vorsteuer		Haben
❷	2.280,00		

Soll	2800 Bank		Haben
AB	...	❸	14.280,00

	Konto	Soll/EUR	Haben/EUR	
2.	0870 Geschäftsausstattung 2600 Vorsteuer an 4400 Verbindlichkeiten aus L.u.L.	12.000,00 2.280,00	 14.280,00	
3.	4440 Verbindlichkeiten aus L.u.L. an 2800 Bank	14.280,00	 14.280,00	
4.	6500 Abschreibung auf Sachanlagen an 0870 Geschäftsausstattung	539,00	 539,00	*monats-anteilig!*

5. Abschreibungen sind Aufwendungen. Sie schmälern den Gewinn und damit die gewinnabhängigen Steuern (z.B. Einkommen- oder Körperschaftsteuer).

Aufgabe 4 Beginn der Abschreibung im ersten Jahr der Nutzung

Anschaffung des Lkws am ...	Abschreibungsbetrag im ersten Jahr der Nutzung bei Anwendung der ...	
	linearen Methode	degressiven Methode
20.01.20..: $^{12}/_{12}$	5.160,00 EUR	11.610,00 EUR
14.08.20..: $^{5}/_{12}$	2.150,00 EUR	4.837,50 EUR
20.12.20..: $^{1}/_{12}$	430,00 EUR	967,50 EUR

DIGITAL+

Projekt: Unternehmensplanspiel Taxi

Planspielunterlagen mit Lösungen befinden sich beim digitalen Zusatzmaterial zum Lehrerhandbuch.